HOW
TO
CASH
IN
ON
YOUR
HIDDEN
MEMORY
POWER

HOW TO CASH IN ON YOUR HIDDEN MEMORY POWER

By

William D. Hersey

Prentice-Hall, Inc.
Englewood Cliffs, N.J.

Library of Congress Catalog Card Number: 63-21439

PRINTED IN THE UNITED STATES OF AMERICA

Nineteenth Printing . . . . May, 1975

Dedicated to
My wife, *Fairlee*
My daughter, *Donna*
and
My son, *Glen*

Around whom gather my most satisfying memories

ACKNOWLEDGMENT

There are three people to whom I owe a particular debt of gratitude. If it had not been for them, my own hidden memory power might not have been developed and the publication of this book might not have become a reality. In chronological order, they are:

William Lundgren, who was program chairman the night I gave a talk on mutual funds to the Sharon, Massachusetts *Rotary Club.* It was he who started it all when he asked, in innocent candor, if I could duplicate the feat of a previous speaker and memorize the names and faces of everyone present. Until that evening I had never before attempted this.

Augustus H. Sullivan, publisher, of Stoughton, Massachusetts. He heard my first talk on memory, encouraged me with the sound advice based on his years of experience in show business and public relations, and published my first brochure. Through his belief in my ability and constant urging, the first public presentation of *Hersey's Short Course for Short Memories* was given.

James Mosely, mailing list broker of Boston, Massachusetts. He first suggested my name to the publisher as a potential author.

None of us stands alone.

I stand where I am today because of these three men. To each, I will always be deeply grateful. . . .

WHY THIS BOOK WILL
ENRICH YOUR LIFE

Have you ever paused to think about the reasons why a trained memory is essential to success?

If you have, you will have realized that today's business world requires "experienced" people.

"Experience" is one's ability to remember, evaluate, classify and successfully use the knowledge to which he has been exposed during the course of a business career. The sound judgment required of people employed in business is founded on their ability to remember experience and then to apply these memories successfully.

It is as simple as that.

Therefore, when one is able to focus all of the forces of his mental powers on a problem and arrive at a successful solution, his personal ability becomes the "stock in trade" he has to sell. The more knowledge he has at his command, the more his "stock" is valued. Consequently, the more of his knowledge he is able to put to use, the more he will earn.

This is why the people with trained memories are the ones who succeed.

Yes, memory *is* the heart of business and social success. Those who have so-called "good" memories are the ones who benefit. They collect the cash and the prestige in the offices, the factories, in public office, and in the community. From the production line to the salesman in the field to the school P.T.A., memory is the vine on which the golden fruit of success grows. Only those who have the trained ability to remember are the ones who pick the choicest fruits.

Memory is *not* a mystical hocus-pocus. It is *not* a trick. It is a power which is now hidden within you. This power can be tapped. My simple method will show you the way. All you have to do is follow the easy rules.

Once you have learned how to tap your hidden memory power, you will discover that your mental capacity and your money earning ability have been multiplied. Not only that, but your influence over others will be greatly increased.

Your hidden memory power, once properly tapped, will enable you to progress through long sales presentations and speeches *without notes,* and without faltering. You will remember seven-digit telephone numbers, appointments, schedules, even foreign words and entire contents of books, magazines and catalogues.

With your memory power this book will show you how to use, you will remember every name and face you want to remember. Facts, figures, data, financial statements and anything else you want to retain, *you will remember!*

This book will show you how by showing you the the secrets of how to organize your memory processes. Yes, this book will prove that you are *not* absent-minded and that you do *not* have a "bad" memory.

No such thing as a "bad" memory exists. We either have a trained or an untrained one. It is as simple as that. Anyone who wants to remember *can* train his mind to remember!

How I Discovered the Age-old Secrets of How to Unlock My Hidden Memory Power

Because of a so-called "bad" memory, what should have started out as a pleasant business trip from Boston to Philadelphia soon became a monotonous and dull train ride.

I had *forgotten* to bring along a book to read.

When I stopped the porter and asked him if he had a book or magazine, he laughed and promptly returned with a book on how to improve your memory. "Can't be much good, sir," he told me. "The man who was reading it got off and *forgot* it."

Out of curiosity and for lack of something better to do, I opened the book and began to read.

I had always taken an interest in self-improvement books, but like most people, I was inclined to be content simply to read *about* how the other fellow had done it rather than apply his successful principle to myself. Then, when I read that the author claimed I could improve *my memory,* I found myself scoffing. Who was he to tell me that I could improve my ability to remember?

Nothing was more ridiculous. As far as I was concerned, my memory was the world's worst. It was like a sieve. As humans, we tend to be smug in our conceit. I was guilty too.

We "know it all" and go through life complaining about our "bad" memories, but never complaining about how stupid we are for holding to such a myopic viewpoint.

But all that was about to change. Suddenly I was growing aware of something in the pages of that volume which I had never before stopped to think about. There is no such thing as a "bad" memory! We either have a trained or an untrained memory.

I thought about that for a while. It made sense. Maybe the author of that book did have something. I began reading in earnest.

By the time the train arrived in Philadelphia, my head was buzzing with a swarm of ideas. Though the book I had just finished reading left a lot to be desired, it had started me off in a new direction of study which was soon about to change my entire life!

Within the next few days I began to devise and adapt a memory system to suit my own needs. I spent hours in reading and research and those were well spent, for within a week I was able to remember *everything* I had determined to memorize systematically.

Once you make these time-tested secrets yours, you too will sparkle with a newly-found self-confidence. You too will find yourself picking the golden fruits of success which have rarely before been within your reach!

If I could—at age 43—learn how to tap my hidden memory power and cash in on it, so can you.

Within the next hour you will discover the incredible but true secrets which will unlock the treasure chest of knowledge for you.

You will be staggered by the limitless possibilities to profit in the new world you are about to discover. . . .

WILLIAM D. HERSEY

CONTENTS

Acknowledgment, vi

Why This Book Will Enrich Your Life, vii

I   What Memory Power Will Do for You, 1

What Is Memory Power? 3   *Is There Such a Thing as a "Bad" Memory?* 4   *The Secret of Memory,* 4   *How Good Are Your Powers of Observation?* 5   *How Good Are Your Powers of Concentration?* 7   *Why an Organized System Is Necessary in Order to Remember Accurately,* 7

II   How to Develop a Thinking-Machine Memory, 10

The Three Secrets of a Thinking-Machine Memory, 11 *How to Develop Mental Storage Places for Things You Need to Remember,* 12   *How to Remember a List of Things to Do,* 18   *Review Questions,* 20

III   The Secret of How to Remember Numbers, 21

How the Number Code Works, 23   *Test Yourself to See How Quickly and How Well You've Learned the First Half of the Code,* 25   *How a Factory Foreman Started Using the Code and Benefited at Once,* 26   *Mastering the Second Half of the Number Code Is Fun!* 26   *Test Yourself to See How Expertly You've Learned the Second Half of the Number Code,* 28   *How Ralph Markham Raised Himself*

III   The Secret of How to Remember Numbers (*Cont.*):

*from Failure to Success When He Learned the Code, 30
Review Questions, 31*

IV   How to Deposit Memories in Your Mental Safe Deposit Boxes, 32

*The Cash Deposit Formula and How It Helps You Deposit
Memories for Later Recall, 33   How to Concentrate, 33
How to Associate, 33   How to Use Your Sight and Hear-
ing Properly, 34   Why You Shouldn't Try to Remember
Verbatim, 34   How to Exaggerate, 35   How to Think
in Pictures, 35   How to Think in Pictures that Are Oddi-
ties, 36   Why Silliness Makes Recollection Easy, 36
How to Convert Ideas Into Concrete Images, 37   How to
Understand Thoughts, 38   The Secret of Learning, 39
How to Classify the Things You Remember, 39   Review
Questions, 41*

V   The Secret of a Trained Memory, 42

*How to Train Your Memory to Function Automatically Like
a Data Processing Machine, 42   5 Ways to Make Your
Memory Function Automatically, 43   How to Test Your
Mental Images for Distinctness, 43   How to Test Your
Mental Images for Vividness, 44   How to Test Your
Mental Images for Clarity of Detail, 44   How to Time the
Speed of Your Memory, 45   How to Check Yourself for
Accuracy, 45   How to Review and Take Inventory, 45
How to Practice and Drill Your Mind, 45   Why a Data
Processing Machine Is Like a Human Brain, 46   The 5
Divisions of a Thinking Machine or Trained Memory, 47
Input: What It Is and How It Works, 47   Symbolic Logic
and How It Is Applied, 48   Information Storage: How It
Works, 49   Programming: What It Is and How It Works,
52   Output: What It Is and How it Works, 52   Review
Questions, 53*

VI   How to Remember Number Series and Statistics, 54

> *How to Remember Telephone Numbers, 56   How the Number Code Enables You to Remember Phone Numbers and Area Codes, 57   How a Yarn Broker Increased His Income by $5,000 a Year Remembering Phone Numbers, 59 How to Develop a Money-making Memory for Rate Tables, 60   How Chuck Dean Cashed in on His Knowledge of Rate Tables, 62   Review Questions, 62*

VII   How to Remember Financial Statements and Catalogues, Prices, or Data, 64

> *How I Memorize a Bank Statement, 65   How a Public Relations Man Landed a New Account as a Result of His Ability to Memorize Financial Statements, 69   How to Develop a System for Remembering Price Lists, Catalogues, 70   How a Car Salesman Sells an Average of 8 New Cars a Week Because He Knows Costs, 70   How a Shoe Salesman Benefits from His Memory of Prices, Sizes, Numbers, 73 How to Remember a Catalogue Page by Page and Cash in on This Knowledge, 74   How a Jobber Uses His Mental-Catalogue Memory to Defeat Competition, 75   Review Questions, 79*

VIII   How to Memorize Stock Prices, 81

> *How I Memorized the Entire List of Closing Prices on the New York Stock Exchange, 82   A Real Estate Salesman Earned $7,500 the First Week He Memorized Stock Prices, 86   Review Questions, 89*

IX   One: The Secret of Remembering Names, Faces and Facts About People, 90

> *Why It Is Important to Observe Faces and Hear Names Spelled in Order to Remember Them, 91   How to Observe*

IX One: The Secret of Remembering Names, Faces and Facts About People (*Cont.*):

Properly the Faces and Names of People, 91   *How to Concentrate on a Person's Face,* 92   *How to Select a Prominent Feature to Remember,* 93   *How to Associate the Name with the Face,* 94   *Why It Is Important to Hear the Sound of a Name,* 97   *You Have the Cash, Now Deposit It,* 98   *How to Cash in on These Techniques in Your Everyday Life,* 98   *How a Club Woman of 65 Memorized the Names and Faces of 43 People After Only One Hour of Instruction!* 99   *How a Clothing Store Salesman Tripled His Income as a Result of His New-found Ability to Remember Names, Faces, Facts About Shoppers,* 100   *How the Ability to Recognize Faces and Remember Names Does More Than Open Doors,* 103   *Review Questions,* 103

X Two: The Secret of Remembering Names, Faces and Facts About People, 105

How Advertising Men Cash in on the Techniques of Controlled Association, 118   *A Few Tips on How to Remember Unusual and Everyday Names,* 118   *How to Sharpen Your Ability to Observe People Closely,* 119   *How Joe and Tony Silva Win and Hold Customers in Their Gas Station,* 121

XI The Secret of Remembering Groups of People, 123

How I Remembered the Names of 100 or More Persons in Less Than 45 Minutes, 124   *How I Got Started on Learning Large Groups of People,* 125   *Important Tips to Remember About Meeting Groups,* 126   *What to Do Before Meeting a New Group for the First Time,* 127   *Why It Is Important Not to Get Groups Within Groups Mixed Up,*

XI   The Secret of Remembering Groups of People (*Cont.*):

128   *How to Avoid Confusing Occupations of Groups of People,* 128   *How to Remember a Roster of Names, Addresses and Facts About People,* 130   *Review Questions,* 132

XII   How to Use Your Memory as a Diary Planner, 134

How to Control Ideas and Thoughts Before They Elude You and How to Record Them in Your Mind, 135   *How to Remember Birthdays, Anniversaries and Other Important Dates,* 138   *How to Develop a Perpetual Calendar in Your Mental Diary Planning System,* 140   *How to Keep Track of Time in Your Mental Diary,* 141   *How Danny Morehead Was Promoted to Radio Station Manager due to His Phenomenal Ability to Remember Program Time Slots,* 142   *How to Remember Appointments and Schedules and Record Them in Your Mental Diary,* 143   *Review Questions,* 145

XIII   One: How to Use Your Memory for Self-improvement, 147

How to Use Your Memory Power to Overcome Absent-mindedness, 148   *How to Protect Yourself from Being Absent-Minded—Tie Mental Strings Around Your Mind,* 149 *What to Do When Your Mind Goes Blank and You Lose Your Train of Thought,* 150   *How to Use Your Memory Power to Help You Concentrate When Under Fire,* 151 *Build a Fence Around Yourself When Concentrating,* 152 *How to Fence Memory Power in While Solving Problems and Learning or Reading,* 152   *The Hersey Memory Power-Fence, and How to Use It for Deep Concentration,* 153   *How Ted Marsh Learned the Memory-Fence Formula and Used It to Make a Fortune,* 156   *Review Questions,* 160

XIV Two: How to Use Your Memory for Self-improvement, 161

How Eddie Kraft Used the Fence Formula to Begin a Career of Law at Age 51, 161 How the Memory Power-Fence Formula Helps You Reach Decisions and Break Bad Habits, 162 How to Use Your Memory as a Calculating Machine, 163 How to Use Your Memory as an Adding Machine, 164 More About Mental Calculation, 166 How Claire Wells Was Promoted to Department Head When She Learned How to Use Memory Power for Mental Calculation, 166 How to Use Your Memory Power to Break Bad Habits, 167 How Paying Attention Helps Self-Improvement, 168 How to Use Your Memory as a Life- and Time-Saving Device, 169 Review Questions, 171

XV How to Use Your Memory for Greater Profit on the Job, 172

How Your Memory Power Can Help You Improve Your Handwriting, 174 How Your Memory Power Can Help You Improve Your Spelling, 174 How to Keep Your Spelling Ability Up to Date, 175 100 Business Words Most Frequently Misspelled, 177 100 Words Most Commonly Misspelled by Educated People, 178 The Hersey Better Spelling Formula, 179 How Ernest Ritter Won a Promotion to Editor When He Learned These Rules, 182 How to Increase Your Vocabulary of Spoken Words, 183 How an Effective Vocabulary Wins Friends, 186 How an Effective Vocabulary Breaks Bad Language Habits, 187 How to Be Positive, Not Negative in What You Say, When Using Effective Language, 188 How Effective Speech Makes Commonplace Expressions Obsolete by Using New "Twists," 189 How to Create Novel Ways of Expressing Yourself, 189 How to Have Something Original and Interesting to Say at All Times by Planning Ahead, 190 How to Always Have a Good Word or Compliment for the Other Fellow, 191 How to Always Be Ready to Talk

XV How to Use Your Memory for Greater Profit on the Job (*Cont.*):

About Things the Other Fellow Wants to Hear, 191   *How to Mean What You Say by Showing How You Are Sincerely Interested in Him,* 191   *How to Use New Words and Expressions Socially and in Your Work,* 192   *How to Make Your Goodbyes Become Unforgettable Remembrances,* 192   *Review Questions,* 194

XVI Everyday Uses of Your Memory Power, 195

How to Use Your Memory Power to Become a Super-Secretary, 196   *How to Use Your Memory to Build a Professional Following of Clients,* 201   *Review Questions,* 203

XVII How to Be a Hero to Your Children, 204

How to Be a Hero to the Children by Helping with Their Homework, 204   *How to Use the Number Code to Remember Dates and Mathematical Constants and Statistics,* 212

XVIII How to Remember Speeches, Sales Talks, Presentations, Jokes and Anecdotes, 214

How to Think Out and Plan in Advance What You Want to Say, 215   *How to Apply Your Memory Power in Public,* 219   *How to Link the Thoughts You Want to Express,* 220   *How to Know Your Audience,* 222   *How to Personalize Your Talk by Using Know-How to Awaken Them with a Joke,* 223   *Review Questions,* 226

XIX How to Have Fun With Memory Power, 228

How to Memorize the Contents of a Magazine, 228   *How*

XIX   How to Have Fun With Memory Power (*Cont.*):

to Have an Entertaining Memory for Playing Cards and Tricks, 230   How to Use Your Memory Power to Win at Poker, 233   Poker Hand Probabilities and Odds, 233 The Tables of Poker Hand Probabilities, 234   Here Are Other Ways to Have Fun with Your Memory Entertaining Audiences, 237   You'll Never Again Have an Excuse for Saying, "I Forgot!" 239

XX   The Hersey Number Dictionary, 240

HOW

TO

CASH

IN

ON

YOUR

HIDDEN

MEMORY

POWER

What Memory Power Will Do for You

"Badness of memory every one complains of, but nobody of the want of judgment."
—LA ROCHEFOUCAULD

Do you want a memory like a thinking machine? Do you want to possess the ability to instantly and automatically recall facts and faces and names that heretofore you've been unable to remember?

Do you *really* want this and the rewards that comes with it?

Would you like to earn more money? Reach a goal? Achieve an ambition? Get what you want out of life quickly and completely?

You will need the driving ambition, naturally; but, you must already have the ambition or you wouldn't have opened this book.

On the pages of this volume are the secrets of the ages, secrets which have been brought up to date to make it possible for you to develop a powerful memory. These secrets are *not* new. Simonides, a lyric poet of the island of Ceos, 535 B.C., is supposed to have discovered mnemonics (pronounced *nee-MON-icks*), or the art of memory. This is untrue.

Simonides secretly traveled to Egypt and "borrowed" the ideas he later enlarged upon from the hieroglyphics and symbols which were used to teach mnemonics (*nee-MON-icks*) by the Egyptians.

The oldest records of the world's peoples were *not* written on parchment or inscribed on stone. They were written in the faithful *memories* of the people who handed down their heritages from father to son, century to century. The Bible is one example, the Koran another. The memories involved therein were indeed miraculous.

1

Historians and scholars who have studied the sacred *Vedas* or *Vedic* hymns of ancient India have been astounded at their accuracy. The memories of those ancient Hindus which date back for 30 centuries, before 2000 B.C., are amazing. The chanted hymns recount a history of civilization which is truer and fuller than any accounts which could have been recorded on stone or papyrus scrolls. Imagine, sacred hymns, learned by heart, containing all this!

How did the ancients remember so prodigiously? What were the secrets they have known since time immemorial? Were these the same secrets known to Hortensius in 115 B.C., the celebrated Roman orator and contemporary of Cicero, who was able to attend a public sale and at the end of a whole day recite in regular order the names of all the buyers, the articles sold, and their prices, with perfect exactness?—Or to Seneca, in 65 A.D., who could recite 2,000 names after hearing them uttered once? —Or to Ebn-Sina, the 10th century Arabian philosopher, who, at the age of 10, could recite the entire *Koran* by heart? And at age 14, the entire works of Aristotle?

And to Themistocles, who knew every one of the 30,000 citizens of Athens by name?

And to Scipio Asiaticus, who could address every one of the 243,704 arms-bearing Romans by name?

And to Michaelangelo and Leonard da Vinci, who, when youths, could accurately draw detailed portraits of people after meeting them only once?

And to Napoleon, who not only knew the names of every one of his officers, but as well knew the thousands of details of the maps of Europe?

Yes, these great men and countless hundreds of others knew the secrets. But what of the secrets? Why had they eventually become lost to mankind?

From the time of Pliny until the time of Shakespeare, little was heard of the mnemonic art of remembering. The barbarism of the Middle Ages swept away all emphasis on study. Gradually, as the use of Latin diminished, the books teaching the systems in Latin, the language of Cicero, fell into disuse. Only a select few among the educated of those times were able to pore over the scientific works of which were nearly all written in Latin. And few of these men were able to understand the strange mnemonical systems which would have helped them remember what they read or learned.

Finally, when men became dependent upon the written word, they found little or no need to commit teachings to their memories.

In 1730, Dr. Richard Grey, Rector of Hinton, in Northamptonshire, England, published a system in English under the Latin title of *Memoria Technica*. This produced a sensation. Yet, the memory system was impracticable.

Dr. Grey's discovery, which was based on his findings in the study of the ancient Hebrew vowel-less language, reactivated interest, however, in the art of memory.

Not until 1807 did a new teacher of mnemonics appear in the civilized world. He was M. Gregor von Feinaigle, a native of Baden. His was the first workable system to be employed by Englishmen. He lectured for several years at the Royal Institution, London, and in the provinces, performing remarkable mnemonic feats together with his pupils.

Feinaigle became so famous that even Lord Byron paid him homage in his famous *Don Juan*, while speaking of the extraordinary memory powers of his Donna Inez: "For *her* Feinaigle's were an useless art," etc.

It is a curious fact that the slang word *finagle*, which means to contrive, to manage, to figure out a way by unethical or unusual means, was derived as a result of Feinaigle's fame.

Once Feinaigle's system was published, others imitated and improved it. M. Aimé Paris provided the most practical improvements, and finally, Francis Fauvel-Gouraud published his *The Art of Memory*, in 1845. It is Gouraud's number code which is still in use by students and practitioners of mnemonics today. This is the code I have adopted.

Now these secrets are available to you. Here are the methods which will make it possible for you to develop a phenomenal memory. Once you master these easy-to-understand methods you too will win what you want.

It's indisputable.

Knowledge *is* wealth. The ability to retain knowledge and then to employ it enables the possessor to achieve *whatever he wants* in life!

What Is Memory Power?

Your memory is the "bank" of your mind. The experiences through which you live, the facts and ideas you accumulate, and the teaching you master are all stored in the "vaults" of your memory "bank."

Memory *is* the depository of the golden coins of knowledge. It is the seat of intelligence, the library of the mind.

You recognize others with your memory. You remember facts about people and things with your memory. You *reason* with your memory. You can't think or reach decisions without a memory. In fact, no civilization, no human life can exist *without* memory.

Stop and think about this for a moment.

During this very instant you are using your memory. Though you are not aware of it, you are depositing thoughts and ideas in your mind. You are probably depositing an average of ten thoughts every minute in your memory "bank."

In 48 years 250,228,800 thoughts will have been placed in your mind!

Incredible, isn't it? But it's true. Now, what *is* memory power? Basically, we must understand what memory actually does as a faculty of our minds. *It consists of remembrance and the ability to recollect.*

Remembrance is passive memory. It is accomplished without effort.

Recollection is active memory. To recollect thoughts requires methodical or systemized effort. And there you have it!

As you see, memory *power* is the ability to recollect our thoughts *accurately* and *at will.* The degree at which this is accomplished is the measure of our memory power!

Is There Such a Thing as a "Bad" Memory?

No. But I used to think I had a bad memory until I discovered how to employ a system to train my memory. Now it is *impossible* for me to forget anything I deliberately want to engrave in my memory.

There is no such thing as a "bad" memory—only a trained or untrained memory. *Anyone,* no matter how young or old, as long as he has learned to speak, can be trained to remember with photographic accuracy.

The Secret of Memory

The word, memory, has been derived from the Greek *mneme,* or *Mnemosyne* * (pronounced *nē-mos'-i-nē*). As you may know, Mnemosyne

---

* Mnemosyne and the other Muses were myths which existed only in the imagination. The belief that your memory depends upon a gift is just as much a myth as Mnemosyne. You *can* improve your memory immediately and profitably.

is the Goddess of Memory, the mother of the nine muses we read about in Greek and Roman mythology. The muses are looked upon as the patron goddesses of music, song, poetry, fine arts, science and history, all intended to promote the civilization of man. The word music is derived from this origin.

Each of the muses was depicted by the ancients in sculpture. When their statues are studied, one observes the thought-provoking details of what each represents. For example, the traditional pose of Mnemosyne indicates the silent, mysterious action of memory.

Clio, the first muse, is shown seated, wearing a laurel wreath, holding forth a parchment roll. It is obvious she represents History.

Melopomene and Thalia, represent Tragedy and Comedy by the familiar masks they are holding. The others are also shown in poses typifying the muses they indicate. One must *observe* each statue in order to get the idea.

It is what we *observe* that shows us the idea behind each statue.

So it is with all things we wish to remember. We must visualize and observe before we can remember. That visualization must be directed to finding the meaning or idea of what we want to remember. We must see the details and be aware of them.

The first secret of memory, therefore, is in knowing how to observe.

Before we go any further, let's see how well you observe things.

How Good Are Your Powers of Observation?

The ability to *observe or hear* can be developed to a powerful degree. Most of us fail to practice the habit of careful observation. Many of the details of what we gaze upon escape our notice because we are in the habit of not paying attention to detail.

Quickly now, glance at each of the sketches shown below and see if your powers of observation are good enough to pick out the errors at your first quick glimpse.

List below each thing missing from each picture:

1._____   6._____   11._____   16._____
2._____   7._____   12._____   17._____
3._____   8._____   13._____   18._____
4._____   9._____   14._____   19._____
5._____   10._____   15._____   20._____

Now, cover the illustrations with a sheet of paper, taking care to conceal the answers you have written in above. Then list every sketch you can recall, briefly describing it. Try to recall as many of the drawings as you can without pausing to go back and fill in those you may have missed.

As you have just seen, recalling those pictures took some effort. A score of 50 is very superior; 35 is average. But don't feel discouraged if you've missed more than you feel you should have. Before you finish reading the next chapter, not only will you be able to recall each picture, but you shall also be able to call them off in perfect sequence, forwards, backwards, or in any order!

The ability to observe is strengthened through practice. The more you "see" the more you will remember. However, this is not enough. First, you must learn to *concentrate* on what you are seeing. In other words, you must determine the *idea* behind, or the purpose of, what you are studying.

How Good Are Your Powers of Concentration?

Charles Darwin cited this example which clearly illustrates what is meant by concentration or intellectual effort. He relates a story of an animal trainer who, before deciding to purchase an ape, always rented the animal for several days. If the wild animal trainer noticed in the course of his teaching the ape tricks that the beast was easily distracted, perhaps by the roar of an animal in another cage, or a fly buzzing, he returned the ape and considered him to be unteachable.

In order to determine the idea behind what you are studying, you must therefore fix your entire attention on the matter at hand. The importance of concentrated attention cannot be overstressed.

Why an Organized System Is Necessary in Order to Remember Accurately

When you observe something you want to recollect later, you must go about it in a systematic manner. The very act of observation is somewhat like making out a mental "bank deposit slip" which you deposit, through the act of concentration, in the vaults of your memory bank.

Let's carry the analogy further to illustrate the vital importance of this memory law.

Answer to picture quiz, page 6. The missing features:

1. Mouth	11. Trigger
2. Eye and brow	12. Tail
3. Nose	13. Leg
4. Spoon	14. Shadow
5. Chimney	15. One ball
6. Ear	16. Net
7. Filament	17. Left arm
8. Stamp	18. Speaker
9. Strings	19. Arm reflection
10. Metal tip	20. ◇ in upper inside corner.

Score 5 for each illustration you are able to recall.

1.＿＿＿	6.＿＿＿	11.＿＿＿	16.＿＿＿
2.＿＿＿	7.＿＿＿	12.＿＿＿	17.＿＿＿
3.＿＿＿	8.＿＿＿	13.＿＿＿	18.＿＿＿
4.＿＿＿	9.＿＿＿	14.＿＿＿	19.＿＿＿
5.＿＿＿	10.＿＿＿	15.＿＿＿	20.＿＿＿

When you actually make a cash deposit in your bank, you are following a systematic procedure. The deposit slip must be properly filled out, the bills sorted, change counted, checks endorsed, etc. When the teller takes your deposit, he checks it, allocates the money to the proper department and sends your deposit slip up to the bookkeeper. Then your deposit is properly recorded in your account.

But what would happen if your bank permitted its customers to make deposits and withdrawals without putting their names and account numbers on the deposit and withdrawal slips or on their checks? And suppose the bank officials took all the cash that was deposited and dumped it in wheelbarrows which they then emptied into the vaults? And suppose investment firms did the same thing with securities and bonds and other valuable documents? And suppose manufacturers and retailers and wholesalers didn't bother to keep systematic records of their stocks and accounts and funds? Everything would be in one sorry mess, wouldn't it?

If this were the case, who could produce a financial statement that would serve as credit "power" with which to grow?

Well, this is precisely what happens when you deposit—in a haphazard and disorganized fashion—the valuable things you need to remember in your *memory bank!* The ability to recall a name or fact or phone number at the snap of a finger is to have the ability to produce memory *power.*

When one has the reputation of being a mental wizard, and then cashes in on it when he needs to, that man has memory power! His mind isn't cluttered with disorganized thoughts. He has on deposit in his memory bank the power to win whatever he wants in life! When he needs to withdraw the precious coin of knowledge to cash it in, he does so instantly.

These are only a few hints of some of the things memory power will accomplish for you. Once you turn the page and begin the next chapter, you will be turning over a new page that will change your life!

II

How to Develop a
Thinking-Machine
Memory

"Let all things be done decently and in order."
—I CORINTHIANS 14:40

Unless a definite plan or systematized method of procedure is adopted and followed, no government, business, or institution can be successfully operated and managed.

So it is with all things.

In order to develop a thinking-machine memory you *must* adopt a system and then follow it. The method I have employed has enabled me to successfully perform many mental feats that others thought were sheer wizardry. This is hardly the truth. I merely practiced a memory or mnemonic (*nee-MON-ick*) system. You are about to learn this same system. Just as a man with poor vision uses eyeglasses to help him see better, so you and I can use these mnemonic devices to improve our ability to remember.

Apply yourself diligently. Concentrate. The time you spend carefully studying the principles on the following pages will enable you to develop and then cash in on the power of a thinking-machine memory.

Remember, a code of laws becomes your "servant" as soon as you understand and master it. But you are not the master of any set of principles until you work to put them into action! Once you do this, the art of memory will be your obedient servant.

The Three Secrets of a Thinking-Machine Memory

How many times have you heard someone say, *"That reminds me!"?* How many times have you seen or heard something that prompted you to snap your fingers and cry out the same thing?

When this happens we are reminded through a process which is called *non-controlled association.*

Until we see something that enables us to recall something else, we are virtually memoryless. We are forced to struggle and grope for that "lost" thought.

In order to develop the ability to recollect information at will, we must therefore use a system which makes it possible for us to pinpoint the exact memory and pluck it out. This is done through *controlled association.*

Controlled association is made possible through an orderly arrangement of storage places in one's mind in which *permanent* images are engraved. The thoughts to be remembered are then deposited, or assigned to the permanent places in a manner that connects them.

After this is done, we virtually peer into our memory bank, reach into a designated storage vault and re-collect the data on file. The reason why we are able to produce this deposited information speedily and with unfailing accuracy is because of these three secrets:

1. We have a bank storage vault in our minds in which we store our memories.
2. We have learned how to deposit our memories in our mental memory banks.
3. We have learned how to use our reasoning powers as data processing machines.

The three secrets of a thinking-machine memory which I am about to explain to you are incredibly simple, *provided you unleash your imagination.* Once you do this, the riches of the world will literally be yours for the taking. *Knowledge is wealth.*

Your mind will become the bank in which a whole new world of riches, of ideas, facts and learning will be on deposit for you to cash in at will!

**How to Develop Mental Storage Places
for Things You Need to Remember**

Here are the names of 20 objects found in most homes. Think of the ones in your own home and imagine them in this order:

In Your Kitchen	*In Your Bathroom*
1. Sink	11. Bathtub
2. Stove	12. Lavatory
3. Chair	13. Medicine cabinet
4. Table	14. Mirror
5. Refrigerator	15. Towel

In Your Living Room	*In Your Bedroom*
6. Rug	16. Bed
7. Easy chair	17. Bureau
8. Lamp	18. Wastebasket
9. TV set	19. End table
10. Window shade	20. Alarm clock

Read this list over and mentally *see* each one of these familiar objects in *your* own home. Next, associate them in sequence. For example, in your kitchen there are five items. In your living room there are also five items, numbered from six through 10. In your bathroom, the bathtub stands for number 11, the medicine cabinet stands for number 13, and the towel for number 15.

In your bedroom, the bed stands for number 16, the end table for number 19, and the alarm clock for number 20.

Now I'm going to show you how to use your imagination to associate images of things on a shopping list with the pictures of those things in your home which are so familiar to you. When you follow these instructions, you will prove to yourself that you do have an imagination and that you do have the ability to remember.

Here is a shopping list. In a moment I will explain how to remember it by associating each item on this list with the objects in your home.

1. Buy some mustard
2. Six pounds of hamburger
3. Molasses

  4. Facial tissue
  5. Grapefruit
  6. Corn flakes
  7. Eggs
  8. Spaghetti
  9. Window cleaner
 10. Coffee
 11. Ginger ale
 12. Onions
 13. Dog food
 14. Orange juice
 15. Cream
 16. Crackers
 17. Butter
 18. Soap powder
 19. Beef liver
 20. Matches

Please follow my instructions carefully. I want you to see each of these pictures with your imagination. It may sound "screwy," but do this exercise. It is of tremendous importance in developing your memory.

  1. Your kitchen sink full of mustard. You are actually washing dishes in it. See it now!
  2. Your stove with a gigantic hamburger on it. This hamburger is a yard square and six inches thick and you are cooking it on all four burners. See it now!
  3. Your kitchen chair covered with a pool of molasses. If you sat down in that, you'd never forget it. See it now!
  4. Your kitchen table with a gigantic box of cleansing tissue on it. These are at least a yard square and incidentally they'll be mighty handy in wiping up that molasses. See it now!
  5. Your refrigerator loaded with grapefruit. When you open the door, 50 grapefruit roll out on the floor. See it now!

Now don't look back but what do you see in your mind's eye when I say sink, stove, chair, table, refrigerator? Did you see those pictures? I'll bet you did. Let's try the next five items.

  6. Your rug is covered with corn flakes six inches deep. They crunch as you walk through them. See it now!

7. Your easy chair has six dozen eggs on it. If you sat on them, you'd never forget it. See it now!

8. Your lamp is decorated with fringes of spaghetti! See it now. The pull chain, the electric cord, all made of spaghetti.

9. Your TV set is turned on and there is a vivid commercial for a window cleaner. It is so vivid that the little man rubbing the window is actually reaching out into your living room and spraying you with his spray gun. See it now!

10. Your window shade with your wife shredding it in a coffee grinder and telling you that unless you buy the coffee, she'll brew the shade in the coffee pot!

Now think back. What did you see with sink, stove, chair, refrigerator, rug, easy chair, lamp, TV set, window shade? If this isn't coming back to you, make more vivid pictures. *See it now.* Take five more.

11. Your bathtub full of ginger ale. Whoever heard of bathtub ginger ale? See it now!

12. Your lavatory filled with onions. You're peeling them there and your tears fill the bowl. See it now!

13. Your medicine cabinet filled with cans of dog food. Every shelf of it! See it vividly, see it now!

14. Look in your mirror and see yourself drinking an enormous glass of orange juice, at least two quarts of it. See that reflection now!

15. See your towel covered with cream, dripping with cream! See it now!

Now look again into your mental file case and see the pictures you made with sink, stove, chair, table, refrigerator, rug, easy chair, lamp, TV, window shade, bathtub, lavatory, medicine cabinet, mirror, and towel. You're doing fine. Five more and you will have proved to yourself that you can be trusted to shop for 20 things at the supermarket and not buy a lot of impulse items.

Picture your bed filled with crackers. If you've ever eaten crackers in bed, you'll have a vivid recollection of how scratchy and annoying this is. See and feel it now!

Your bureau drawers are filled to overflowing with butter. Pounds and pounds of it melting in every drawer. What a crazy place to keep the butter. See it now!

Your wastebasket is filled with soap suds from the soap powder. You see yourself dipping a bubble pipe into it and blowing bubbles. See it now!

Your end table is piled high with 10 pounds of raw beef liver on it. Can you picture yourself reaching out in the middle of the night and putting your hand on that clammy liver? See it, feel it now!

Picture your alarm clock bursting into flames. It is on fire because when it went off, it struck a match. See it now!

Now write down what you saw with each of these items:

1. Sink _____	11. Bathtub _____
2. Stove _____	12. Lavatory _____
3. Chair _____	13. Medicine cabinet _____
4. Table _____	14. Mirror _____
5. Refrigerator _____	15. Towel _____
6. Rug _____	16. Bed _____
7. Easy chair _____	17. Bureau _____
8. Lamp _____	18. Wastebasket _____
9. TV _____	19. End table _____
10. Window shade _____	20. Alarm clock _____

Stop now and think a few minutes about what you have just done. At first this seemed strange to you. However, you have succeeded in associating a picture representing an object on your shopping list with a picture of something you couldn't forget because of your long familiarity with it.

This method of associating pictures representing items on a shopping list with items in your household may also be applied to memorizing the points in a sales talk or a speech.

Think of how much more confidence you will have when you know you can't possibly forget what you want to say on any occasion! Incredibly simple, isn't it? Yes, that's all there is to it. Now you know the principle of the first secret: *Have a permanent storage place in your mind in which to store memories.*

And this is the first step to take in the development of a thinking-machine memory. You see, when man uses an electronic brain, data is stored in the memory bank of the machine. When the machine is asked a question, it immediately locates the answer to that question by finding it in the place where it has been stored.

When you have stored the things you want to remember in their proper places, you are able to come up with the right answer.

Another way to think of your memory is to liken it to a safe deposit box vault. For instance, you might locate your kitchen sink, stove, chair, table and refrigerator in the first five bank vault spaces and imagine them arranged in orderly rows. The point is, you must become familiar enough with these "locations" and objects to enable you to recall that number 4 is a table and number 14 is a bathroom mirror quickly. When you are able to think of these mind pictures like this, they *represent* the numbers. Once you are able to do this, you are then able to recall the list of errands or for that matter, any list of things you want to recall, in or out of sequence, backwards and forwards!

Now, close your eyes and go back over the list of things you were supposed to "buy." Go over the list backwards and forwards. Amazing, isn't it? You can recall every item without a mistake.

Remember, as you see yourself participating in doing something ludicrous and ridiculous with the objects in your permanent memory bank you are also vividly seeing the things you want to remember. Once you become accustomed to seeing these images in your memory bank it will be second nature for you to connect anything you want to remember and deposit these things for safekeeping until you want to recollect them.

Now memorize this list of images in sequence and assign them places in your memory where they will always be found when you want to recall them.

1. hat
2. hen
3. ham
4. oar
5. whale
6. shoe
7. key
8. wife
9. pie

An easy way to connect them in sequence so you won't forget their order, is to *visualize* like this:

1. See your favorite *hat* in the first place.
2. See the *hen* in the second place using your *hat* in the first place, as a nest. You are shooing the *hen* out.

3. Instead of returning to her second place, the *hen* lands atop the *ham* in the third place and lays three eggs on it.

4. You grab the *oar* from the fourth place, swat the *hen* and she flies back to the second place where she belongs. The three eggs the *hen* has laid on the *ham* in the third place makes the *ham* slip into the air and land right in the mouth of the *whale* in the fifth place. You jump down, return the oar to the fourth place where it belongs.

5. Then you leap upon the *whale's* back and take the *shoe* from the sixth place and swat the *whale* with it. The *whale* disgorges the ham which flies back to the third place where it belongs.

6. The *whale* in the fifth place swats you with his tail and knocks you into the air. You drop the *shoe* in the sixth place where it belongs.

7. Then you tumble head over heels onto a huge pile of *keys*. You select a *key* from the seventh place and creep over to the door to your house and put the *key* in the lock.

8. But your *wife* in the eighth place spots you coming home at 8 A.M. and she seizes the *pie* from the ninth place and lets you have it right in the face.

9. You return the *pie* to the ninth place and kiss your *wife* in the eighth place, return the *key* to the seventh place, the *shoe* in the sixth place is yours so you put it on, then you avoid the *whale* in the fifth place, wipe off the *oar* in the fourth place, put the *ham* in the oven in the third place, feed the *hen* in the second place, and dust off your *hat* in the first place.

As you can see, fixing the sequence of these objects in your mind *is* easy. Later on, I will explain why each of these objects were chosen in this list. For now, just remember that it's easier to remember *images* than abstract numbers or words.

Now let's make another practical application of what you have just learned. Here's another list of errands to remember. Connect these nine items with the nine objects you have just remembered.

1. Go to the hardware store for a pound of ten-penny nails.
2. Drop off your suit at the dry cleaners.
3. Drop off the books at the library.
4. Have the prescription filled at the drugstore.
5. Stop at the bakery for some bread.

6. Pick up your repaired watch from the jeweler's.
7. Buy some hamburger from the butcher.
8. Have the car serviced at the station.
9. Cash a check at the bank.

All you have to do in order to remember this list is to associate each item in the same manner as you associated the first list. I am requiring you to memorize this list deliberately. It is important that the principle be perfectly clear. Now, I will again explain how to do it.

How to Remember a List of Things to Do

When you connect the things you want to do with the basic objects in the compartments you've visualized, it is possible to remember them in any order, backwards, forwards, or out of sequence. But first, here's how to connect them. Use your imagination like this:

1. See your *hat* bulging and overflowing with nails. It is so heavy you can hardly carry it. The nails are sticking out through the hat, damaging it. You hear yourself saying it isn't worth a *dime* because you've just ruined it by carrying all those *ten-penny* nails in it.

2. You see yourself carrying a *hen* into the dry cleaning store and the clerk chasing the *hen*, which is wearing your suit, all over the establishment. You hear the *hen* clucking and saying it doesn't need its suit of feathers dry cleaned.

3. You see yourself carrying an armload of *ham* into the library. You see the librarian and all the people in the library making faces because you're all greasy from the hams. You see the library in an uproar because the librarian is calmly rubber-stamping the ham.

4. You see the druggist mixing your prescription with the *oar*. Instead of a mortar and pestle, he's using the mortar and the *oar*. The handle of the oar is so long and unwieldy that he's knocking all the bottles and jars down as he uses the *oar* to mix your prescription.

5. You see yourself standing in the *whale's* mouth buying bread from the baker who tells you this is his way of beating the high rent situation. You see the smoke rising from the whale's spout which is the chimney for the baker's oven.

6. You see yourself testing your repaired watch at the jeweler's by

pounding it to pieces with the *shoe*. You are pounding it and grinning at the jeweler, complaining that he didn't do a good job because all the works are coming out. He puts the works in the shoe
and you pay him.

7. You see yourself at the butcher's watching him grind up *keys* in
the meat grinder. You imagine yourself eating that meatloaf and
breaking your teeth on the ground-up keys.

8. You see your *wife* crawling out of the hood of your car. You see
the wife wiping the oil dipstick on your car with her apron and
tasting the gasoline with a tasting spoon.

9. You see yourself endorsing a *pie* and cashing it at the bank. The
teller cancels it with a rubber stamp and the juicy pie splashes
you both.

Since you have now learned the first 9 place assignments of objects
which are going to become part of your permanent mental filing system,
make a clear visualization of these familiar objects:

		10. toys
11. tot	12. twine	13. thumb
14. tire	15. till	16. dish
17. duck	18. dove	19. tub

For number 10, see yourself buried under a mountain of *toys*. Or
perhaps see some *toys* which are familiar to you. For number 11, visualize
the *tot* of a friend or neighbor's, or perhaps your own *tot*. For number 12,
picture a huge ball of twine. Number 13, your *thumb*. Number 14, an
auto *tire*. Number 15, the *till* or cash register in a store with which you
are familiar. Number 16 is a *dish*. This is easy to remember when you
visualize a *dish* which is familiar to you. For number 17, picture a *duck*,
either life-like, or perhaps like a cartoon. Number 18, see the *dove* of
Peace. Number 19, visualize your bathtub filled with water, or perhaps
some other tub with which you are most familiar.

Now associate the list by using your own imagination.

Remember, the secret is to stretch your imagination. Really
s-t-r-e-t-c-h i-t! Picture each object in the spaces on the first wall at your
left.

After you have engraved each image into its respective place in
sequence, review the entire list twice, first forwards, then the second
time backwards. Say aloud to yourself, *1 is a hat, 2 is a hen, 3 is a ham*, etc.

Easy, isn't it?

You have now mastered the first step in the development of your hidden memory power. As you now understand, you merely deposit a series of fixed images in your memory bank and then through a process of *controlled association* you visualize the things you want to recollect in a ludicrous or ridiculous manner, always tying them in with the permanent images.

Review the questions following and then test what you have just learned by asking a friend or relative to call out a new list for you to remember.

REVIEW QUESTIONS

Circle the correct answer:

1. What is the *first thing* to do if you are to develop a thinking-machine memory?
   (a) Learn how to memorize   **(b)** Adopt a memory system   **(c)** Study mnemonics.
2. What is the first secret of how to develop a thinking-machine memory?
   (a) Let your imagination go   **(b)** Don't let your imagination go.
3. Controlled associations are easy to remember when they are:
   (a) Ridiculous and ludicrous   **(b)** Not ridiculous or ludicrous.

Answers: 1. b   2. a   3. a.

III

The Secret of How

to Remember Numbers

"Nothing is secret which shall not be made manifest."

—LUKE 8:17

We are all familiar with time-saving abbreviations, codes and various forms of shorthand.

The names of states, for example, are abbreviated so frequently that we have no difficulty recognizing Fla. as Florida, Me. as Maine, and S.C. as South Carolina. We go a step further and recognize instantly the organizations represented by these abbreviations: AA, AAA, BPOE, and IOOF.

Often, this form of mental shorthand creates words that eventually become part of our everyday language. *Snafu* is an example, from Navy usage meaning "situation normal, all fouled up!"

Retail stores use codes such as the following to conceal wholesale prices and other information from retail buyers.

1	2	3	4	5	6	7	8	9	0
C	O	S	T	P	R	I	C	E	X
N	A	K	E	D	G	I	R	L	S
C	U	M	B	E	R	L	A	N	D
S	A	V	E	Y	O	U	R	X	T
A	M	P	F	E	C	T	I	O	N

All types of businesses use various numbers to refer to the forms and procedures in their office systems. For instance, I once worked in an office where a form No. B-86 was used to record the transfer of merchandise. Whenever we wanted to transfer some goods, we simply said, "B-86 that to Albany," or wherever it was to be delivered.

Everyone uses codes and abbreviations to save time, materials and effort. One of the most extensive code systems used today is the Gregg Shorthand method. Another is the Stenotype machine used by court reporters and others for taking fast dictation. With these systems a stenographer is able to take down, verbatim, long letters, complex instructions, legal testimony, and other types of dictation. Considering that the average radio or TV commercial lasting one minute averages 125 w.p.m., and the average employer dictates at a rate of speed of about 100 w.p.m., a competent knowledge of the shorthand system is a must if the secretary expects to keep her job.

So it is with all things. We must understand and know our business tools and how to use them. Knowledge of shorthand is a tool. When it is known thoroughly and can be put into use skillfully and expertly it pays.

Since you have already learned the first 19 words which name the objects in the safe deposit compartments in your memory bank, you *already know* part of the secret of how to remember numbers!

The arrangement of letters in those words *also* has another meaning. It forms a number code.

The code you are about to complete learning might well be called a system of "mental shorthand." This code was first invented by Gregor von Feinaigle who introduced it in Paris in 1807. It was later perfected by M. Aimé Paris in 1823. Carl Otto, a Danish mnemonist, simplified it, translated it from French into German and introduced it on the continent about the same time another man, Francis Fauvel-Gouraud came to America and also hit upon the same idea. It was Gouraud's system, first taught in 1844, which has been in use since then.

This code can be learned in a few minutes.

It will unlock tremendous new areas of memory power within you! You will be able to instantly remember all numbers, prices, classification and serial numbers, seven-digit phone numbers and even entire financial statements once you master this easy code.

This is the most important chapter in this book.

Pay close attention and learn these easy rules. This should be super-easy because you are already prepared with a basic knowledge of the numbers from 1 to 19.

How the Number Code Works

Suppose you are driving along a highway and see some license plates with the following letters on them instead of numbers. See if you can make words out of these letters by adding the vowels:

a - e - i - o - u

Or the consonants:

w - h - y

For instance, R K S becomes *Ra*K*eS.* S L T could become Sa*LT.* Write your answers in the spaces provided.

1. D G _____	6. G T _____	11. C T S _____
2. M T _____	7. R M _____	12. B L T _____
3. R D _____	8. S L _____	13. R S H _____
4. B D _____	9. P L T _____	14. C H S T _____
5. F T _____	10. J T _____	15. B R N _____

The exercise you have just completed illustrates how much easier it is to remember complete words than groups of letters. You remember from the previous chapters that it is easier to remember concrete pictures than abstract words. Numerals are abstract digits. It is impossible to remember them in long or complicated sequences unless they are translated into *picture words.*

As you already know, the following words represent numerical equivalents in the form of objects or words you have visualized.

ha*T*	he*N*	ha*M*
oa*R*	wha*L*e	*SH*oe
*K*ey	wi*F*e	*P*ie

For the number one we substitute the consonant "T." When you need a word picture for the digit "1," you can use the word "*T*ea" or "*T*ie" since all vowels are wild and have no numerical value.

The consonants "W," "H," and "Y" are wild also. This is easy to remember when you say to yourself: "*W-H-Y are the vowels a, e, i, o, u wild?*"

To simplify the explanation, the consonants or letters with numerical values or equivalents have been *italicized* and capitalized.

In the first compartment of your memory bank is the word haT, the picture word for the number "1." Your picture word for the number "11" is ToT. If you want a word picture for the number "111," it could be TighT Tie. You find it easy to remember that T equals "1" when you remember that T has one down stroke.

An important thing to remember is that it is the consonant *sound* and not the way the word is spelled that counts.

For the digit "2" use the consonant "N." Notice that the "N" has two down strokes like the roman numeral II. The word picture heN equals "2." Another word could be Noah. Another could be wiNe. Notice how easy it is to remember when you recall that the vowels and W-H-Y have no number values.

Your word picture for "22" is NooN. Another word could be NuN. And as you already know, "12" is TwiNe and "21" is kNighT. You see the illustration of the rule that it is the *sound* that counts in the word kNighT. Here the silent consonants are not counted because they literally are not heard.

"3" is the equivalent of the consonant sound "M." Note that with a little stretch of the imagination the "M" resembles the roman numeral III. Additionally, the written "M" has three loops and three down strokes. You already know that haM is the word picture for "3." Other words can be heM, hoMe, May, hyMn and so on. Your memory bank image for "33" is MoM. The Hawaiian dress MuuMuu is another choice.

What's the picture words you remember for the following 13 _____ 23 _____. See how easy it is?

An easy way to form words is to go through the *a, e, i, o, or u and w, h, y,* letters mentally, in that order, testing them to see how they fit between the consonants. You will be amazed at how quickly you will form words which are apropos to the situation.

"R" is the consonant which is equivalent to "4." It is remembered easily when you recall that the written word fouR has four letters. "R" is the fouRth or last letter of the word fouR. With some applied imagination you can picture the resemblance between "4" and "R." Your word picture for "4" is oaR. It could also be eaR, haRe or aRRow.

This brings us to another rule which is easy to remember. When a double consonant such as in the word aRRow is used, it is only counted as *one* consonant.

For the number "44" the word you have already learned is waRRioR. Your word for "14" is TiRe; "34" is MaRe; "24" is NeRo.

An interesting fact about the roman numeral "L," which means 50 but in this code is the equivalent of "5," is this curiosity. The original of the "L" symbol is the human hand! In the market places of ancient Rome, goods were bought and sold in much the same way as they are sold today at our auction sales. The bidders usually kept silent and relied upon hand signals. The outstretched palm, fingers close together, tips pointing up, thumb out straight, was the first "L." Our "V" for victory sign meant "5" to the ancient Romans and thus the derivation of "V" the roman numeral. "VI" was indicated on one hand by popping up one finger beside the "V" of thumb and forefinger. "VII, VIII" also were hand and finger signals.

For the digit "5" a word picture in addition to whaLe could be wheeL or hoLLy. "55" could be LiLy or whaLe-oiL. Your word picture for "45" is ReeL. AeRiaL, RaiLway and RaiL are also equivalents for "45."

Test Yourself to See How Quickly and How Well You've Learned the First Half of the Code

Here are a series of numbers. Make your own word pictures for each. If you first write down the consonants with a space between the letters it will be easier to find the vowels that fit. For instance, T—T with the space between the letters helps you to visualize the words as you picture the vowels between them. You will find the words forming themselves!

11___12___13___14___15___16___17___18___
19___20___21___22___23___24___25___26___
27___28___29___30___31___32___33___34___
35___36___37___38___39___40___41___42___
43___44___45___46___47___48___49___50___
51___52___53___54___55___

If you were to stop right here you would be able to make practical use of what you have learned so far for numbers involving the first five digits.

How a Factory Foreman Started Using
This Code and Benefited at Once

Jack Murray, a cable plant foreman who was in one of my classes when I taught the first half of this code in split sessions, started putting what he had learned to work *before* he learned the second half!

Jack was so eager to tell me how he had cashed in that he almost tripped over his own feet the next evening when I arrived. The fire of enthusiasm was in his grin when he told me his story.

"You know, Mr. Hersey, I didn't believe this number code could be put to work so quick. I thought it would take me months to learn it. Just wait'll you hear what happened!"

Then Jack went on to tell me that a rush order came through for some wire harness assemblies for Raytheon. The order number was 24520. In a flash he was able to create a visual picture which could be associated with Raytheon's priority order. *New wiRe LiNeS.*

"I didn't know if the S was a zero or not, but it seemed to fit so I used it," Jack continued. "I was able to refer to that order without looking up the number when I had to discuss it with the supply room, the front office, the shipping and other departments. Ordinarily, I would have had to fumble around and look up the order, but I didn't have to do that, not once! And I had to call it off at least 15 times this morning."

This is just one of the many time-saving usages you too will be able to get when you put the number code right to work. Start using it immediately and keep right on using it. Soon you'll master it. Before you know it, you'll discover it really is the most valuable tool there is in the development of your hidden memory power.

Mastering the Second Half of the
Number Code Is Fun!

Jack Murray used some common sense logic which was almost second-nature to him when he utilized the "S" for zero. His instinctive usage of this consonant proved once again to me that the old masters who originally invented the code were geniuses!

The "S" sound and the "C" sound, as in "cipher," stand for zero or naught. Again, an easy way to remember this is to recall that the "S" and the "C" sounds, *as in "cipher," stand for "cipher"* which *is* "0" or zero!

Believe me, it's thrilling to see people starting to cash in on this so fast. Once they grasp the idea behind the system and make up their minds to put it to work, they suddenly discover that it's really fun. And that fun multiplies every time they cash in.

Now you begin to see how important this number code can be to you in remembering telephone numbers, financial figures, order and serial numbers, and in building the second vault of 50 compartments in your memory bank.

Further on, I'll show you how I used this same method to memorize the closing prices on one thousand stocks in less than five hours!

Right now, let's go on to the next five numbers.

For the digit "6" the "*J*" sound or the "*Sh*" or "*Ch*" sounds are employed. This is fun to remember when you think of the hissing sounds of a jet swishing through the sky. Too, the pronunciation of the "J" and the "Sh" sounds are similarly formed in the mouth. You might think of the "J" as a flipped-over "6" or perhaps as the handle of an umbrella which you are holding to shield yourself from the swooshing "Ch's" and "Sh's" of the flying J's. Some word pictures for the "6" are heDGe, Jaw, Jay, hitCH, huSH and waGe. "66" could be JuDGe or perhaps CHowCHow. "16" could be TiSSue (note the SS "sh" sound). "56" could be LaSH or LoDGe.

"7" looks like a hooK with a stretch of the imagination. Sometimes a hooK is used as a Key. Looking at the "7" another way, we could picture it as a deformed "K." The consonant sound of "K" or the hard "C" is the substitute for the number "7." A word picture in addition to hooK or Key could be Cow. "7" could be CaKe. "71" could be CaT. Remember, it is the "K" sound that counts.

For the digit "8" the consonant sound of "F" is used. "F" is written somewhat like the figure "8." Your word picture for the figure "8" is wiFe. Others could be Fee, haLF, hooF, or waiF. The pronunciation of the letter "F" is easy to make when you say aloud to yourself w-i-F-e, then *hear* the way the "F" sounds. "V" is also used as a substitute for the numeral "8" because it not only has the "F" sound, but becomes the plural of "F." wiFe—wiVeS, KNiFe—KNiVeS, etc. wiVeS equals "80." KNiFe equals "28." KNiVeS equals "280." "82" could be either FaN or PHoNe since it is the "F" *sound* that counts. "38" could be MuFF. (Again only *one* counted sound although there are 2 F's.)

The consonant "P" is the substitute for the digit "9." This is easy to remember when you imagine that you are seeing the "P" reflected in a mirror and you see it in reverse as a "9." A word picture for "9" in addition to *P*ie could be hoo*P*. "99" could be *PiPe*. "29" could be *NaP*. "49" could be *RoPe*.

The consonant "b" is the alternate for "9" and this is easy to remember when you recall that the "B" is formed the same way in the mouth as "P." Additionally, the "B" as in *B*oy when written in the lower case looks like an upside-down "9." "b" = "9" "p" = "9." *B*oa or *B*ow can be used as "9's." *B*oa*T* is "91." *P*u*B* is "99." *P*u*BL*i*C* is "9957." See how simple it is?

Now this is one important thing to remember. The consonant sound "d" or "D" is formed the same way as "T," the equivalent for the number one. It should not be confused with the "B." When you use your imagination and remember that the "9-year-old *B*oy is always *equal* to another *P*iece of *P*ie, oh-*B*oy!" and that "ho*T T*ea always ai*D*s the o*DD* wi*D*ow to find her equal in 1 (one) man," you will never confuse the "t-d" and the "p-b" relationships.

As I explained before, "0" is the symbol for cipher or zero which mean the same and therefore are logically interchangeable. "S" and "Z" and "C" which sound alike as in *cipher* are equivalent to "0." si*Z*e, si*SS*y, sau*C*e and i*C*e each are equivalents of "0." Your word for "10" is *T*oy*S*. "00" could be *Z*oo*S*. Your words for "20" and "30" are *N*oo*S*e and *M*e*SS*iah. "30" could also be *M*oo*S*e or *M*i*C*e. "40" could be *R*o*S*e.

Test Yourself to See How Expertly You've Learned the Second Half of the Number Code

Here's an exercise in the form of a test that will not only show you how easy it really is, but which will also give you a chance to practice. Again, work from left to right. Be sure to leave enough spaces between the consonant sound equivalents to help you place the vowels to form words.

16____	26____	36____	46____	56____	66____	76____	86____	96____
17____	27____	37____	47____	57____	67____	77____	87____	97____
18____	28____	38____	48____	58____	68____	78____	88____	98____
19____	29____	39____	49____	59____	69____	79____	89____	99____
10____	20____	30____	40____	50____	60____	70____	80____	90____
61____	71____	81____	91____	62____	72____	82____	92____	
63____	73____	83____	93____	64____	74____	84____	94____	
65____	75____	85____	95____	66____	76____	86____	96____	
69____	79____	87____	89____	88____	99____	98____	100____	

Fun, wasn't it? Now here is the breakdown for the number code for your review. At the back of this book is a "number dictionary" giving you 1,000 words. Later you can use this dictionary as an aid in learning the picture words for countless other combinations. However, you *must* learn this list of basic words. Here it is, beginning from 0 and ending with 100.

But first, remember, it is the sound that counts. For example, *ph* as in *phone* has the "f" sound, therefore *PHoNe* equals 82.

1	2	3	4	5	6	7	8	9	0
t	n	m	r	L	J	k	f	P	s
d					ch	ck	v	B	z
					sh	hard g	ph		soft c
					soft g	hard c			
					dg	Q			
					tch	ng (hard)			

0. Zoo	20. NooSe	40. RoSe	60. CHeeSe	80. oFfiCe
1. haT	21. kNighT	41. heaRT	61. SHaDow	81. FooT
2. heN	22. NooN	42. hoRN	62. JohN	82. VaN
3. haM	23. NaoMi	43. RaM	63. JaM	83. FuMe
4. oaR	24. NeRo	44. waRrioR	64. JaR	84. FiRe
5. whaLe	25. NaiL	45. ReeL	65. JeweL	85. FiLe
6. SHoe	26. NiCHe	46. RaJah	66. CHoo-CHoo	86. FuDGe
7. Key	27. NaG	47. RaKe	67. JoCKey	87. FoG
8. wiFe	28. kNiFe	48. whaRF	68. CHeF	88. FiFe
9. Pie	29. kNoB	49. RoPe	69. CHiP	89. ViP
10. ToyS	30. MeSsiah	50. LaCe	70. KiSs	90. BuS
11. ToT	31. MeaT	51. WaLleT	71. KiTe	91. BoaT
12. TwiNe	32. MoNey	52. LioN	72. Gun	92. PeNny
13. ThuMb	33. MoM	53. LaMb	73. CoMb	93. BuM
14. TiRe	34. MaRe	54. LuRe	74. CaR	94. BeeR
15. TiLi	35. MaiL	55. LiLy	75. eaGLe	95. BaLl
16. DiSH	36. MaTCH	56. LeaSH	76. CouCH	96. BeaCH
17. DucK	37. MiKe	57. LaKe	77. CaKe	97. BiKe
18. DoVe	38. MuFf	58. LoaF	78. CoFfee	98. BeeF
19. TuB	39. MaP	59. LoBby	79. CaB	99. PiPe
				100. DoZeS

The secret of how to remember numbers is now yours. The rest is up to you. Once you apply this knowledge and develop the habit of making up words for every number you want to remember you will never forget a telephone number, address, price or serial number. Here's how one of my students cashed in on the number code and later was promoted to sales manager because of his ability to remember numbers.

How Ralph Markham Raised Himself from Failure to Success When He Learned the Code

At 55, Ralph Markham considered himself a failure. He had worked for 22 years in an automotive supply house, but because of his poor ability to remember numbers, he was still just a parts clerk. Time after time he had been bypassed when a better job opportunity was available. Other men who were adept at remembering the complicated filing and serial number system were the ones who always seemed to get the coveted promotions Ralph felt he deserved.

He always lost out because he was too slow in his work. He had to take time out to double-check or look up the numbers he should have known.

Then he decided to do something about it. He came to one of my classes and before enrolling, told me that he doubted if he could ever learn. "You can't teach old dogs new tricks," he said, still dubious.

"This is not a trick, Ralph," I said. "I'll personally guarantee that if you apply yourself and learn my code for remembering numbers, you will succeed in your job."

Well, Ralph *did* apply himself. Within *ten days* he was able to call out hundreds of numbers without consulting the catalogues or inventory control sheets.

"I really doubted that it could be done," he told me weeks later after he had been promoted to parts department manager. "Then I happened to notice that the classification number for Mufflers was 38540. I was amazed. *MuFfLeRS* equals the number! And that was a number I could never in a million years remember!

"Other coincidences cropped up too. For example, in the *TRuCK TiRe* department, the vendor and classification numbers equal the words —147-14! Fuel Pumps were listed under 859-90, so I merely called them *FueL PiPeS!*

"Suddenly, a job I had gradually grown to hate became fun overnight! For the first time in 22 years I actually enjoyed my work! Within a week I was able to call out most of the numbers everyone else had to stop in order to look up. Before long my boss took notice. He wanted to know what had gotten into me all of a sudden. He couldn't get over how everyone was asking *me* for the numbers instead of taking the time to go through the cards."

Yes, Ralph now holds the managerial job he should have had years before, all because he applied himself and put the number code to work with the memory system you have learned so far in this book.

No matter what your age, or what kind of job you have, this number system will also work for you too!

Now here are some things to review. Don't skip over them. Study diligently.

REVIEW QUESTIONS

1. What makes it possible to remember numbers by translating them into words?
2. Why is the ability to remember numbers so important in everyday life?
3. Which are the "wild" letters that do not have numerical equivalents?
4. Which are the two consonants which equal No. 1?
5. What is the rule to remember about the "t" "d" relationship and the "p" "b" relationship?
6. What words can you make up from your address, telephone number, social security number, and license tag number?
7. Can you invent words which describe the serial numbers of the following items?

No. **0751-2** Refrigerator _____

No. **314-01** Gear _____

No. **741** Target Rifle _____

No. **1390** Wristwatch _____

NOTE: Review the preceding pages whenever you cannot answer a question without hesitation. It is important that you thoroughly understand the text before going on to the next chapter.

By all means, memorize the basic word list of the first 100 words. You should stop at this point and commit this list to memory, following the same procedure as outlined previously.

Answers to No. 7:
ICe CoLD heN refrigerator (No. 0751-2)
MoToRiZeD gear (No. 314-01)
aCcuRaTe target rifle (No. 741)
TiMePieCe wristwatch (No. 1390)

IV

How to Deposit Memories in Your Mental Safe Deposit Boxes

> "We REMEMBER the facts, and we can also RECALL THEM into the mind at pleasure. The former is MEMORY; the latter is that modification of it which we call RECOLLECTION."
>
> —ABERCROMBIE
> *On the Intellectual Powers*

Now you begin to see that memory is in reality a *power*. In everyday life he who has the gift of a trained memory possesses the one indispensable requisite for leadership and success. He who leads, or wants to lead, must be skilled in the use of the power of his memory.

So it is in all things. One must be skilled in a systematic way of doing things if he is to use his power at full capacity.

There is a simple method to use which will enable you to deposit memories in your mental safe deposit boxes. For ease of remembering, I have named this the *CASH DEPOSIT* formula.

Just as there is a regular procedure to follow when making out a bank deposit slip to put money in your bank, so must you also follow some rules when banking your memories. Here it is. Study this for a few moments, then read the detailed explanations. After that, put it to use for several days until you have mastered the idea and then forget it. Mind you now, this is the first and *last* time I'm telling you in this book to forget something! Just remember to use the *CASH DEPOSIT* formula until you are adept at memorizing, then discard it.

The Cash Deposit Formula and How It Helps
You Deposit Memories for Later Recall

Concentration	Concentrate on what you see or hear.
Association	Associate with your permanent box images.
Sight	See your associations in action.
Hearing	Hear and listen to better understand and see.
Deposit	Deposit only enough to help you remember.
Exaggerate	Exaggerate every thought to see it better.
Pictures	Pictures, not abstracts, are remembered.
Oddities	Oddities, the odder, the better.
Silliness	Silliness makes recollection super-easy.
Ideas	Ideas must be concrete interpretations.
Thoughts	Thoughts must be understood clearly.

How to Concentrate

Visualize yourself inside your memory bank with your sole attention on the safe deposit boxes into which you are depositing the ideas you want to remember. You must *see* the picture of the actual place the memory is to be housed. As time progresses, you will become more and more adept at this and before you know it, your entire concentration processes will be focused on what you are committing to memory.

Concentration is nothing more than hard thought which is fixed upon one thing at a time. Erase everything else from your mind except that which you are seeing or hearing. Do not permit your thoughts to stray.

Finally, see *yourself* physically depositing that memory in your mental memory bank. When you are able to do this, you *are* concentrating.

How to Associate

Always see one object doing something to or in connection with the next object. Get into the act. For example, if you want to remember to buy paint and a brush, you might see yourself holding your *hat* which is full of paint. The *hen* is in the next compartment holding a paint brush in her foot. When she flies up to dip the brush in the paint in your hat, the paint splatters you.

When you use this technique of controlled association with fixed objects in fixed places, it's practically *impossible* to forget anything you have properly deposited in your memory bank.

How to Use Your Sight and Hearing
Properly

You must clearly see and hear before you can make a memory deposit you will be able to withdraw later. Focus your sight on the object to be remembered and see it in your imagination. Hear it, or perhaps taste or feel it. But in any case, allow your senses to get into the act.

Remember the old gag kids still pull by sucking on lemons while standing before a bandstand upon which musicians are playing wind instruments?

When you permit your senses to become involved, the impression is always keen and not easily forgotten. Feel that pie thrown into your face, feel the hot juices and sticky mess oozing down. See yourself full of pie and you won't forget.

Why You Shouldn't Try to Remember
Verbatim

The secret of remembering is in the memorization of the general thoughts behind the thing you want to recall, rather than in the word-for-word memorization.

When you are fixing your attention on all the words, you misunderstand or fail to comprehend the ideas behind those words.

Relax, listen carefully and concentrate on what's being said. Remember only the key phrases and deposit only a word or two at a time. When you follow this procedure, you will be amazed at how much you are able to repeat by rote.

In other words, only digest an *outline* of what is being studied. Deposit in your memory the "cue" words only.

Relax. Do not try to grasp every word. Assume a devil-may-care attitude and select only the key words or idea images of what you want to remember.

We often fail to remember because we worry about forgetting or else try to remember too much. Deposit the idea and go on to the next. Then go back and review the first deposited idea.

How to Exaggerate

We think in pictures. Therefore, we must learn to use words as tools to conjure up the pictures. When we embellish these mental photographs by exaggerating the size, shape, quantity, we make it indelible.

Notice how difficult it is to forget an image of that pie hitting you in the face and the filling oozing down over your clothes? That image can be made even more unforgettable when you see yourself being baked in a gigantic pie.

The rule is simple. Merely overstate, intensify and magnify your mental image. That's all there is to exaggeration.

How to Think in Pictures

Look at this list of words and try to concentrate on each word for at least five seconds.

hero
brave
coward
cowardice
dunce
ignorance

You see it's easy to *visualize* a hero, but difficult to form a picture of an abstract word such as brave. You can see an image of a cringing coward, but it's difficult to form a picture of cowardice, or ignorance. You can see a picture of a schoolboy sitting in the corner wearing a dunce cap, but you can't think of an image or mental picture that fits with the word *ignorance*. Therefore, you must link the abstract with the concrete word in order to form a clear mental image. For example:

I see a *brave hero,* beaming proudly, arms folded across his chest, one foot resting on the chest of a vanquished enemy. He is being showered with bouquets and applause.

I see a *cowardly coward,* cringing beneath a bed, shivering with fear, trembling in terror. This is *cowardice.*

Get the idea? Simple, isn't it?

How to Think in Pictures that Are Oddities

Carrying the exaggeration a little further, let's suppose you want to remember a man who is a sports car enthusiast. You can conjure up an image of this man that you'll never forget by imagining that he has a body like a sports car, wheels for legs and headlights for eyes. This is an oddity.

Another oddity would be to visualize someone with a bad temper with a volcano for a head blowing his top. Still another would be an image of a woman whose reputation as a gossip is notorious. How would you see her? With a huge megaphone permanently attached to her mouth, of course!

How many oddities can you image from the following suggestions?

A watchful boss or teacher
A straw boss
A person who always complains of being ill
A greedy person
A stubborn person
A busy housewife

Naturally you'll see the watchful boss or teacher with eyes in back of his head, the stubborn person with the ears of a mule, the busy housewife with six pairs of hands, etc.

When you practice thinking in exaggerated pictures containing oddities, it will be virtually impossible to forget. Try it by starting now, and be convinced!

Why Silliness Makes Recollection Easy

Hickory-dickory-dock are the words that make up the nonsense rhyme that recalls automatically: *the mouse ran up the clock. Rub-a-dub-dub* reminds us of *three men in a tub.*

These are silly nonsense words that make recollection easy through nonsensical association. The same principle as applied to remembering things in everyday life is extremely effective. For example:

There's tightwad Joe who owes all that dough and never lets go of my big toe when I ask him for my dough.

Mary, Mary quite unwary, how do you want to go?

Jack be nimble, Jack be quick, tell me Jack, how's your friend, is he still sick?

A is for alibi that I'll need if I don't bring home something to read.

Abracadabra do, three things I must do, etc.

As you see, you must utilize the silly nonsensical thoughts with which you are most familiar in order to create vivid images to deposit in your memory bank. In other words, you associate the things that you want to remember with other things you have previously remembered. If you are able to make up a nonsense image, perhaps visualizing three people you want to remember as the "three men in a tub," you would couple this image and recollect it clearly by saying: "rub-a-dub-dub," etc.

When you master the art of using the inane and silly thoughts which are so deeply instilled in all of us, the recollection is easy because remembering becomes *fun*. (Reread the quote from Abercrombie on the first page of this chapter and contemplate this for a few moments.) Silliness and nonsense convert difficult-to-remember facts and serious things into amusing mental images which become a pleasure to recall.

Nothing in life is so dull or serious that it can't be made into something that's fun to remember. When something is humorous or incongruously ridiculous, recollection *is* easy because it's fun!

How to Convert Ideas Into Concrete Images

To remember an abstract idea is difficult, if not altogether impossible. Therefore, it is vital to visualize an image or mental picture that immediately recalls to mind the abstract idea you want to remember. We have already discussed this briefly under the section on *how to think in pictures*.

Let's take the same list of words and add abstract "idea" words to them.

Patriotic brave hero
Traitorous coward
Foolish ignorant dunce

To see a *patriotic brave hero,* I visualize a *patriot,* Patrick Henry making his famed speech. He is brave and a hero and I picture that clearly.

To see a *traitorous coward,* I picture *Benedict Arnold.* He is hiding under a bed and the people he has betrayed are coming toward him with muskets.

To picture a *foolish ignorant dunce,* I visualize a boy from my school days who was so foolish that he preferred to remain a dunce and after clowning his way through the fifth grade three times was finally expelled.

Of course you should draw upon your own store of knowledge in order to convert abstract words or ideas into concrete images. Now test yourself on these:

> The face that launched a thousand ships
> Freedom to worship
> Imagination is the air of the mind
> The worst fraud is to cheat yourself
> Confidence is to have hope and trust

As time progresses, you will become more adept at the technique of converting abstract ideas into concrete pictures you can *see* in your mind's eye. Be patient. Make a concerted effort and you'll discover how easy it is!

How to Understand Thoughts

The two phrases, *the worst fraud is to cheat yourself; confidence is to have hope and trust,* are *thoughts* more than they are ideas. In order to understand them, you must first reduce them to the germ of an *idea* or *meaning.* What does the first phrase mean? *Don't cheat yourself.* Cheat means fraud and fraud is the worst kind when you cheat yourself.

Now that you understand the *idea* behind the thought, let's reduce it to an image. You see yourself holding a bag of gold in your right hand while your left hand steals into the bag when you aren't looking and cheats you. Or you can see yourself being cheated by a merchant in the image of yourself.

Understanding the thought behind the second phrase is easy. To visualize yourself sitting on the seat of a unicycle with a gigantic quarter for a wheel atop a hope chest is one way of representing the thought. You can see the word *trust* on the enormous coin-wheel and you are able to register the entire thought in your mental safe deposit box.

Basically, we cannot deposit anything in our memory banks until we reduce it to something we *understand,* then to something we can *see* or *visualize*. To try depositing thoughts we do not understand is like trying to deposit foreign money in our bank accounts. We must first *exchange* the strange money and convert it into standard, familiar currency.

The Secret of Learning

You cannot expect to learn anything simply by shoving it into your mind. Merely shouting at a baby who ventures too close to a fire doesn't teach the baby that fire is hot. Unless he has once been subjected to the pain of heat, the word *hot* is meaningless. Therefore he cannot learn what *hot* means.

On the other hand, if he has accidentally tasted some hot milk, or perhaps has burned himself on a cigarette or a hot stove, *he knows that hot hurts!*

And this is the secret of learning.

All learning is accomplished by adding things you do not know to things that you do know.

Think about this for a few moments. Now you understand the fallacy of trying to cram information into our minds verbatim, without understanding or *connecting* what we were trying to learn with that we had already learned.

Let's suppose you have a bill to pay. The amount is $14.92. What is the connection that immediately springs into your mind? Columbus discovering America in 1492, of course! That's all there is to it. The secret of learning is in adding things you do not know to things you already know.

How to Classify the Things You Remember

When you make a deposit at your bank you follow a definite procedure. Remember, you either make a savings deposit or a checking account deposit. The teller will require that you fill out the proper deposit slip. If you are depositing your money in a Christmas Club Savings Account or in a regular savings account, you must fill out the proper deposit slip. Likewise with the regular or special checking account. In other words, a deposit you make at your bank is classified, then divided. This is done obviously to simplify the keeping of records and to control the banking system.

Your memory bank functions best when the memory deposits you make are classified and then divided. Here's how it works.

Suppose you have to go over five different catalogues in order to select a list of items you want to buy for a home you are having built.

The contractor gives you a catalogue of electrical fixtures from which you are to make a selection.

You immediately picture the contractor wearing a *hat*. This is your connection with the first place in your memory bank. Next you visualize the hat lit up like a chandelier. He is wearing a chandelier for a hat. A chandelier is an electric device, therefore you have arrived at the classification of the catalogue.

But you are to choose nine different items. Where will you place the memories of those things? That's easy. You form an additional memory bank in the place where the contractor is seen wearing the chandelier for a hat. It is classified and divided like this:

ELECTRICAL DEVICES—*hat*—(First classification)

1. transformer	2. inductor	3. magnet
4. relay switch	5. lightning-rod	6. charger
7. coil	8. fuse	9. plug

To the objects you see in each memory safe deposit compartment under the classification of Electrical Devices, you attach the things you want to remember.

Next, you receive a catalogue from the plumbing contractor. You imagine him holding the *hen* by its feet trying to loosen a pipe fitting by using the open beak of the hen as a monkey wrench. The memory bank under this category will be classified and divided like this:

PLUMBING DEVICES—*hen*—(Second classification)

1. toilet	2. nipple	3. male fitting
4. wrench	5. lift pump	6. chisel
7. hacksaw	8. file	9. pipe

As you see, there really isn't much to classification. When you use common sense and group related items that naturally go together, then associate them, you have a basic nomenclature, or division of memory storage places into which you may index and file away countless numbers of thoughts.

Remember, you must first make the classification, then make it ridiculous before it can be made to stick!

Review Questions

1. Why must the **CASH DEPOSIT** formula for depositing memories be followed?
2. What is the test of concentration?
3. Why is association so important a factor in any memory system?
4. How must you use your senses in order not to forget?
5. Why is it important **not** to be tense or ill at ease when mnemonizing?
6. What is the rule of exaggeration?
7. What is the rule for developing the knack of thinking in pictures?
8. Why is it that oddities, ridiculous and silly things are easily recollected?
9. What is the rule to follow when you want to convert an abstract idea into a concrete object? Why must you not try to remember abstract things before translating them into concrete things?
10. What is the secret of learning?
11. What is the purpose of classification?
12. Have you formed mental images of numbers 20 through 29?

V

The Secret of

a Trained Memory

"I have a room whereinto no one enters
Save I myself alone:
There sits a blessed memory on a throne,
There my life centers."
—CHRISTINA G. ROSSETTI, *Song*

The dictionary defines the meaning of the word "train" as an orderly arrangement; a connected sequence; a regular order. A *trained* memory, in the sense that it is used here, means *a memory that has been made proficient as a result of drilling and practice*. It is a memory that has *formed habits which in turn result in dexterity of remembering and recollection*.

The only way a typist can become expert is by typing. The only way a pianist can become a good or a great artist is by playing. The only way an athlete can excel is by training. And the only way a masterful memory can be developed is by *training*.

This is the secret: in order to train your memory to function like a data processing machine you must train your mind to receive thoughts automatically. The memory safe deposit boxes must become so familiar to you that you can visualize them instantly, *without effort*. Once this degree of training is achieved, you will have a trained memory!

How to Train Your Memory to Function Automatically Like a Data Processing Machine

An automatic response is one that is more or less self-acting. When the basic list of memory storage compartments is so thoroughly known to you that you are able to instantly recall any number of any compartment, you have progressed through the first stage of development.

The second stage which makes it possible for your mind to function like a data processing machine is reached when you are able to remember with clock-work precision. When you are mnemonizing without being aware of the processes, and are following a habitual routine of translating the data and depositing it in the vault boxes, you've achieved the goal!

A push-button memory is possible once you've caused a self-acting reflex to be built into your memory system functions. You can develop the power of your memory by following this formula:

5 Ways to Make Your Memory Function Automatically

1. Test your mental images for
   a. distinctness
   b. vividness
   c. clarity of detail.
2. Time the speed of your memory.
3. Check yourself for accuracy.
4. Review and take inventory.
5. Practice and drill your mind.

How to Test Your Mental Images for Distinctness

Visualize yourself in your memory bank. Study the first compartment and examine the *hat*. Is it clearly seen? Can you see its form and shape, size and texture, color and quality? If not, make the image strong and distinct. Take a look at your *hat* again. Fix it in your mind as the symbol for number one.

Next, look into the next compartment. Is the *hen* distinctly seen? Can you hear her distinctly cluck-clucking? Can you feel her feathers? Perhaps smell her?

Turn away and look at the ham. Follow the same procedure.

When you take your time and examine each object for distinctness, you fix it so firmly in your mind that it's impossible for you to make a mistake.

*How to Test Your Mental Images for
   Vividness*

Look at your *hat* again. Is the color vivid? How does the material feel when you touch it? Can you see the worn places on the *hat?* Can you actually feel it on your head?

Examine the *hen* again. Is the color of her feathers, beak and feet vivid and realistic? Does she seem alive, really alive? If not, make her come to life.

When you deliberately take an examination of your memory bank for vividness you literally are checking to see that all the objects in the spaces are real and alive. Merely ask yourself, does it live and breathe so vividly that I can sense as well as see it?

*How to Test Your Mental Images for
   Clarity of Detail*

Once again examine the *hat.* Can you find details you've missed on the previous two examinations? How does the brim look to you? Is it even on all sides or is it out of shape? How about the shape of it? Is the crown just right or is it somewhat battered? After all, it is your favorite hat.

Now check the size of it. How does it feel on your head? Is it tight, or loose? How about the texture? Does it feel smooth or rough? Is the color fading in places? Is it a good hat, a cheap one, or a moderately priced one?

Ask yourself all these questions, then take another look at the hen. Can you see the color of her eyes, the arrangement of her feathers, the details of her feet, the lively look about her as she scratches around in that compartment number two?

As you see, the test of a mental image for distinctness, vividness and clarity of detail isn't complicated at all. Once you make this test, you will have a permanent image symbol you'll never mistake or hesitate in recalling.

When you link to these permanent images the things you want to remember, the attachment will be powerful and lasting with little chance of forgetting.

How to Time the Speed of Your Memory

Look at the second hand on a watch or clock. Begin when the hand moves by the noon mark and call off in order the first 29 objects in your memory bank. Did you make it in 29 seconds? If you did not, make the time test a second and third time.

After you have made it in 29 seconds, see if you can better that record. Later on, you can make the test backwards by odd numbers and then forward by even numbers.

How to Check Yourself for Accuracy

If possible, have someone listen to you as you reel off the order of the objects. The main thing is to *visualize* each number of each compartment as you call out the object. You must be 100 per cent accurate before repeating the process again. When you make a mistake and confuse the order of the boxes, begin again after correcting yourself.

The test for accuracy is in *seeing* each object as you name it. You must see it, however swiftly, in order to *be* accurate.

How to Review and Take Inventory

Call out the numbers of your mental safe deposit boxes at random and quickly name each object. Once during the review of your list make the mental image test for distinctness, vividness and clarity of detail.

Be like a bank examiner examining your memory bank. It is the most precious possession you have. Guard it well and see that each object is in its proper place.

How to Practice and Drill Your Mind

Boring repetition or recitation isn't the way to practice or drill your memory. Make it interesting. See how many new things you can remember to link with your basic list of objects. Test yourself, time yourself and then try to improve your accuracy and speed of recall.

The more you use your memory bank filing system as a data processing machine that stores information and the more you fill it with things to remember, the more effective and proficient it will become. The old adage, practice makes perfect, adheres here too. Once you have achieved a method of practice that has resulted in speeding up your ability to recall, continue to drill your mind regularly. Your memory bank becomes more powerful the more you use it. Remember, practice by making up games with yourself. Make your memory practice *fun*.

Why a Data Processing Machine
Is Like a Human Brain

Believe it or not, your brain has an enormous capacity that no computer memory machine can even begin to approach!

If it were possible to build a computer with the same memory power and reasoning power contained in the human brain, it would require a tremendous building.

Think of that for a minute.

Your brain can store from *ten million* to *one quadrillion* different memory "thoughts." Now you see why psychologists tell us that we only use less than one per cent of our potential brain power.

Here is why your brain is like a data processing machine: *It operates on the same premise.* A typical magnetic "memory" machine such as that used in a commercial bank to file records has a bank of "memories" or information on the "scanners" inside it.

When we feed the machine questions in the form of punched cards or tapes or other methods, the machine then goes to work. If it is in a bank where each account is kept on tape, it can give the balance of an account within seconds. If it is in a department store to provide management with sales data or other records, it can give the answers at once.

The data processing machine is controlled by circuits which enable it to "read" the stored information, come up with a logical conclusion and supply the answer wanted.

So it is with your brain, particularly when you use a systematized method of storing memories. When you scan the vaults in your mind for the information you've put away you are literally doing what the machine does. Only you can't do it as fast. But you can do it *better* and just as accurately!

And this is the secret of a trained memory: You are able to recall any memory that has been stored away previously when you are able to select the stored information with clock-work precision.

This is possible only when you know thoroughly every compartment in your memory bank and can process information in the twinkling of an eye. When you follow the principles explained on the previous pages, 5 Ways to Make Your Memory Function Automatically, before you know it you will have a trained, push-button memory!

The 5 Divisions of a Thinking Machine or Trained Memory

Continuing the analogy of the comparison of the human brain to the electronic calculator or computer, we find another set of similarities. I have listed the different functions of the machine and shown how they compare to the human mind.

It is surprising to note that we are using the same processes when we do the following:

- a. Input—we receive the data
- b. Symbolic logic—we employ logic
- c. Information storage—we remember
- d. Programming—we utilize instructions
- e. Output—we disperse information

Input, What It Is and How It Works

There are two types of electronic computers: The digital computer that *counts* numbers (like an adding machine) and the analog computer that *measures* a quantity (like a fuel gauge or voltmeter).

In the digital computer is an arithmetic unit or accumulator that gathers information, and when activated after being fed data or a question to be answered, acts on the data and supplies the answer in seconds.

An analog computer, like the digital computer, is not complex. Its main components are amplifiers and passive networks of resistors, condensers, and inductors. When the proper amplifiers are connected to the networks, any problem can be resolved. For instance, the Air Force Air Traffic Control system uses an analog computer to track aircraft and schedule their landings. This machine enables a control tower to land planes at the rate of one every 30 seconds so they do not get in each other's way. The computer calculates the proper flight pattern for each plane while other machines insert values indicating wind velocity and direction, the proper runways which are clear of traffic, then compares the course of the aircraft with the theoretical path it has plotted and relays corrections.

Your brain can accomplish the same tasks.

When you know how to receive information and then channel it to the stored knowledge in your memory bank, this is input. Your input of data is absorbed with machine-like precision because your memory has been trained properly to receive information. This has been accomplished through the practice of the rules on the preceding pages.

Therefore, this is the first division of a trained memory.

A print reader, operating on the same principle as the ones now being installed by the Post Office Department to read addresses on mail, is the ultimate in man-made input devices. It translates the words it reads on the printed page into computer language. You do the same thing when you search for stored information in your memory. In other words, your input process consists of using a form of mental shorthand to record information so that you can scan your memory bank and locate the desired information.

Symbolic Logic and How It Is Applied

Computers, like the trained human memory, are made up of simple circuits which are grouped and arranged according to the rules of symbolic logic.

Logic is basically the establishment of the truth of a fact or idea. Symbolic logic is the science of thought that establishes that what is true in one statement is true in all equivalent statements or propositions: For example:

1. All A is B. (All apples are fruits.)
2. Some A is B. (Some apples are winesaps.)
3. No A is B. (No apples are minerals.)
4. Some A is not B. (Some apples are not winesaps.)

These four examples are undisputed truths. Though they sound idiotic there is a reason for stating them here. Working only from those statements it is possible to deduce a number of additional truths.

For instance, if we change No. 1 into Nos. 2, 3, and 4, we see which are true and false:

1. All apples are fruits.
2. Some apples are fruits.
3. No apples are fruits.
4. Some apples are not fruits.

As you see, if we assume that No. 1 is true, then No. 2 is true *always;* however, Nos. 3 and 4 are obviously false *always.*

Any textbook on logic can explain this further. The point is, we apply symbolic logic by establishing symbols in our memory banks which represent facts or truths we have learned.

Employing logic we can form a statement like this:

All apples are fruits, and that
Mackintosh is an apple; then we deduce without a doubt that
Mackintosh is a fruit.

We apply symbolic logic when we think; however when we know the rules of logic, we are able to reach decisions based upon our knowledge of the rules. But more about that later in another chapter. The point is a trained memory uses the rules of symbolic logic as a foundation of its system.

The processes of a trained memory are controlled by logic. We employ it both logically *and* illogically; logically *or* illogically; logically *and/or* illogically. A machine cannot do this. Only man can accomplish it!

As I stated on the first pages of this book, it is necessary to understand the idea behind any and all facts before you can remember them accurately. Likewise, this is true when you are mastering a new method of doing something. As you have just seen from the analogy comparing your memory to a machine, your mind really is capable of far more than the machine! You not only can employ logic, but you can also apply the *illogical.* It is this facility that is the real secret of a trained memory.

Information Storage: How It Works

A computer, again like the human mind, requires several types of information storage, or memory. This is determined by whether the speed of recall or the amount stored is more important.

While the computer has a small, high-speed memory for instant insertion and disbursement of small amounts of data, so does the human brain. And the brain also has a larger information storage unit for information of a larger or more complex nature. So does the machine. Finally, there is a mass storage place in both the human brain and the computer memory machine for the accumulated knowledge which is arrived at by deduction.

An example would be, "Don't eat a poisoned apple!" We know that an apple is edible, but also that poison is deadly. Therefore our "sense" tells us through logic and memory comparison that we must not eat a poisoned apple. The machine reaches the same conclusion when the information which has been stored in the "brain" is compared against the "question" fed to it. Of course, the decision reached by the machine is reached by going through a complex path of switches which are nothing more than a simple series of yes-or-no switches.

Get the idea? The brain really is quicker than the machine!

Now, we progress to the stage where the machine becomes swifter than the human brain. Reaching the depths of the information storage with problems of a highly complicated nature, we find that the human mind cannot deduce answers as swiftly as the machine. This is because the machine, operating at an incredible speed, is able to "scan" the planes of its memory unit and come up with the solution to an equation within mere minutes that would ordinarily take an Einstein a century to deduce.

We are not concerned with this type of lightning calculation. Let's leave that to the machines. The point of all this is that we're concerned only with the ways and means which will make your life more productive, successful and happy through the development of your hidden memory power.

The use of your memory storage bank does work on the first and second level at a great rate of speed. However, on the third stage, it works more slowly. For simplicity's sake, we're only concerned with the first level in this book. But I point out these comparisons in the hope that it may leave you with a better understanding of the nature and power of your memory.

One curious fact, however, should not pass unnoticed. In the electronic brain, memory storage is contained in "places," either static (latching relays or punched cards) or dynamic, where the data circulates through an amplifier. The same thing takes place in your brain. Our older memories are contained in the subconscious or static form and the recent ones in the conscious or dynamic form.

When we establish a memory bank in our minds, in effect we are forming a memory unit. The list of 100 basic words you have already learned is the main unit. To this we can add many secondary lists. It is easy to expand your mental file spaces or memory shelves as fast as the need arises without having to know all the peg words in the number dictionary.

Let's assume you have learned the first 100 words. These are easy to memorize as you have proved for yourself, and they have become what I refer to as the standard list of 100 words. This may meet your needs for a long time. However, you may suddenly want just a few words over 100 or perhaps another complete list of 100 words. You can get these additional words by two simple methods.

By the first method you use an adjective in front of the standard word. If you want a number series from 100 to 200, you could make it up by using the adjectives "Hot," "Wet," or "White" in front of the standard words. You can also make other hundred series by using the following words to supply the first digit and putting them in front of the standard words.

1. Hot, Wet, White	Example:	111 White tot
2. New, Win, Own	Example:	212 New tin
3. My, Aim, Hem	Example:	313 My team
4. Wire, Hairy, Hire	Example:	414 Wire tire
5. Yellow, Oily, Wheel	Example:	515 Yellow till
6. Huge, Ashy, Wash	Example:	616 Huge tissue
7. Hack, Gay, Weak	Example:	717 Gay tack
8. Heave, Few, Wave	Example:	818 Wave taffy
9. Happy, Boy, Wipe	Example:	919 Wipe tape
10. Dice, Dizzy, Hideous, Dose	Example:	1010 Hideous toes

This can also be a useful way of remembering three digit numbers quickly. Use an adjective for the first digit and the standard word for the next two digits.

The second method is to use words for the numbers 100 to 200 which are natural associations with the words in the standard list. Let me illustrate.

Standard List	Secondary List
1 Hat	101 Cap
2 Hen	102 Chicken
3 Ham	103 Eggs
4 Oar	104 Stroke
5 Whale	105 Spout
6 Shoe	106 Lacing
7 Key	107 Door
8 Wife	108 Mother-in-law
9 Pie	109 Crust
10 Toys	110 Dolls

Your secondary associations might be entirely different from mine. I have found this type of list useful when I found a magazine or an article or series of speeches that ran somewhat over 100 pages or points. The process can be extended indefinitely.

Looking over your equipment, you can now see that the standard list gives you 100 words. The use of adjectives multiplies this so that you can have 1,000 words.

You could set up a secondary list based on each of those thousand words and have 2,000 words, pegs, or mental pigeonholes. On top of all this the number dictionary gives you words for a thousand numbers. Each of these would be used with one of the adjectives to multiply your pegs to 10,000 almost at once, if you need it.

I don't suppose for an instant that everybody needs all that I'm giving you. However, I hope you will consider it all so that you will know what to look for if you need help.

Programming: What It Is and How It Works

The term *programming* merely means giving instructions to the computer. An abacus is the original digital computer. When the modern Chinese of today use this simple device, which consists of strung beads on a series of parallel wires, they are very often able to tabulate and compute faster than an accountant using an electric calculator.

Because the beads are moved from one end of the wire to the opposite end, the abacus has a form of *memory storage*. When the beads are shifted, it can be said that the abacus is "programmed."

Oddly, this ancient device was the prototype of the modern digital computer in which relays and pulses take over the function of the beads.

In other words, to "program" is to ask a problematical question which can be answered by the stored information in the brain.

Another way of putting it is this: You understand the limitations of your mind and the rules it has learned, therefore you "program" your questions to conform to those principles. You know the steps you must take in order to solve the problem and you take them with clock-work precision. This is brought about through a clear understanding of the rules learned. When this is mastered, you have a trained memory.

Output: What It Is and How It Works

Output means the retranslation of your mental shorthand into everyday thoughts and language. What happens is this.

You have mastered the first 29 basic words in your memory compartments. If you were asked what was the sixth object in the sketches on page 6 at the beginning of this book, you should immediately visualize one of your favorite shoes. This is the shoe you substituted for the sixth compartment of your memory bank. And in this shoe you have visualized the one-eared rabbit.

Perhaps to better remember this, you may have envisioned the rabbit trying to hop around with the shoe and perhaps it was a one-eared lady rabbit who had given birth to a dozen little one-eared bunnies who were falling all over themselves trying to get out of the shoe.

You retranslate these memory images into one word: *rabbit*. This is output. Output means the retranslation of what you have logically or illogically planted in your memory storage compartments into sensible answers.

These, then, are the secrets of a trained memory. Regardless of what you plan to do with your hidden memory power once it's developed, it pays to remember this chapter.

Review Questions

1. What must you do if you are to train your memory bank to function like a data processing machine?
2. Name the five ways of making your memory function automatically.
3. What is the test of a mental image for distinctness? For vividness? For clarity of detail?
4. How do you time the speed of your memory?
5. Why should you check yourself for accuracy? Why does this build confidence in your ability to recall everything correctly?
6. Why is a data processing machine like a human brain?
7. Name the five divisions of a thinking machine or trained memory.
8. How is *input* similar to both the machine and the human brain in the sense it is explained in this book?
9. How is *symbolic logic* applied?
10. How does *information storage* work?
11. What is *programming* and what is meant by the term?
12. What is meant by *output*?

Review the list of 100 basic words until you know them so well you can call them out forwards and backwards.

VI

How to Remember
Number Series
and Statistics

"At Hiroshima
When the *Asia Foe* was *paralyzed*
By the death bomb that *coughed hell's* spit-fire
Over Hiroshima
The maimed and the wounded moaned and cried:
'Bow to your *maker, kneel,* Samana!
Pray for the vanished in the *atom's-fume* pyre
Of Hiroshima.' "

———————————————————————

What does the above free verse have to do with the topic of this chapter? Strangely enough, everything. When you examine the italicized words you find that they give you the following statistics:

Date of bombing	= ASia Foe PaRaLyzed	= 6 August 1945
Killed by blast	= CouGHeD heLl'S	= 78,150
Maimed or wounded	= MaKeR, kNeeL	= 37,425
Missing	= aToM'S—FuMe	= 13,083

And now *They* kNow the oFfiCiaL View: 128,658 (total) casualties. As you can see from this graphic illustration, the application of the number code is unlimited. Of course it isn't necessary to compose verse in order to link the dates and statistics with the facts pertinent to them. But what is important to learn is the fact that nearly *all* the facts you wish to connect with numerical equivalent words *can be* coupled with meaningful phrases.

What better descriptive phrase is there which tells when the Asia Foe was paralyzed? In the word A*S*ia, the "sh" sound stands for 6, the 6th day. *F*oe is the "f" sound for 8, the 8th month, August. Pa*R*a*L*yzed stands for 945, the year. Notice that the numeral "1" denoting the thousand has been omitted because it's hardly likely that anyone would make a thousand year error in citing any historical date.

The phrase "death bomb that Cou*GH*e*D* he*L*l'*S* spit-fire" is self-explanatory: 78,150 killed by the death bomb!

Another rule to remember in composing descriptive phrases of the words you want to couple is this. When you use connectives or words that enable you to make up understandable sentences, these words are *not* counted. Before we go further, I think this little parody on the nine parts of speech from a 19th century third grade reader will serve to remind you of some rules you may have forgotten.

THE NINE PARTS OF SPEECH

1. Three little words you often see
    Are ARTICLES—*a, an,* and *the.*
2. A NOUN's the name of any thing,
    As *school* or *garden, hoop* or *swing.*
3. ADJECTIVES tell the kind of noun,
    As *great, small, pretty, white* or *brown.*
4. Instead of nouns the PRONOUNS stand—
    Her head, *his* face, *your* arm, *my* hand.
5. VERBS tell of something to be done—
    To *read, count, sing, laugh, jump,* or *run.*
6. *How* things are done the ADVERBS tell,
    As *slowly, quickly, ill,* or *well.*
7. CONJUNCTIONS join the words together,
    As men *and* women, wind *or* weather.
8. The PREPOSITION stands before
    A noun, as *at* or *through* the door.
9. The INTERJECTIONS shows surprise,
    As *ah!* how pretty—*oh!* how wise.
    The whole are called nine parts of speech,
    Which reading, writing, speaking teach.

The reason I have introduced this little verse is not only to remind you of the parts of speech which you will use in forming your numerical sentences, but also to demonstrate a mnemonic device which is a powerful memory aid.

Now let's illustrate how this can be put to practical everyday use.

How to Remember Telephone Numbers

The cash value of the time you save by memorizing telephone numbers can easily be enough to pay your telephone bill.

It takes an average of one minute to dial information and request a number and an average of 72 seconds every time you open a telephone book, riffle through the pages and locate a number, then make a note of it before dialing.

Figure up what your time is worth to you in dollars or cents per minute and there you have it. It costs you money in lost time and effort, not to mention the frustration of making mistakes when you dial the wrong number because you got it wrong.

Take a good look at the telephone dial illustration and compose a new word to represent the exchange. Use the letters on the dial under the three digits of the prefix. Form a word which has a *meaning* to you.

Here is the way your dial looks with 3 letters under each hole except number 1 (one) and "Operator." *

1 —		6 MNO	
2 ABC		7 PRS	
3 DEF		8 TUV	
4 GHI		9 WXY	
5 JKL		0 —	

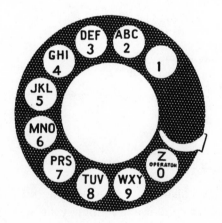

---

* The "Q" and the "Z" are the 2 missing letters. This is a good test of one's observation. Most people cannot tell you which letters are omitted.

Now let's suppose your number has been changed to 773-1432. Could you forget your number if you remembered *PRE*sident *TRuMaN*?

You see, you are right back to a simple word and four-digit memory proposition. The rule is simple. Merely adapt the letters on the phone dial for the prefix and compose numerical equivalent picture words for the remaining digits.

Of course, this simple rule is flexible. You may think of a better word by making all the letters of the dial work for you instead of using them in conjunction with the number code. Here's one a Miami, Florida, mortgage company uses tied in with an advertising message:

FOR FREEDOM FROM DEBT, DIAL FREEDOM
And here is their number: 37 3-3 3 0 6

An organization dedicated to helping people in desperate straits who are bent on suicide, urges them to dial: FRIENDS
And here is their number: 37 4-3637

Not all of us are so fortunate to be able to preselect our phone numbers or to be able to develop special words which we would prefer. Therefore it is up to us to apply our imaginations.

How the Number Code Enables You to Remember Phone Numbers and Area Codes

You know how to make words out of numbers. Let's apply that knowledge and a little imagination.

Area Code 617   = "Show-dog"
3-digit prefix 285   = "Anvil"
4-digit number 7705 = "Cake sale"

To remember this number I picture a show dog displayed on an anvil in the middle of a table at a cake sale. If I didn't need to remember the area code, I would merely use "anvil" and "cake sale" and make a pictorial association between the two.

When the telephone companies switched from prefix words to all-digit phone numbers it became difficult to remember numbers without transposing or forgetting digits. Because a picture word is easily retained, the number code permits you to make *all* phone numbers into image words which are appropriate.

You may make these into ridiculous pictures or into those which are appropriate to the person or business with which they are linked. For instance, the number of an animal hospital is 277-2030. Glancing at my number dictionary which is in the appendix of this book, I find "Hancock" for 277 and "nose" for 20 and "moose" for 30.

The picture I visualize is *John Hancock putting his John Hancock on the nose of a moose at the animal hospital.* I see myself taking the moose out of the animal hospital into the bank next door to try to cash the check which John Hancock has signed on the nose of the moose.

Occasionally you will come across a number which spells a significant word. I know an anesthetist whose number is 1120. When I saw it for the first time I immediately thought of the vowels to go between the letters: "D D N S." I came up with the word "deadens." He "deadens" pain.

0700 is the number of a mental hospital. I started thinking of the letters which would go between the consonants: "S K S S" and came up with "psychosis." The prefix to this number happened to be IV-4. From this I composed the word "ivory" because I once heard someone refer to the human head as "ivory." *Ivory psychosis* certainly is appropriate.

You will find that using the first 100 key or basic words in pairs, paired-up with the two pairs of digits, is the quickest method of stringing together phrases. To avoid reversing the order of the words, it is best to form your picture with the first pair of numbers in the equivalent word at the left of the mental picture and the other at the right.

6581 comes out "Chili" and "Foot." The action taking place in your mental images counts too, so if you visualize someone putting chili on their foot, you can't possibly reverse the digits. Amusingly, this particular number once came up in connection with a rather fat gentleman who had a frozen face and a cold personality. I have always referred to him as "Mr. *Chilly Fat.*"

Take the phone book and try it out *now.*

Many times you will find that the exchange is the same for most of your calls in a locale, so you only need to remember the last four digits. A representative list of three-digit prefixes can be found in the number dictionary at the back of this book. You will find ample suggestions there which will enable you to develop appropriate image words.

Another method which is quickly learned is to make a sentence or phrase in which the first consonant of each word is the key to the number.

Here is how I memorized a banker's number: 6—Just
                                              9—Pay
                                              1—The
                                              3—Money

If this had been a lawyer, I might have pictured him advising a client, "*Just Plead, Then Moan.*"

The important thing to remember about telephone numbers is this. You must take your time at first in the translation of digits into words or phrases that associate with the people or firms with which they are linked. You can make a fun thing out of this when you try. And making up words from numbers can prove to be more of a "game" than crossword or anagram puzzles. Here are a few numbers some of my students have been using:

FISH MARKETS   BRUSH SALESMAN
8 6   3 47 10   9 4 6   0 5 0 3   x

PARTY TOASTS   TRAIN STATION
9 41   1   0 1 0   1 4   2 0 1 6   2

How many numbers are you able to convert into meaningful image-words?

If you wish, you can count *only* the first three or four digits of a word when forming numerical equivalent words. As you become more adept you will find that the number dictionary at the back of this book will stimulate your imagination and enable you to think up additional words. When you are remembering three digits and a word such as PaRaLyzed (945) is really equivalent to "94501," you won't make the mistake of adding the extra digit if you knew when you selected it that you only needed to remember three digits.

The words above each contain more than three digits. This is because my students gave a great deal of time and thought to developing these number words. If you will note, in "Brush Salesman" there is a final "x" beneath the N or "2" equivalent, since it is not needed to represent a digit.

How a Yarn Broker Increased His Income
by $5,000 a Year Remembering
Phone Numbers

When Harry Paynter joined one of my classes he had an almost un-believably poor memory for phone numbers. Even though he had to use the same numbers over and over again, Harry was unable to remember them. As a result he had to depend upon his notebook in order to recall them. And every once in awhile the notebook would be mislaid. As an independent yarn broker who earned his livelihood calling on knitting mills and manufacturers, this was disastrous.

After adapting the memory system and the number code explained in this book, Harry began *overnight* making interesting and unforgettable words out of the numbers he had to remember. Now he is able to telephone his mills, processing plants and customers from his home office or from telephone booths along the highways without wasting time to hunt for a lost notebook. He went from a total inability to recall numbers to perfect and accurate retention by using the number code.

When Harry told me his story about two years after he had attended my classes, he added that he had increased his income by more than $5,000 a year! Here, for example is just one of the numbers he has committed to memory, and what yarn broker could forget such an association?

Area Code: 201 (nest) Prefix: 014 (sweater) 7450 (girls)
"A nest of sweater girls."

How to Develop a Money-making Memory for Rate Tables

When you have developed the ability to translate numbers into words with ease, you will find that you can remember series of sequences of numbers with little effort.

This is accomplished by storing each connecting idea in its proper memory deposit box in your mental bank. When you know the sequence of your memory compartments you are also able to store away thoughts *in* or *out* of sequence and still get them right, then be able to call them off in proper order. This is important when you only have time to study portions of a table. For instance, the following table used by a life insurance company is only part of the whole. If the entries under 20, 25, and 30 were out of sequence, the other entries could be remembered and fitted into place at a more convenient time.

However, any chart with which a salesman works constantly can and should be memorized in its entirety because it enables him to recall important facts which close sales at the blink of an eye. When an agent knows his data for costs, cash values, and amounts which can be purchased for $10.00 monthly at certain key ages, he can use the knowledge to close sales.

The man who is able to demonstrate such an ability and such a thorough knowledge of his business is the man who is respected by his clients.

And when a potential customer sees for himself that the man with whom he is doing business knows his business backwards and forwards, he buys with confidence. No one likes to buy from a man who has to fumble and stall and spend valuable time "looking up" prices and information.

Now here is a sample table and the code words I selected and filed in my memory storage compartments:

| Age | Annual Premium | Cash Values per $1000 | | | Amount Purchased by $10 Monthly |
		10 yrs.	20 yrs.	Age 65	
20	$12.58	$ 98	$229	$606	$9100
25	14.69	114	264	585	7793
30	17.34	133	303	560	6602

Now here are the code words:

20	12.58	98	229	606	9100
20	TiNy LoaF	BeeF	NuN Buoy	CHoiCe aGe	BoaT houSeS
25	14.69	114	264	MuSeuM	585
25	TaR SHiP	DaughTeR	iNJuRy	7793	LeVeL
30	17.34	133	303	KiCK BuM	560
30	TaKe MoRe	To MiaMi	JuDGe SoN	6602	LoDGeS

And here is how I added the connecting words to make up the ridiculous sentences which were then filed in each proper memory storage compartment:

"At *twenty* a boy has a *tiny loaf* of *beef*. He sits on a *nun buoy*."
"At a *choice age* he bought the *boathouses* for *ten dollars*."

"On *twenty-five tar ships* my *daughter* sustained an *injury*. It was on the *level*, and she was still able to *kick* the *bum* for ten dollars."

"At *thirty*, a young man has to *take more to Miami* to live in a *museum* or else he lodges with the *judge's son* for ten dollars."

You see, transposing abstract and meaningless digits into phrases and image words that make sense can be fun and profitable fun at that! Here's how a highly successful insurance salesman puts this technique to work and cashes in on it.

How Chuck Dean Cashes in on
His Knowledge of Rate Tables

Chuck Dean uses his thorough knowledge of his rate tables in the most subtle way there is. He uses this technique when his prospects are completely unaware of it during casual conversation.

Knowing that it isn't good taste to bring business into social situation discussions, Chuck usually bides his time until someone makes a crack about his career of insurance.

When an acquaintance laughs and comments: "So you're in insurance, eh? I suppose you're going to tell me I'm worth more dead than alive?" Chuck smiles and replies: "As long as you mention it, did you know that you could be worth $100,000 *more* for just $100 a month?"

He then discreetly gets the prospect to talk about his business or something else of interest to him. Frequently this leads to the invitation, "How about dropping by my office tomorrow? I'd like to hear more about how I could be worth $100,000 for $100 a month."

If your business is insurance or if it relies on rate tables, you can cash in on your rate tables with your hidden memory power just as Chuck does. Your accurate knowledge of the sales tools at your disposal —your key figures and the ability to use this knowledge at the right moment *without hesitation*—stamps you as a man who knows his business. And people like to do business with a man who *knows* what he's talking about.

REVIEW QUESTIONS

1. In order to remember statistics or series of numbers what is the first thing to be done?
2. Have you memorized the parody *The Nine Parts of Speech*? If so, have you memorized it according to the series and linking them to your memory compartments such as No. 1—*hat*, see ARTCLES, *a, an, and, the*

No. 2—*hen*, NOUNS, *name anything, school, garden, hoop, swing*

No. 3—ADJECTIVES *kind of noun, great, small, pretty, etc.*?

If not, do so. You will be surprised at how this will aid you in composing word sentences later on. Besides, you will benefit from the practice of remembering this parodized list.

3. When remembering telephone numbers it is perfectly okay to utilize any system or combination of the number code and the telephone prefix names. Is this (**true**) or (**false**)?

4. Without referring back to the page where the picture of the telephone dial is shown, write in this space the one missing letter of the alphabet which is *not* found on the dial. _____. Now list the letter shown in the illustration which is *not* on your telephone dial. _____.

5. Why does it pay to memorize rate tables and other pertinent data in your business or profession? List how many ways you can cash in when you develop this hidden memory power and put it to work:

1.	2.	3.	4.
5.	6.	7.	8.
9.	10.	11.	12.

6. If you have not listed at least six ways you can benefit, go back and reread this chapter, paying particular attention to how these techniques may be applied to make your career and personal life more rewarding. Then try to list at least 12 things you will gain.

7. How many salesmen, businessmen or professional men do you know who possess the ability to cite facts and figures without consulting notes or catalogues? When you meet a person who is able to do this, how do you rate him? Think about this for a time and ask yourself why.

VII

How to Remember
Financial Statements
and Catalogues,
Prices, or Data

*The illiterate Anglo-Saxon swineherd knew that
he would be put into a higher tax bracket if
he owned more than 12 pigs. To be on the
safe side, he would tell the King's tax collector,
"Endleofen," and point one finger at his toes.*

*He couldn't count past ten so he pointed at his
toes and indicated "one pig left." This is how the
word "eleven" found its way into our language.*

The business or professional man who
doesn't take the trouble to have those statistics which are important to
him at his fingertips is oftentimes no better off than the illiterate swineherd
or an aborigine who points at his toes and indicates "one left." When a
person doesn't know what he's *supposed* to know, he fails to make a favorable impression.

We have progressed a long way since the days when ignorance was an
accepted thing. Now it is possible, with the memory aids you have learned
so far, to commit everything you need to know to your memory!

The man who can instantly quote every asset or liability of his own
business, or that of another business, gives an immediate impression of
being expert in his field. He knows how his figures stack up against a
competitor's. He knows his business thoroughly without pausing in the

middle of a sales presentation to look up a fact or figure and while so doing, lose control of the interview.

There is no better way for any man to impress others than to possess a thorough knowledge of significant data, no matter how complicated. There is no more effective way to win plus-business than to demonstrate a knack for remembering seemingly complex and involved figures.

The techniques to be used in the memorization of a financial statement are similar to the other procedures which you have learned on the pages of this book; however, they involve a more intricate and time-consuming method of mental picture painting and careful association. But this isn't important. The benefits you will derive after you have spent the time in committing the things you *should know* to memory, are what really count.

How I Memorize a Bank Statement

You are about to see how I apply the techniques in this system to enable me to remember a complete financial statement. In order not to confuse this with the regular figures in my memory bank, I have devised a separate bank of *18 rhyming memory compartments.* You will notice that my memory compartment words rhyme with the number. Here's how it works:

1. gun		10. den
2. zoo		11. leaven
3. tree		12. shelves
4. door		13. thirsting
5. hive		14. fording
6. sticks		15. lifting
7. heaven		16. sweet-16
8. weight		17. seven-teens
9. wine		18. waiting

These rhyming words and how they are associated are shown below:

NO.	RHYMING WORD	ITEM	HOW ASSOCIATED
1.	gun	Cash and Due from Banks	*Gun*man taking the *cash due me from banks.*
2.	zoo	U. S. Government Securities	A lion in a *zoo* guarding *Uncle Sam* and a huge stack of *bonds.*
3.	tree	State & Municipal Securities	The *governor, mayor* and *council* up a *tree* with *bonds for leaves.*

NO.	RHYMING WORD	ITEM	HOW ASSOCIATED
4.	door	Other Bonds and Securities	A vault *door* with other *securities bonded like wallpaper* to it.
5.	hive	Loans & Discounts	A banker I know pulling a *loan* for me from a *hive on a counting disc.*
6.	sticks	Banking Premises, Fixtures, Furniture and Vaults	Picture a bank made out of *sticks rustic-style* by the second little pig in the Big Bad Wolf nursery story.
7.	heaven	Other Assets	*Angel* on a cloud counting up *other assets.*
8.	weight	Total Assets	A series of *weights* opposite me on a balance or beam scale giving my *total assets.*
9.	wine	Liabilities	A *liar* drinking up my *wine* and saying he's not *liable* for the bill.
10.	den	Time Deposits	A *time* bomb being wound up by a grinning fox in a *deposit* box *den.*
11.	leaven	Demand Deposits	A *baker* sprinkling yeast onto the *deposits demanding* that they *leaven* and grow like other "dough."
12.	shelves	Reserves	A company of Army team *reserves* sitting on the bank *shelves* held in *reserve* during the Army-Navy game.
13.	thirsting	Unearned Income and Other Liabilities	A man crawling out of a desert with his *tongue hanging* out stealing a *water cup* labeled *"unearned income"* and screaming he'll sue for *libel* if I say he did it.
14.	fording	Capital	I see myself *fording* the Potomac River going toward the *Capitol* Building.
15.	lifting	Surplus	I see myself *lifting* a *surplice,* a huge robe and trying to get it off over my head.
16.	sweet-16	Guaranty Fund	At a *sweet-16* birthday party you can *guarantee fun!*
17.	seven-teens	Undivided Profit	*Seven-teen*ers know all the answers at their age. They are *undivided prophets.*
18.	waiting	Total Liabilities	*Waiting* at a gate while staggering under the weight of bills *totaled* and labeled: *"Total liabilities."*

I have taken you through this formula step-by-step to show you the basic format for remembering a financial statement. Of course, I have abbreviated the descriptions of my associations. As you can see, you may make up your own associations linking your images with your background and experience.

This completes the first part of how to memorize a financial statement.

Now, before going further, read this sentence: "Dinty saloon raccoon leg." Now put in a few extra words to remember it as: "In Dinty's saloon I saw a raccoon with a wooden leg."

Those are the words I wrote on the blackboard at the close of an afternoon seminar for secretaries at the University of Connecticut. I had not explained what the words meant to the group. I merely asked them to remember the words.

The next morning I wasn't at all surprised to find that nearly every-one recalled them. Then I explained that if I had written this figure on the board:

$$\$121,052,472.57$$

no one would have even tried to remember it. It was too big a number, too abstract, and had no association with anything else within the confines of their experience. Those words happen to represent the Total Assets and the Total Liabilities on the bank statement in the following example.

You are about to see the entire statement with each group of picture words I used. Only words with exactly the correct number of digit-equivalents have been selected.

NO.	RHYMING WORD	ITEM	AMOUNT			
1.	gun	Cash and Due from Banks	$20, NoSe	557, LiLaC	467. ReJeCt	73 GuM
2.	zoo	U. S. Government Securities	21, NeT	842, FeRN	116. ToaDiSH	94 BaR
3.	tree	State & Municipal Securities	17, TwiG	228, Noah NaVy	167. wooDCHuCK	28 kNiFe
4.	door	Other Bonds and Securities	1, hiDe	917, PaDdiNG	679. CHeCKuP	51 LooT
5.	hive	Loans & Discounts	57, LaKe	550, LiLieS	129. DaNuBe	41 RaDio
6.	sticks	Banking Premises Fixtures, Furniture and Vaults	1, Tie	718, GoDiVa	580. LeaVeS	63 JaM
7.	heaven	Other Assets		238, NyMPH	331 MaMmoTh	.07 SaCK
8.	weight	Total Assets	121, DiNTy	052, SaLooN	472 RaCCooN	.57 LeG
9.	wine	Liabilities				
10.	den	Time Deposits	19, TuB	350, MuLeS	859 PhiLiP	.06 SaSH
11.	leaven	Demand Deposits	84, FiRe	135, whiTeMeaL	075 SCaLe	.16 DiSH

NO.	RHYMING WORD	ITEM	AMOUNT			
12.	shelves	Reserves	2, wiN	189, DiVvy UP	580 LoaVeS	.78 CoFfee
13.	thirsting	Unearned Income and Other Liabilities	7, Key	774, CoCKeR	551 weLl LaiD	.90 BuS
14.	fording	Capital	2, Noah	200, NieCeS	000 SiSsieS	.00 SeiZe
15.	lifting	Surplus	2, New	800, FeZzeS	000 iCehouSeS	.00 oaSiS
16.	sweet-16	Guaranty Fund	1,	000, remembered as $1 Million birthday gift	000	.00
17.	seven-teens	Undivided Profits	1, Tie	602, JaSoN	405 wReStLe	.67 JaCK
18.	waiting	Total Liabilities	121, DiNTy	052, SaLooN	472 RaCCooN	.57 LeG

When it comes to remembering the numbers, I simply added them to the basic formula for remembering the outline of the statement. For example:

1—gun—Cash and Due from Banks	I visualize myself grabbing the *gunman* by the *nose* because he was trying to take the *cash due me from the banks* and shoving a *lilac* in the muzzle of his *gun* and *rejecting* his attempt to shoot the *lilac* out of the *gun* by sticking it in place with some chewing *gum*.
2—zoo—U. S. Government Securities	I see a man with a *net* sneaking up on the *lion* in the *zoo* who is guarding *Uncle Sam* and the stack of *securities*. The man with the *net* is hiding behind a *fern* tree. He has the head of a *toad* and he looks *toadish* and I take one of the *bars* out of a zoo cage and clobber him with it.

See how much fun it really is to link the numerical-equivalent words to the images you have already learned? Stop now and see if you can *paint your own mental pictures* to represent the items and the amounts. See if you can pictorially associate *"Dinty Saloon Raccoon Leg"* with item No. 18 indicated by the word *waiting* and *total liabilities*.

Go through the entire list in this manner without referring to the pages you have just read, relying solely on your safe deposit box words that rhyme. Stop after every third item and repeat the previous entries to make sure you are keeping the images strong and the pictures distinct in your memory bank.

Once you develop the ability to handle more extensive associations such as those you've just seen, you will be able to develop your own "formulas" for remembering other statistical outlines and formats into which you can then insert the equivalent number picture words.

With a little practice, before you know it you *will* become increasingly adept. This is the shortcut to the development of a powerful money-making memory! Learn the fundamentals well and put them to work for you without delay.

How a Public Relations Man Landed a New Account as a Result of His Ability to Memorize Financial Statements

Shortly after Larry Hilliard mastered the simple method of how to memorize a financial statement, he put it to work as a sales tool.

A particularly promotion-minded Savings and Loan Association was on the top of Larry's prime prospect list. Aside from the money he would make as a result of landing it as an account, he stood to benefit from the prestige and contacts. This was why Larry enrolled in my "Short Course for Short Memories" program. He was particularly interested in learning how to remember long series of numbers.

Within a month after he mastered the number code, Larry found himself face to face with the association's board of directors. While he was delivering his presentation, a vice president he had not been able to convince interposed a question. "Tell me, Mr. Hilliard, why do you believe we should continue to spend $100,000 annually on public relations? Our competitors seem to be doing just fine on budgets *below* $50,000."

This had been what Larry was waiting for. He smiled and replied: "It isn't what *I* believe, gentlemen. It's what your financial statement, as opposed to your competitors' statements, shows. Your record of growth far exceeds theirs in ratio to promotion funds spent." At that Larry launched into a discussion which incorporated the use of a large blackboard upon which he jotted down figures which supported his rebuttal.

The bankers looked on incredulously.

A recess was called and Larry's figures were checked against those of the institution's competitors and when it was all over, Larry unanimously got the approval of the board—and the account.

"Any man who knows that much about our business, as well as our competitors' business, *deserves* to handle our account!" said the vice president who had formerly been against making a change at that time.

No matter what your business is, a thorough knowledge of statistics pertaining to that business is vital. But even more important to the man who really wants to get ahead *is* his ability to know those figures cold.

When you put your mind to it and master this technique, you'll be amazed at how many opportunities there are for you to cash in on your memory power.

How to Develop a System for
Remembering Price Lists, Catalogues

The man with a money-making reputation for knowing his business usually is successful because of his ability to remember the prices of what he sells. Nothing builds greater faith in a salesman than when a man demonstrates his knowledge of what he sells by quoting prices accurately from memory.

Retail sales people fail to realize it, but when they have to pause to turn over a price tag or look up a cost in a catalogue, they lose control over the sale. The reason control is lost is because the customer's mind is allowed to stray, and he instinctively feels the salesman doesn't know what he's talking about. After all, how can you believe a man who must take time out to look up a price?

Makes sense, doesn't it?

How a Car Salesman Sells an Average
of 8 New Cars a Week Because
He Knows Costs

Automobile salesman Fred Brunell virtually doubled his income when he hit upon an easy method of remembering not only the prices of the cars he sells, but comparative costs of competitive cars as well!

Besides this, he knows the breakdown for each individual item: how much it costs with or without the radio; how much the deluxe model is *less* than a competitor's with the same equipment; how much *less* his power steering unit is than the next three competitors'. Fred's ability to cite all these facts without a moment's hesitation spells his success. He knows that most of his sales are closed on a minor sales point. He knows that when his competitor is charging $33 *more* for a power brake unit than he is, this can become the turning point in a sale.

This is the system Fred has developed which not only enables him to remember *all* of his prices, but those of his competitors' as well.

First, the formula for remembering the prices. Fred looks at each car in this order, using the number code to classify eight basic models:

1. *D*eluxe model
2. *N*ext model
3. *M*y favorite model
4. *R*oyal one that's fit for a king
5. *L*ifetime model
6. *S*harpest car in the line
7. *K*ing's ransom model
8. *F*inest of the fine

Station wagon
Convertible

In this manner Fred classifies his cars. He knows that he can't afford to lose any potential customers because of what he *didn't* show the customer. The method works even when a car is out of stock or on order. He can't forget. The very car his customer might be after might be the one the dealer is temporarily out of. Therefore, Fred uses this list to remind the customer of the complete line. The numerical equivalent consonants at the beginning of each phrase are his memory joggers.

Carrying this a step further, he then associates the model *numbers* with the cars. Here are three examples to give you the idea:

1. *D*eluxe model No. 201 = Deluxe and ho*N*e*ST*
2. *N*ext model No. 301 = Really cuts the *M*u*ST*ard
3. *M*y favorite No. 485 = A masterpiece by Ra*P*hae*L*

Next, Fred thinks of himself as a mechanic mentally undressing or stripping the car. He looks at the roof of the car and that's where he visualizes the basic price less the extras. Also, the roof of the car indicates the model and style. From there he proceeds over a check list like this:

1. Roof. Style and basic price.
2. Radiator. New type coolant or anti-freeze.

3. Engine. Style, horsepower, etc.
4. Transmission. Attached to the engine. Next logical.
5. Power brakes. Logically, you have to stop the engine.
6. Power steering. You have to steer the car.
7. Radio. Now you're inside looking around.
8. Tinted windshield.
9. Electric windshield wipers to wipe the tinted windshield.
10. Windshield washer.
    etc.

The point is that Fred always uses the same check list. Now, he goes through his prices like this:

No.			
1–Custom convertible	$3222.00	*MoNey* and *oNioNS* and *iCe* on the roof.
2–Coolant or Anti-freeze	6.20	*oCeaNS* can't replace this.
3–Special V-8 engine	137.60	*aToMiC JuiCe* is what runs the engine.
4–Automatic transmission	220.90	*aNNouNCe PaCe* when you step on the gas.
5–Power brakes	43.20	*RaM heNhouSe* if the brakes fail.
6–Power steering	81.70	*FaT KiSS* one-armed lovers love that steering!
7–Push-button radio	58.50	*LiFe LaZy* and push button music too.
8–Tinted windshield	21.55	*NuDe LuLu* can be seen through these windows.
9–Electric windshield wipers	13.70	*ToMahawkS.*
10–Windshield washers	7.75	*GoGGLes* you won't need with this.
11–Padded instrument panel	21.30	*NuDe MiSS* could (could not) use the padding.
12–Wheel covers	19.20	*TaP NoiSe* when you tap on these.
13–Courtesy light group	14.80	*TaR FaCe* could really use this.
14–White sidewall tires	37.00	*MeCCa'S* the place these will take you to.
15–Transportation	83.00	*FuMe oaSiS* because you have to pay this.
TOTAL	$3988.40	*MoPe FiVe yeaRS* while you pay for this!

Once Fred has his basic prices memorized, he computes the cost of the car "extras" and breaks them down showing the total cost of the complete package *less* each "extra." For example:

Power Steering = 81.70 = *FaT KiSs* minus equals (cost of car *less* unit) = *FaT KiSs* — *MayBe SieGe KiSs* = $3906.70

As you see these word equivalents are easily remembered when they are filed mentally in order. From this basis, Fred Brunell constructs his most troublesome competitors' weakpoints into selling points. An example is merely added to the word link like this:

Cost of Competitor A's Power Steering Unit $123.10 = *DyNaMiTeS*
Cost of Competitor B's   "   "   " $134.00 = *TuMoRS*
Cost of Competitor C's   "   "   " $146.10 = *TRaGeDieS*

And this is how Fred links them together:

A *FaT KiSs MayBe* a *SieGe KiSs* and when you *DyNaMiTeS TuMoRS* it's *TRaGeDieS!*

Poor grammar, yes, but you can't beat this for remembering all these comparative costs! No wonder Fred Brunell is able to cash in on his memory power to the tune of more than a car sale a day!

As you have seen, the construction of a mental catalogue may be a little time-consuming, but it pays off in real dividends.

How a Shoe Salesman Benefits from His Memory of Prices, Sizes, Numbers

When Bill Hurst, a shoe salesman in a ladies' shoe salon heard me talk about applying the number code to the memorization of styles and prices he laughed. "Too much work," he scoffed. "Besides, I'm too busy. I'd never find the time to do all that."

I challenged Bill to give it a try, explaining that the secret was not in trying to learn the code and then trying to apply it in one day, but to accomplish it little by little over a period of several weeks. I then suggested that he begin the application of the code gradually, as he showed his merchandise to each customer. The idea was to get the "feel" of the shoes and commit them to memory every time he brought out a pair to be tried on.

Within several weeks Bill dropped in to tell me how amazed he was.

"It really works!" he said. He then went on to explain that as he began learning more and more of the stock by rote, he also began to close more sales!

Because of his unerring memory he was always able to snap his fingers and say to a hesitant shopper, "You know, Miss, I just happened to think: We have a very similar style and model that's a special today. It's only $10.98 and there's one pair left in your size. Just wait until you try them on!"

This is how Bill "personalizes" himself and succeeds in getting his customers to remain in a buying mood while he goes into the stock room to look for the shoes. He does not lose customer contact or "rapport" by making the mistake of saying "I'll go see what else we have."

Instead, he knows what he does have. Thanks to his conscientious use of the number code, Bill does not forget.

His words to me were: "Why, it's just as logical as putting the shoes in the right places on the shelves. All I have to do is put the styles and prices on my mental shelves."

Think of your job and the many ways this memory system will enable you to do it better. Then apply yourself and before you know it, you'll excel too!

How to Remember a Catalogue Page by Page and Cash in on This Knowledge

The salesman who knows his products or services so well that he does not have to falter in the middle of a sales presentation to look something up is the man who stands head and shoulders above his competition.

In today's competitive market place where often the same lines of popular priced merchandise or trade brands are carried by rival firms and offered to the trade at the same discounts, it is the salesman *alone* who makes or breaks the firm for whom he works. And of these men, the most successful are those who do not waste their customers' precious time by hemming and hawing and not knowing as much as possible about what they sell. Yes, these are the men who know their business and demonstrate that ability time and again by showing their clients instead of telling them how expert they are.

Here's an example of how one of these highly successful men uses his memory as a selling weapon.

How a Jobber Uses His Mental-Catalogue Memory to Defeat Competition

Dan Crawford is one of those traveling men so often referred to in the trade as a "wagon jobber." As he travels through his territory calling on prospects he is just one among many others who drives a walk-in van loaded down with merchandise.

Before he took my memory course this used to bother Dan. But no more. Today he uses the wholesaler's catalogue as a weapon to defeat competition. He doesn't have to carry armloads of samples into the business establishments along his route. Instead, he hands his prospect a catalogue and then walks away, saying: "Mr. Buyer, I see you're low on men's tee shirts. If you'll turn to page 51 you'll find the new style we're carrying on the right hand side of the page."

His prospects blink in surprise and open the catalogue, unable to get over their incredulity at Dan's thorough knowledge. They sit and watch and nod their heads as they hear him rattle off prices in grosses or quantities ranging from single units to dozens. It is his remarkable ability to quote prices without referring to the catalogue which astounds them.

"How come you never have to look up a price?" one of his customers asked Dan.

"I sell more of what I carry," he replied modestly. "That's how I'm familiar with what's on every page."

But this is barely half the truth. Because of his thorough knowledge of his business, which is calling on small town department stores, notion stores, ready-to-wear shops and general stores, Dan is able to "mosey" around each store in an off-hand manner without being hamstrung with a briefcase full of catalogues. This is how he is able to "see" where his customers' stocks are low and thus be able to "see" the pages of the catalogue in his mind to offer suggestions. As Dan stations himself on the other side of the store calling out which page number to look at, he eliminates his competition entirely.

The cordial welcome he receives everywhere he goes is astonishing. Merchants greet Dan like a long-lost friend. He is to them a sort of modern merchandising man who doesn't sell, but "suggests" merchandise.

Think of the time and effort any salesman can save, to say nothing of impressing his prospects, when he memorizes his catalogue of most important sellers and can quote at random.

It doesn't matter if you sell electronic components or printed blotters, if you take the trouble to develop a memory like a mental catalogue, you will be the gainer.

You have learned how to use your 100 memory storage compartments and you have learned how to apply the number code too. This is all you need to know in order to memorize a catalogue or at least, the important parts of it. In the "niche," No. 26 in your memory bank, you have remembered the following which are from page 26 in your catalogue:

In the "niche" you have placed four samples of men's shoes.

Imported high-riser	$19.94 =	*ToP PaiR* because the next shoe which is a
French Toe-Bal	9.94 =	*ViPeR* has been scared out by a continental
Continental Step-in	8.94 =	*PeePeR*
Italio Wing-tip Blucher	11.94 =	*DaT PaiR* from Italy who can't speak without "blutch-ering" up English

On the "fume," No. 83, you have tied seven ladies' watches which are illustrated on page 83 of your catalogue. You see standing on those watches which resemble steps rising up on a "fume" of mist or a cloud, seven beautiful girls. They are:

Miss America	$39.33	*MoP MaMa* gives the mop to mama who is
Dolly Madison	54.95	*YeLLow ReBeL* she screams at Jackie who is
First Lady	65.45	*JeLLy RoLL* is her present to Princess Grace the
Leading Lady	78.65	*CoFFee JeLLy* fattening which she gives to
Self-Wind Sport	43.95	*RuM PaiL* who spills it on starlight eyes
Starlight Thrift	21.95	*NighT PaLL* is what she has from starlight.

These illustrations have been presented briefly to show you how effectively an entire catalogue can be committed to your memory bank. Now here is a list of items which you may practice with. Form your own imagery and picture how you would make up ridiculous sentences which you can remember. *Don't be afraid to unleash your imagination! Don't tell yourself that it is easier to remember the things without this system. Try it and see.*

On page 42 which is your memory safe deposit box No. 42, word equivalent _____. Remember the following: (Write in your own words)

Lingerie

1. Sweet Dream Bra	$5.95–LaPeL	_____
2. Maidenette Bra	2.00–NieCeS	_____
3. Long Line Bra	8.95–FaBuLouS	_____
4. Deb-Teen	1.92–DeePeN	_____

Men's Underwear (Page 51) Write in your memory compartment number-word_____

1. Tee Shirt	3 for	2.05–3 iNSuLts	_____
2. Mid-L Shorts	3 for	2.65–3 iNSHeLL	_____
3. Undershirts	3 for	2.35–3 (on a) New MaLe	_____

Men's Jackets (Page 57) Write in your memory compartment number-word_____

1. Ex-Heavy Wool	9.94–PePPeR	_____
2. Zip Pullover	5.97–aLPaCa	_____
3. Corduroy	7.84–QuiVeR	_____

Furniture (Page 70) Write in your memory compartment number-word_____

1. Three-piece Sectional	139.90–DuMP PieS	_____
2. Sofa, Chair & Ottoman	119.85–TiDy uP VeiL	_____
3. Corner Table	12.95–TiN PaiL	_____
4. Arm Chair	34.95–MaRRy BiLLy	_____
5. Platform Rocker	39.95–hyMn BiBLe	_____

You must practice to get your full value. Now continue practicing with these. Do not skip through this chapter without practicing!

Housewares (Page 13) Write in your memory compartment number-word_____

1. Cast Iron Cookware	2.97–heN PeCK	_____

2. 6 qt. Dutch Oven w/lid   14.95–waTeR BowL _____
3. Pressure Canner Cookers 24.95–NeweR PaiL _____
4. Canister Set   6.97–SHoPPiNG _____
5. Bread Box (King-size)   7.69–KeTCHuP _____

_____

"Cast Iron Cookware" and "henpeck" certainly bring violent images to my mind. How about you? And, I repeat. Do not skip through this chapter *without* taking time out to practice. Don't be too eager to continue until you digest this. You will have fun during the last half of the book if you do!

Automotive Supplies   (Page 97) Fill in the proper memory bank number-word_____

Rebuilt Carburetor	5.80–oLiVeS _____
Fuel Pump	16.65–DiSH JeLLy _____
Tail Pipe	2.59–New LiP _____
Piston Ring Set	9.15–hosPiTaL _____
Dual Exhaust System	14.50–waTeRLooS _____
Valve Spring Guide Set	13.75–TiMs CooL _____

_____

Tools   (Page 17) Fill in the proper memory bank number-word_____

Cordless Electric Drill	59.90–hoLe PiPeS _____
Sander	25.50–NaiL hoLeS _____
Power Shop	269.50–eNJoyaBLe Seesaw _____

_____

Now you have had an opportunity to practice using what you have learned so far. You can see how it becomes easier as you practice and you can also understand the *how* of why this system works. The rest is up to you.

Practice is the keynote. Ask yourself this question: As you looked at the code words for the prices, did you make pictorial associations between them and the articles? If you didn't, go back and do so. Remember, if it works this easily for you on these more or less uninteresting items, think of how much more effective this will be when you start remembering the things in which you are genuinely interested.

Again, let's see how you do with this list. Commit it to memory, then jot down the items in the exact order they are given here on a separate sheet of paper. Okay, let's go shopping!

		Code Word
Soap powder	.35	*MoP*
Corn Flakes	.27	*YaNKee*
Coffee	.91	*PoT*
Napkins	.28	*kNiFe*
Vanilla	.77	*CaKe*
Sugar	.53	*LiMe*
Bananas	.14	*TRay*
Cocoa	.42	*iReNe*
Salt	.29	*NiP*

As you see, it's very easy to become so familiar with the code that you can think of words quickly which represent digits. You are about to learn, as I have, that it is much easier to associate the word signifying the price with the name of the article.

You are on the way to success. The rest is up to you. You have the know-how and there is no excuse for not understanding the techniques of developing your hidden memory power. All you have to do now is apply yourself diligently. Practice and learn to use your memory bank and the number code.

Make a game out of everything you do. Don't just sit around idly when you're waiting to keep an appointment. Think. Practice what you have learned on these pages. Not only will you be able to create a deep and favorable impression upon everyone you meet, and be better equipped to increase your income and go places in your career, but also you will be able to make your memory pay off in hundreds of other ways.

Take your cue from the success stories of Dan Crawford and shoe salesman Bill Hurst and automobile salesman Fred Brunell and PR man Larry Hilliard. Learn how to remember financial statements and catalogues, prices and data which are important to you. Learn *how* by accepting the challenge and doing it!

REVIEW QUESTIONS

1. Why is it so important to remember statistics when you can refer to a statement, chart or price list just as easily?

2. Why was the rhyming word list used to remember the outline of the financial statement? (one—gun, two—zoo, three—tree, etc.)

3. Can you remember without referring back to the financial statement the amusing phrase which represented the total assets and liabilities of the sample bank statement? If so, write in the figures: _____

4. Why was it necessary for Fred Brunell to first construct a formula to remember his prices when all he had to do was look at the cars he sells?

5. If you were actually memorizing a catalogue which contained a 100 pages do you believe you could do it? If so, would you have to remember it by making notes and consulting those notes, or would you be able to rely solely on your memory bank?

6. If your answer to question No. 5 was that you *could* rely solely on your newly developed memory bank, go on to the next chapters. If not, ask yourself *why* you feel this way. Then review the first seven chapters again.

VIII

How to Memorize

Stock Prices

"A land of promise, a land of memory,
A land of promise flowing with the milk
And honey
Of delicious memories!"
—Alfred Lord Tennyson

Most investment brokers are capable of quoting important prices exactly. Their keen interest leads to natural retention of the prices for the most frequently traded stocks. If you are interested in learning how to quote prices for any number of stocks, this chapter is made to order for you.

The ability to quote prices without resorting to checking the board is an ability that instills customer confidence. An investor feels he is on surer ground when he does business with such a wide-awake fellow. This attitude of confidence leads to freer and easier spending as a matter of course.

If you will follow my explanation carefully and try to do the exercise I am about to show you, this technique will be swiftly mastered. You also will develop more "mental muscle" with which to tackle other feats of strength and power.

It doesn't matter how involved or complicated your business is—you can use the money-making principles in this book to solve them. To prove this point, I'm going to show you how I performed a mental feat that at first seemed impossible!

How I Memorized the Entire List of Closing
Prices on the New York Stock Exchange

My reputation for memory often prompts people to challenge me to attempt something which has never been done before. One of the things I was asked to do was memorize the entire list of closing stock prices on the approximately 1,200 stocks traded on the New York Stock Exchange.

My first reaction was that it could be done, but I had my doubts as to its practicability. For one thing, I believed it would take so long that it would have no worthwhile value. But then I got to thinking about it.

I realized I didn't have to memorize and then recite the entire list. I only needed to make an association between the name of the stock and the price so that when I heard the name mentioned, I would immediately think of the pictorial image I had associated with the price.

Stock prices represent a special problem since they are quoted in whole dollars plus eighths or quarters or halves. For instance, 35-$\frac{1}{8}$, 36-$\frac{1}{4}$, 42-$\frac{1}{2}$. After looking over the sheet, I also realized that most prices were under $100 per share. Therefore, I concluded that if I translated all the fractional remainders into eighths and treated the numerator as a whole number, I might be able to use words for the numbers from 001—1000 that I had worked out for the number dictionary which is at the back of this book.

(Originally, I had devised this dictionary in order to memorize 10 issues of *Life* magazine which at that time was running about 100 pages per issue. I will show you how to do this in a later chapter.)

Using this method, 35-$\frac{1}{8}$ becomes the number 351 or "mallet." 36-$\frac{1}{4}$ becomes 36-$\frac{2}{8}$ or the number 362 or the word "mission." 46-$\frac{1}{2}$ becomes 42-$\frac{4}{8}$ or the number 424 or "Rainier."

The next step was to think of a picture to represent the stock to be remembered. First on the list was Abbott Laboratories. My picture happened to be that of a friend named Abbott who worked in a large white laboratory. The price at the time was 71-$\frac{5}{8}$. This became 715 or "cattle" so I visualized my friend Abbott experimenting on cattle.

Here are a few more examples selected at random from that list.

Stock	*Picture*	*Actual Price*	*Price as Whole No. & Word*	*Visual Association of Word with Stock*
Admiral	Navy Admiral	14-3/8	143-drum	*Admiral* beating a a big bass *drum*
Bath Iron Works	Big iron bath tub	53-1/2	534-Elmer	*Elmer* the bull *bathing* in that tub
Bendix	My Bendix washer	64-1/4	642-Churn	*Churning* butter in my *washing machine*
Celotex	Celotex ceiling	28	28-knife	A big *knife in a ceiling*
Cluett Peabody	An *Arrow* shirt made by them	81-5/8	815-fiddle	A violinist using a starched *Arrow* shirt as a *fiddle*

There were some price problems also. Some stocks were over $100 and others were less than $10. This is how I handled those over $100.

I knew that with American Telephone at 121, if I used the picture word "donut," I could rely on my basic knowledge that AT&T was not 12-1/8. If it were 121-3/4 I simply added another word for "6," JAY and pictured a bluejay eating a donut on a telephone wire.

On the other hand, with a lesser known stock it is possible to make up a new word. Financial Federal was just a new name to me at the time. The price was 154, code word "tailor." I merely pictured a "big tailor" for that one. I could have used "tailor" for that and "dealer" for 15-1/2.

Stocks under $10 per share I decided to code with a zero in front. A stock at 1-5/8 became first 01-5/8, then 015, or the word "stool."

Benguet, a gold mining stock, closed at 1-5/8. My visualization was easy. I saw people sitting on stools at a "banquet" table mining gold.

When I first tested this idea, I discovered that I could memorize about 60 prices in 20 minutes. But I soon found out that it was tougher than I'd imagined. I didn't know what some of the names represented and therefore couldn't make a vivid picture quickly enough to represent the stock. I went through the list making pictures wherever I could. I did not try to make the picture represent the actual business the company was in. Notice in the example how I used my Bendix washing machine as a symbol for Bendix Aviation.

As I found stocks for which I had no pictures, I checked them off and looked them up in the stock guides later. After I learned what kinds of businesses they were I was able to make mental pictures.

Quite a few stocks started with the word "General." So I visualized an image of General Grant and had him smoking a cigar for "General Cigar," baking a cake for "General Baking," and so forth.

At this point I'd like to remind you that it's best to use whatever image you can draw up from the well of knowledge and experience in *your* background. This is the key to developing a powerful memory: linking new images with the old images you already know. So don't try to remember the images I use. Instead, cultivate the habit of conjuring up your own mental pictures and develop your imagination in that direction.

When I first decided to master the entire list of stocks, there was a strong incentive for me to do this because it had never before been done. I can now do 1,200 stocks in less than five hours.

I must admit that I haven't practiced extensively, simply because I can't think of a reason why anyone would have a need for remembering all those prices, except perhaps to make an impressive appearance on a national television show.

However, it is good exercise. It gives you a chance to practice your mastery of the number code. So try no more than 20 of the 32 prices listed below right now to help develop your money-making mental muscles. After writing in your own code word in the below exercise, make your own association. You may never need to remember stock prices, but this is an excellent setting-up exercise.

Stock	Price	Price as Whole No.	Picture Code-word From Number Dictionary	Association of Word with Stock
American Optical	68-½	684	_____	_____
American Telephone	121	121	_____	_____
Armour Packing	44-⅝	445	_____	_____
Bayuk Cigars	47	47	_____	_____
Bell & Howell	49-½	494	_____	_____
Bethlehem Steel	40-½	404	_____	_____

Stock	Price	Price as Whole No.	Picture Code-word From Number Dictionary	Association of Word with Stock
Chrysler	47-⅛	471		
Congoleum	10-⅛	101		
DuPont	202-½	2022 (Use 2 words)		
Eversharp	33-⅝	335		
Firestone	39-⅞	397		
General Baking	6-⅜	063		
Greyhound	25-¼	252		
Hammond Organ	31-¾	316		
Hershey Chocolate	198-⅜	1983 (Use 2 words)		
International Harvester	52-½	524		
A & P	66	66		
International Nickel	80-⅛	801		
Johns-Manville	54-⅝	545		
Merck	79-¼	792		
National Airlines	13-⅛	131		
Owens-Illinois Glass	83-½	834		
J. C. Penney	53-¼	532		
Pepsi Cola	55-⅜	553		
Revlon	69-¾	696		
Sears Roebuck	79-½	794		
U. S. Steel	44-⅜	443		
Standard Oil of N.J.	46-⅞	467		
Texaco	50-⅜	503		
Ward Baking	10-¼	102		
Yale & Towne	31-⅝	315		
Zenith Radio	81	81		

Once you have mastered this method, and then from time to time memorize the stocks which are important for you to remember, you will be astonished at the many ways of cashing in on this knowledge you will find.

One man I know spends three hours every Friday memorizing the closing prices and then puts this knowledge to work on the golf links Saturday and Sunday.

Another man whose business is not in the exchange, but in the mutual funds field, uses his knowledge of the stock prices and their highs and lows as a sales weapon to sell portfolios. Here's how he does it.

Mike McKinney makes it his business to know what's going on in the market, even though he deals in mutual funds. At least once a month, Mike memorizes the prices of approximately 600 stocks. He does this for the sole purpose of being able to have something to discuss when he calls on new prospective investors.

Most of the prospects upon whom he calls, if they have not owned funds, have owned or do own stocks. His understanding of these stocks, and the guesswork and worry through which his prospects are often led, plus his knowledge of their prices, permits him to sell the benefits of owning mutual funds rather than stocks.

He is able to show his prospects the why and the how of the mutual funds success and why it pays them to invest in his diversified offerings in lieu of isolated and often risky board stocks. Mike's knowledge of the market fluctuations pays off because he uses it as a sales tool with which to write new business.

Through this subtle method he is able to show his prospects why it pays to leave the guesswork and calculated risk elements up to the trained experts whose business it is to protect him as an investor.

Remember, no matter what your business is, if it is allied to the investment field, it *does* pay to have a thorough knowledge of stock prices. Strangely, men in other fields *not* allied to the brokerage business also have adapted their knowledge of stock prices to help them earn more money.

A Real Estate Salesman Earned $7,500
the First Week He Memorized Stock Prices

Irv Thorne was a moderately successful real estate salesman who took my memory course of instruction to help him remember his listings and also to remember names and faces of his prospects. Then he discovered a way to cash in on the system by memorizing stock prices. He has made a lot of money because of it!

The majority of Irv's prospects are businessmen and industrialists. His pleasant personality and pleasing appearance always assured him an interview, but beyond that he was in a quandary. There was little he had "in common" with his prospective clients which would lead to "breaking the ice." Then he noticed the obvious: nearly every prospect was a *Wall Street Journal* subscriber. And whenever he called on these men they nearly always were studying the market or talking to others about stocks and conditions.

Irv decided to make it his business to know stocks. He began to take the *Journal* also, and checked off a list of 100 stocks which he scanned every day before making his calls. He followed my system of memorization and within a few weeks could quote the price of most key stocks. When he felt he was ready to put his plan to work, he made a call on a prospect he had seen many times previously. He had a sale-leaseback proposition that was tailor-made for this man, but could never seem to get him to sit still long enough to listen.

Now, with his new knowledge of stocks, he was determined to capture this prospect's attention and hold it long enough to put his proposition across.

As usual, Irv found himself sitting opposite his prospect's desk, "visiting" (as usual) instead of selling. Sipping coffee and idly scanning the *Journal* while hardly noticing Irv, the prospect mumbled a few comments about his holdings.

"I see Armstrong Rubber's up an eighth again," Irv said in a casual manner.

The prospect frowned and hunted for the listing, mumbling something incoherent. Irv then said: "Arvin's down an eighth and Atlas preferred is up a quarter."

After several minutes of listening to these off-hand comments, the prospect suddenly realized that Irv was citing these stocks *without* referring to the listings. He blinked in amazement. "You can remember all that?" he said with incredulity.

Irv Thorne grinned. He then launched into a recitation of about a 100 stocks, quoting each price and making some casual-sounding comment about each. Then the prospect began to ask him questions about other stocks. Irv answered them accurately. The man suddenly looked at the real estate salesman as though seeing him spotlighted beneath a halo of respect.

Within an hour Irv and his prospect were at the site of the industrial building he wanted to sell. A half-hour later, as though hypnotized, the prospect demanded: "Why didn't you tell me about this deal before? A man as clever as you are must surely know this is the kind of investment I want. How soon can we bring our lawyers together?"

What happened to make this sale possible, a sale that netted Irv $7,500 in commissions? He was able to use his new knowledge of stocks as a stepping stone to meeting his prospects on common grounds. Because his prospect was deeply impressed, he listened. And when he listened, he bought. Today, Irv enjoys the reputation of being a man who knows the real estate investment business inside-out. He earned this reputation, strange as it may seem, largely because of his ability to "talk his prospects' language"—the language of the stock market!

This story is an illustration of how your hidden memory power can be put to work for you. There are other instances where still other men cash in on memorization of stock prices.

As you have just learned, appropriate words, phrases and sentences are easy to compose and fun to make up. When you master the basic list of number words, you'll be able to make words which fit the thoughts behind the numbers you want to remember.

It is important to remember that you may count only the first two or three consonants of a long word. It isn't necessary to spend time composing words that fit the number exactly. To do so defeats the system, unless you have a definite reason. An example could be the word "sea-nymph" (Sea-NyMph) = 0.23. The final sound of "ph" is not figured. Your common sense will remind you of the decision you made in choosing the word.

There are many other variations. When you give some thought to how you can incorporate this method to fit your own needs, you will never forget anything you want to remember.

You'll be surprised at how many ways the object lessons in this chapter will enable you to cash in on your hidden memory power. Practice the word code until you know it by instinct—that's the "how story" of how to do it.

Review Questions

1. Why does the ability to quote prices without resorting to notes instill customer confidence in the salesman?
   List three reasons: _____

   _____

2. How many ways can you list which show how the contents of this chapter benefit you?

   _____   _____   _____

   _____   _____   _____

3. When making up numerical equivalent words to represent the ciphers you want to remember, are you allowing yourself the pleasure of making your own associations? If not, go back over the written exercises and compose new words which stimulate your imagination.

4. You have seen how mutual funds salesman Mike McKinney uses this system to sell new prospects by being able to cite stock prices. How can you benefit from being familiar with stock market statistics? If you feel this knowledge will be of no value to you, then think of a way you can cash in on this technique in remembering facts pertinent to you. Here are some suggestions:

   Latest prices of groceries and household staples
   Newspaper, radio or TV "sale" offerings
   Price lists
   Vital statistics
   Sports scores, odds and statistics

5. At this point take out a watch and see how long it takes you to recite the first hundred basic words.
   Time: _____ Number of mistakes, if any: _____
   List of words you found difficult to recall instantly: _____

   _____   _____   _____

6. If you have had difficulty remembering more than four words, go over the list again, make clear mental images and see them in your memory bank's storage places.

IX

One: The Secret of
Remembering Names,
Faces and Facts
About People

"For any man with half an eye,
What stands before him may espy,
But optics sharp it needs, I ween,
To SEE what is NOT TO BE SEEN."
        —JOHN TRUMBULL, *McFingal*

The last line of John Trumbull's, *"To SEE what is NOT TO BE SEEN,"* sums up the secret of remembering faces, names and facts about the people you meet.

However, you don't need "optics sharp" in order to do this. You already are capable of mastering this easy-to-learn technique. And you are already thoroughly prepared to accomplish this with ease. By the time you finish this chapter, if you will read carefully and take the time out to practice the simple exercises I am about to give you, you will never again forget the name or face of *anyone* you meet and want to remember.

The secret of remembering names and faces and facts about people is in the controlled association method of observation which you have already learned. Now you will learn how to apply this to remembering people.

Why It Is Important to Observe Faces and Hear Names Spelled in Order to Remember Them

There is no single factor more important to insuring success as the ability to remember names and faces and facts about the people you meet. In order to achieve this you must first be willing to make a concerned effort to use your ability and imagination.

Once you have mastered the techniques, nothing else will bring you more satisfaction or win you more personal acceptance. All it takes is a little effort and concentration.

Before you can remember a person's face or his name you must first *see* that face and *visualize* how his name is spelled. When you do this, you are then able to make a controlled association between the person's face and his name. It is as simple as that.

As you have already learned, it is important to link the idea behind what you want to remember with a specific object in your memory bank. Now all you will do is link the person's name with his face. That's the secret!

This is why it is important to observe a person's face and hear his name spelled if you are to remember: you cannot remember anything unless you see it.

How to Observe Properly the Faces and Names of People

You learned how to do this in Chapter III. Merely follow the simple *CASH DEPOSIT* formula.

Concentration	*Concentrate* on the person's face. Select some prominent feature inside the framework of the "shape" of the face. Visualize and hear the name and connect it to that feature.
Association	*Associate* the name and the face pictorially so you'll never forget them.
Sight	*See* your association in action.
Hearing	*Hear* the name and what the sound means to you.
Deposit	*Deposit* the ideas and facts you want to remember on the face.

Exaggerate	*Exaggerate* and contort the association out of proportion.
Pictures	Be certain you are remembering *pictures* of concrete things.
Oddities	Do make *odd* connections. The odder, the better.
Silliness	When you remember *"silly"* associations that are fun to remember, people will be glad to see you because you're smiling.
Ideas	Fix concrete *ideas* in your mind, not abstract ideas.
Thoughts	You must *see* the *thoughts* expressed by the people you meet, or your own thoughts as concrete images.

Yes, that's all there is to it. Now here are the rules to observe which will help you master the *CASH DEPOSIT* formula.

How to Concentrate on a Person's Face

When you take the time to look at anyone's face, in a few moments you know a good deal about him because of the impression he makes on you. We are prone to make snap judgments about people every day. And as we judge others, so they also judge us. We are ready to decide if this man is likable or not, or perhaps interesting or not. This is because we are consciously or subconsciously *associating* the memories his face brings to mind.

We see, often without being aware of it, the age of the person, his race, nationality, the state of his health, his nerves, and his disposition or mood. Often we pay too much attention to the mood the person "seems to be in." Instead of concentrating on seeing his face in order to remember it, we are wrongly concerned with making an "impression" on him instead.

This is the major reason why we often cannot remember faces or names.

We are more concerned with making a favorable impression ourselves than with *impressing* the other man's name and face in our memories.

When we meet a stranger for the first time instead of concentrating on fixing his face in our minds, we often concern ourselves with wondering about his mood or attitude. If his face is devoid of expression, we may think his blank look means we aren't impressing him, so we naturally place ourselves on our best behavior and strive to get through to him and leave a favorable impression on him.

Whenever we do this, we usually are unable to recognize him the next time we see him.

Therefore, the first rule to observe is this: *When meeting a stranger for the first time get him to talk about himself. Remark about his "interesting" name or occupation or perhaps about his clothing or some attractive personal effects such as a ring, watch, or necktie. Then, while he is impressing you, look at his face with a view to selecting something on which you can fix your attention and forget about the impression you are making on him.*

How to Select a Prominent Feature to Remember

While he is talking about himself decide upon the most prominent feature on his face which you see first. You needn't be too concerned about the shape of his face, if it is round, oval, square or triangular. Instead, concentrate on the *features* of his face. Decide if any of the following stand out first when you see him:

1. Is his face unusually large or small?
2. Is his hair straight or curly or is he bald or partially so?
3. Is his forehead high and prominent or low or narrow?
4. Is his nose aquiline or straight, large or small, pinched or pudgy?
5. Are his eyebrows thick and bushy, thin, curved or arched?
6. Are his eyes large or small, slanting or narrowed?
7. Is the base of his nose prominent, medium or narrow?
8. Is his mouth wide and generous or narrow?
9. Are his lips full or thin? Which lip is protruding or straight or curved?
10. Are his ears close to his head or jutting out? Are they prominent, pointed, or round?
11. Does the chin have jowls or is it hard, square or jutting, pointed or receding?
12. Finally, what are the colors of his eyebrows, eyes and hair?

As you can see, there are many features upon which you can focus your attention; however, the important thing to remember is to choose what is *to you* the *most prominent* feature. I repeat, the most prominent feature *to you*. Not his hair, for the next time you meet him he may be wearing a hat. Not the color of a woman's hair, for the next time you see her she may have dyed it. Not the complexion of his skin, for the next time you may see him he may be heavily suntanned.

Notice the shape of that outstanding feature and then exaggerate it in your mind, seeing it out of proportion.

When meeting a person with an "average" or "plain" face without any prominent features seemingly evident, look for laughter lines around the eyes or at the corners of the mouth. Perhaps his teeth are prominent or perhaps he has a blemish or tiny crease or dimple in his chin or on his cheek or forehead. Fix your attention on this detail if you can find no others.

The point is, you must first select one thing about a person's face upon which you can "hook" your other associations. Just as you fixed permanent memory images in your mental bank, now you must concentrate on selecting a permanent (prominent or noticeable) feature upon which you can deposit his name and perhaps his address, phone number and other data about him.

How to Associate the Name with the Face

You have learned that abstract things cannot be remembered. Therefore, you must first *hear* his name, get it correctly, have it spelled if possible so you can *visualize* it, then *convert that name into a concrete image.*

Next, *attach the image to the feature you have selected.* That's all there is to it. Here are some examples of how ordinary names may be associated with (1) a pudgy nose; (2) a fat upper lip; (3) a dimpled chin; (4) almond-shaped eyes.

1. Adams — see a picture of "Adam" polishing the apple on the pudgy nose.
2. Baker — see a tiny "baker" kneading dough on that fat upper lip.
3. Charles — see "Charley Chaplin" kicking those clown shoes into the dimple.
4. Davis — see "davits" protruding from the points of those almond-shaped eyes lowering lifeboats.

1. Eaton — see little people "eating" the pudgy nose that weighs a "ton."

2. Frank   — see that fat upper lip inside a frankfurter roll with mustard.
3. George — see "Gorgeous George" wrestling in the dimple.
4. Harper — see "John Brown" trying to escape from those almond-shaped eyes at Harper's Ferry.

Get the idea? *Good!* Now here are some examples of how unusual names can be associated with (1) bushy eyebrows; (2) thin mouth; (3) thick jaw; (4) mole.

1. Ishelman — see a "shell-man" collecting "eye-shells" in those bushy eyebrows.

2. Jorgenson — see the Sons of Italy crossing the thin mouth of the river "Jordan" playing mouth organs. Jordan-organ-sons = Jorgenson.

3. Kimmelman — see a man shoveling millions of rye bread "kimmel seeds" into that thick jaw. The jaw is thick because it's overloaded with kimmel the man is stuffing inside.

4. Lundquist — see some tiny "Londerers" playing "whist" (a game of cards) on that card table of a mole.

5. Manfried — see a man being "fried" by the cannibals who are hiding in those bushy eyebrows.

6. Oglethorpe — see the Norse god "Thor" stuck between those thin tight lips with huge eyes ogling you while the thin mouth is trying to enunciate the word "Oglethorpe" without disgorging "Thor" when spitting out the inflection "pe."

7. Pennypacker — see some tiny little packers packing pennies into that thick jaw. You can hear the pennies clink every time the jaw opens because the penny-packers have overworked themselves.

8. Quackenbush — see a bush growing out of that mole with a duck nesting in it quacking: "Quackenbush, quack, quack."

These illustrations have shown you how I associate names with the features which stand out on the faces of people I meet. The rule is obvious: you must make your own selections of the features and then make up your own associations, remembering to make each association a concrete image and then tie it in with that feature "hook."

When you practice this rule diligently and then observe the rest of the *CASH DEPOSIT* formula, you will never again forget the name of anyone you meet. Now for your review, I will repeat the balance of the formula briefly to enable you to grasp more fully the easy fundamentals of how the method works so uncannily well.

How to See Your Association in Action

If you were to see the following two short filmstrips, which one would you remember? (1) A picture of a body of water such as a bay; (2) A picture of a man swimming through the water.

Naturally you would see the swimming man more vividly. You would be more apt to remember this picture instead of the first because it is occupied with something with which you can identify.

Of the following two illustrations, which one would be more unforgettable? (1) A picture of a man swimming through water; (2) A picture of a man swimming for his life.

Again, you would be more likely to forget the first picture because it is less dramatic and vividly identifiable to you than the second one. But now, which one would be indelibly imprinted in your memory? (1) A picture of a man swimming for his life; (2) A picture of a swimming man being pursued through the water by a gigantic shark whose snapping jaws are within an inch of his body.

You would never forget the second picture, would you? Of course not. But to intensify the image and to make it stand out in your mind even more, could you ever forget this image?

> A picture of a screaming, struggling man trying to escape from the steel trap jaws of a vicious man-eating shark which has just bitten off one of his legs. You see the churning water, scarlet with the spreading stain of human blood. You see the man's severed limb in the shark's mouth a moment before it's swallowed and it once again begins to close in on his doomed victim.

Get the idea? Certainly you do. The point is this. You *must* see your association in the very height of action. The more ridiculous, tragic or silly you make it, the better.

For instance, if you are associating the name Goldsmith with a deep character line etched into the man's face, you would never forget it if you visualize a little blacksmith with bulging muscles driving a gigantic golden spike into that facial crease.

The way to see your associations in action is by visualizing them doing ludicrous or impossible things.

Why It Is Important to Hear the Sound of a Name

Audio-visual is a phrase which is bandied about more and more often these days when salesmanagers and advertising men speak about putting across dynamic and unforgettable sales messages. You must not only *see* an image, but you must also *hear* it to make it more three-dimensional.

But there is another reason why it is important to hear the sound of a name as well as merely visualize it. Often the very key to association is to be found in the sound and not the way it reads on paper. At times the sound alone enables you to visualize a name.

People are annoyed when their names are mispronounced, so it pays to get the pronunciation correct. Here are some examples of names and how I associate them by sound:

Name	Pronunciation	Association or mental image
Strauss	straws	Soda fountain straws stuck in his nose.
Alberghrine	aw-ber-green	A traffic stoplight for eyes in amber and green.
Baughman	bow-man	A bowman shooting arrows into his target nose.
Boyce	boy-sea	A boy bailing the sea out of a chin cleft.
Carreno	car-ren-yo	A car playing with a rented yo-yo on a nose.
Fernandez	her-nan-des	Her "nanny" at a desk sitting on a forehead.
Levine	lev-in	A little man with a lever trying to get in a tightly compressed thin mouth. Lev-me-in!
Oskowski	ox-owe-ski	An ox who owes me those borrowed skis about to ski down ox-owe-ski's long nose.
Quintero	kin-tear-o	My kinfolk tearing little round o's in an ear.
Ryzewsky	raise-yew-sky	Raising a yew tree on his sky of a forehead.
Whetzelstahl	weigh-sell-stall	A grocer weighing and selling horse stalls on a jutting chin.

This really can be fun when you follow this tried and proven rule.

Remember, listen to the *sound* after you get the spelling correct, then make up your own associations to connect to the person's feature you see.

Anyone can learn to do this and do it well when time is taken to form images from the sounds of names.

You Have the Cash, Now Deposit It

Okay, the rest of the formula doesn't need reiteration. You know you must do the following:

Deposit — Deposit the ideas and facts you want to remember on the face. Fix them on that feature and stick them down with concrete images.

Exaggerate — By all means exaggerate and make the association *impossibly* out of proportion. If his name is Fish, see a million fish jumping.

Pictures — Pictures are the very life blood of your memory power. Get into the habit of forming pictures of tangible objects or people and *see* them.

Oddities — If his name is Whigwam, transform his nose into a wigwam! If his name is Rice, transform those lines on his face into terraced rice paddies. If his name is Legge, give him a pair of legs for ears!

Silliness — If his name is Mullins, call those eyes of his June-moon eyes and *see* them. If his name is Simon, see the pie-man meeting him on his fair of a forehead. If his name is Dock, see the mice running up the clock of his face.

Ideas — Remember to listen for the sound of the name and translate it into concrete sounds which remind you of the abstract idea his name resembles. (Later you can use this to remember some of the things he says to you.)

Thoughts — By all means if he strikes you as a "Hoss" with a horse-face, think of him like that and associate his name with it pictorially.

How to Cash In on These Techniques in Your Everyday Life

James Farley is a living legend of the tremendous benefits gained by the facility of remembering names, faces and facts about people.

Long before the nomination of Franklin D. Roosevelt, in 1931, Farley was touring the country speaking to political groups and meeting people. His manner was so sincere and untoward that no one guessed he was making a deliberate effort to remember the faces of thousands of people!

This was a deliberate effort which anyone else could have done too, provided that he followed the same rules I have just explained. I indicate here that this was a deliberate effort on Farley's part because he followed up each acquaintanceship with a personal note. No one without a definite purpose in mind would have taken such pains.

His memory marshalled vast throngs of people to his cause, and people liked him, supported what he stood for, and later supported the man for whom he subsequently campaigned. Yes, people liked Jim Farley because he had shown a personal interest in them. And as a result, they were likewise interested in him and his ideals.

You see it plainly now, don't you? Farley wasn't blessed with a divine gift of a remarkable memory at all. Quite the contrary. He employed the same techniques explained in this chapter. He got people to talk about themselves in order that he might be able to study them and fix their names and faces into permanently recognizable "tags" which he could read at leisure, days, weeks, or even years later!

Please do not think for one moment that I'm downgrading James Farley. I'm indicating how he did it for your edification so that you too might be able to see the proof of the pudding. And when you make a pudding, if it is to come out right, just follow the recipe for success. Use the *CASH DEPOSIT* formula as your recipe. You can't miss.

Now this same ability is within your grasp. You will soon develop it easily and quickly.

You don't have to be a salesman or a politician, a social climber or a club woman in order to develop this facet of your hidden memory power. Just read what Mrs. Harry Walden did.

How a Club Woman of 65 Memorized
the Names and Faces of 43 People
After Only One Hour of Instruction!

Mrs. Harry Walden attended my memory class because her memory was so poor she couldn't even remember the names of all of her grandchildren! When Mrs. Walden enrolled she expressed the fear that she was becoming more forgetful because of advancing age.

The next day, after attending just one hour of my session on "How To Remember Names and Faces," Mrs. Walden went to a woman's club meeting as a guest of a friend.

Though she was somewhat dubious about her ability, she decided to put the technique she had learned to work. Her friend took her around and introduced her to each woman. As she made the rounds, meeting 43 virtual strangers, Mrs. Walden did the exact same things you have learned on the pages of this chapter.

Unexpectedly, she was called upon by the club president to give a short talk on her hobby which was making miniature Ming trees. When she finished her talk, the women besieged her with questions.

Without being aware of it, she addressed her remarks to each woman —the same women she had only met briefly for the first time an hour before—and called each by name!

"Mr. Hersey," she told me the next day, "I was never so thrilled as I was when the club president came up to me after the meeting was over and asked if I would come again and give a talk. It was the most stimulating, the most rewarding experience I have ever had. Everybody told me how interesting I was."

Yes, Mrs. Walden put the secret to work. The reason why everyone enjoyed her and thought *she* was interesting was because she was interested in *them*, and was therefore doubly interesting *to them!*

How a Clothing Store Salesman Tripled His Income as a Result of His New-found Ability to Remember Names, Faces, Facts About Shoppers

For 17 years Harold Fein was just another salesman in a busy clothing store just off Fifth Avenue in New York. Though he was a hard worker and an excellent salesman, he just couldn't seem to get ahead. His earnings averaged $7,250 a year in commissions. And in order to earn that much he would not go out for lunch or dinner at the normal hours because he wanted extra "turns" as the shoppers entered the store. The only way he could wait on customers "out of his turn" would be to substitute for the other eight salesmen while they were off the floor.

Then Harold began to wonder about several of the firm's top salesmen who had "followings." How was it that they were able to develop such huge "followings" and he was not? He did everything they did. He gave every customer a business card whether he sold him or not. And he was a better salesman and he knew the stock better than the others did. But how was it possible?

One day it finally dawned on him. Harold overheard a customer remark to one of the other salesmen from whom he'd just ordered five suits: "Say, the fellow who told you about those topcoats that just came in. He's the one who waited on me the first time I was here last week. He treated me so well I just had to come back."

Harold came out from the dressing room and took a good look at the customer who had just made that comment about him. His face looked familiar, but that was that. He couldn't remember it.

That's when Harold Fein decided to do something about his poorly trained memory. Ten days later, after completing my memory course, Harold was already beginning to cash in on his newly developed memory power. He was recognizing the shoppers upon whom he had waited previous to their return to the store.

He was then able to step forward and greet each customer by name. Invariably the customer would be greatly pleased and impressed because his name was remembered. (And a man's name is certainly his most valuable and most cherished possession.) Moreover, he was flattered to think that Harold considered him important enough to be remembered.

"You couldn't have come in at a better time!" Harold would often say in way of greeting his prospects. "Am I glad you came in today, Mr. Braun. We just received a shipment of those cashmere sport jackets you were asking about last time you were here. And I have a 42 long put aside for you. Here, give me your coat and try it on!"

This is how Harold Fein "staked his claim" to the shoppers, a practice that soon (within five weeks) enabled him to send his earnings soaring to new heights. Within a year, Harold was earning an average of $412 weekly, more than he had ever dreamed of making in his life as a clothing store salesman!

No matter what your business is, or what you do in life, once you possess the ability to observe and then recognize faces and then remember names, you will possess the magic *CASH DEPOSIT* formula of personal success!

However, you may also go one step further. You may associate facts and preferences with names and faces.

Basically, this is relatively simple.

Harold remembers his prospects' sizes by looking at them with his experienced eye. If a man looks like he wears either a 40, a 42, or 44, he associates the words "worse," "worsted," "worser" with the name. He makes up a ridiculous association to help him remember the man's preferences or what he was seeking but didn't find on his previous trip to the store. Here's how he does it:

Customer's Name and Job	Size	Preference	Other Facts
Mr. Carson, lawyer	42–stout	dark gabardine	on diet
Mr. Reynolds, advertising	39–regular	natty wrinkle- less suit	going fishing
Mr. Southey, Chase bank	46–long	conservative, 2- pants	worried about health

Harold looks at Mr. Carson, spots the "ID" (identifiable, most prominent feature) which is a high-bridged nose with a tiny scar and recalls that he imagined an *arena*—a courtroom arena on that tall nose. He instantly remembers a gabby little attorney jumping up and down while pulling lawbooks out of his "kit" briefcase. The lawyer is fat and the briefcase is stout too. All this adds up: a*ReNa* + attorney + gabby + common-sense + "kit" = size 42–lawyer–gabardine–heavy-set men usually prefer dark colors–stout men usually on diets. "Kit" brings to mind "Kit Carson," hence, Mr. Carson.

Of course, this example has been somewhat abbreviated, but the point is obvious. Now pay close attention to how Harold Fein remembers the next two prospects' names and other important facts about them.

Man with prominent forehead which is unusually smooth and shiny reminds him of Reynolds aluminum foil. His name is Mr. Reynolds. The aluminum foil is embossed with artwork and lettering suggestive of advertising. He is an advertising man. The foil-smooth forehead is suggestive of a map. A regular road map, except that there are no markings on it. Size 39–regular. There are no routes on the map because the shape of it indicates a body of water. Water is suggestive of fishing. The reason Mr. Reynolds didn't buy last time he was in was because he wanted to catch the early train in order to go on a fishing trip. The wrinkleless forehead also reminds him of neatness. A natty, wrinkle-free suit.

The man with the high cheek bones and the crow's feet at the corners of his eyes looks worried. About his health, obviously. But perhaps because the crows have left their feet around his eyes at the tops of those high cheek bones and have flown south for the rich long winter with the riches the crows have stolen from the bank. The crows fly south because they were chased by a man with four legs. Crows flew south for the rich long winter. = Mr. Southey, employed by Chase Bank. Wears a 46–long. Wants to buy a suit with two pairs of pants.

How the Ability to Recognize Faces and Remember Names Does More Than Open Doors

I learned that, in my own sales work, the ability to remember names of, and facts about, people not only opens doors, it also *re-opens* them.

Every salesman runs into situations where it just isn't the time to makes a sales presentation. The prospect is either too busy or distracted to pay much attention to what is being offered. Once a salesman tries to force his prospect to pay attention when the odds are against him, the potential sale is often lost forever. The wise salesman doesn't force himself on a prospect. Instead, he paves the way for a future callback. I have always practiced this maxim. Then, later when I returned to see the prospect, I was able to cash in on my memory power because I had taken the trouble on that previous call to get him to talk about himself and his problems.

My new approach is often deliberately staged, though seemingly casual, and it works miracles when I greet the prospect and say: "It's good to see you again, Dr. Miles! When I met you three months ago the day after you had been elected to the school committee—as you recall—you were as busy as a one-armed paper hanger. Tell me, what decision did you make? Did you give up your post as finance chairman in order to be on that committee, or what?"

This never fails to re-open the door.

In the illustration just given, Dr. Miles, at one time brusque and reserved, today is a good friend and a loyal client.

Now let's get down to the brass tacks of developing your ability to remember names, faces and facts about people. Review the questions and begin meeting some new acquaintances in the next chapter.

REVIEW QUESTIONS

1. How would you sum up the secret of remembering the faces, names, and facts about people you meet?

2. Why is it important to observe faces and hear names spelled in order to remember them?
3. Have you reviewed the **CASH DEPOSIT** formula and applied it to the technique explained in this chapter?
4. Why is it important *not* to pay attention to the mood a person seems to be in?
5. Why should we not be concerned with making a favorable impression instead of impressing the other person's face in our memories?
6. List the most prominent features of six people of your acquaintance which have unknowingly (before studying this chapter) aided you in remembering them.

1. _____   4. _____

2. _____   5. _____

3. _____   6. _____

7. How would you connect each person's name with that feature? Their addresses? Their phone numbers? Other facts about them? Write in your brief answers.

1. _____

2. _____

3. _____

4. _____

5. _____

6. _____

8. Have you visualized each association in action? If not, correct the six lines above.
9. Why is it important not only to visualize how a name is spelled, but also to hear the way it sounds?
10. How many ways can you personally benefit from your newly learned ability to remember faces, names and facts about people? List as many as you can.

1. _____   2. _____   3. _____

4. _____   5. _____   6. _____

X

Two: The Secret of Remembering Names, Faces and Facts About People

---

You are about to meet 20 people for the first time. You will observe their faces, remember their names by association, and also remember some vital statistics about them. All you have to do is follow the directions detailed in the first part of this section.

Remember, first get the name correctly and form a concrete picture of it in association with the prominent facial feature you want to remember. For your review, observe my picture (*next page*).

To most people, my name suggests a Hershey bar. The one characteristic which is most outstanding about me is my short, white hair.

Let's exaggerate that white hair and link the Hershey bar with it. Imagine that I have pulled a Hershey bar out of my pocket and started to comb my white hair with it in order to get it nice and brown again.

If you actually saw me do that, you'd never forget it. Nor would you forget my name. Now for the name. Hersey. Note that the "h" is missing from the Hershey bar because "it dropped out while I combed my hair." Now you have the spelling correct. Hersey. But how do you remember the William D.?

That's easy. Think of me having used a dollar's worth of Hershey bars to comb my hair. A dollar bill = Bill and Bill = William. D = dollar. See the dollar bill in my white hair. You won't forget it.

To remember my address, simply think of a name or object "Norton" suggests to you. One of my students associated the character "Ed Norton" (created and acted by Art Carney) like this. He saw me wearing Ed Norton's character tag, that battered hat, to Mass and not taking it off during services. Norton wearing a hat at Mass = Norton, Massachusetts.

Photo A: My name is **William D. Hersey.** I live in Norton, Massachusetts. My address is 68 Burt Street. My phone number area code is 617. The local number is 285-9531.

My address, No. 68 Burt Street is also easy to remember. Another of my students imagined this association. 68 = Chef. Burt Street sounds like "burp" street. Chef cooked up a batch of Hershey bars and hair and—*burrrrp!*

My phone number area code is 617. I think of it as representing a "show-dog." The three-digit prefix 285 is an "anvil." The four-digit main number is "ball bat." To remember this number you can picture a show dog displayed on an anvil in the middle of a table and holding a ball bat.

See how easy it is?

Remember, follow the *CASH DEPOSIT* formula and be sure to exaggerate the feature you observe. Make my hair six inches or six feet long, but exaggerate it in your mind. Then use it as a depository for the name and other facts you want to remember.

Okay, now meet the 18 persons pictured on the next pages. Their names are their real names, but the vital statistics have been changed. Take your time and meet them. But don't try to learn all the information at once. Go through the 18 pictures and practice associating the name with the face. After you have mastered this, it will be much easier to add pictures to represent the other information. I repeat—don't try to do too much at first.

 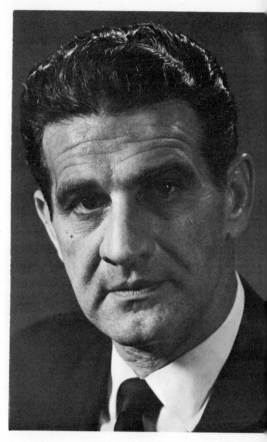

Photo 1: My real name is **Ruth Nadell.** I am a receptionist. I live at 215 Washington Street.

Photo 2: My name is **Monroe Myers.** I am a store detective. I live in Miami. I drive a sports car with the tag number 1-D 3241742.

Write in how you would remember this person.

_____
_____
_____

Write in how you would remember this man.

_____
_____
_____

Photo 3: I am **Annette Foosaner.** I am an actress. Mercury Artists Agency are my agents. I can be contacted at 407 Lincoln Road, Miami Beach, in care of them. The telephone number is Jefferson 2-7270.

Photo 4: I'm **John Stuart.** I'm the collection manager at the Atlas Loan Company, 6201 Rutland Street.

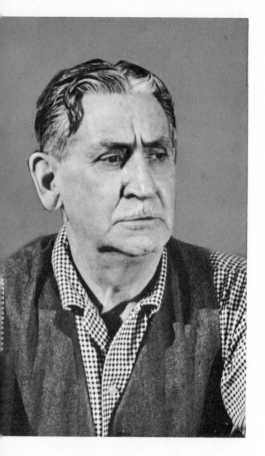

Photo 5: I'm **Eric Apple-white**, the proprietor of my own general store at 740 Main in Johnstown.

Photo 6: I'm a debutante. My name is **Diane Heaton.** Just in case you're interested, my phone number is area code 212, prefix 941, number 3209.

_____
_____
_____

_____
_____
_____

Photo 7: Me? I'm **George Odom.** Occupation? Presently keeping my eye on the town. One of these days I'm gonna get rich, when I finish digging up the yard where I live at 76 Oak Street. Look out now, I never forget a face. Will you forget mine?

Photo 8: I'm **David Aldrich** and that's my real name. I'm a pro ball player. The reason I need a shave is because I'm going to do a razor blade commercial on Channel 12.

_____
_____
_____

_____
_____
_____

Photo 9: I am **Bruce Solomon.** I'm a medical student. When I'm not at the university you can usually find me at the study hall in my dorm at 3175 College Lane. I hope someday to find a cure for cancer and will specialize in internal medicine.

Photo 10: I'm **Elida Deferes.** I'm a professional dancer. Sometimes I do a dance act with my mother, Alicia. Our phone number is 238-0860.

_____

_____

_____

_____

_____

_____

Photo 11: I'm the best dog-goned auctioneer in the business. **Bill Hess,** that's me. Sold 14 cows, 133 sheep and a span of horses within one hour the other day. Some record, huh? When you need a good auctioneer, call me up at 445-3709. Ask for Bill. Bill Hess.

Photo 12: I'm **Edward Ross.** Lawyer. Served as circuit court judge for 8 years. Now I'm senior partner of Ross, Blue, Burns and Cole. Suite 525, Roosevelt Building.

_____
_____
_____

_____
_____
_____

Photo 13: Tony Gulliver is my name. I'm a sound technician with a TV network. My favorite sport is boating and I own a speed boat with the numerals 8976 on the bow.

———————————
———————————
———————————

Photo 14: You caught me at a bad time, unless you want to contribute to the library fund drive. Last year we raised $1,357 at the benefit show. This year we hope to top that by at least $500.

Ruth Bernstein

———————————
———————————
———————————

Photo 15: I'm **Ben Hawkins.**
I'm not going to tell you my
occupation because I'm going
to try and fool you later on.
I'm a tenant of the Normandy
Building at 4916 Duke Road,
but that's all I'm going to
admit.

Photo 16: I'm **Budd Haw-kins.** My dad is Ben Hawkins
whom you've just met. I get
around a lot too. I sometimes
travel to my different jobs.
Last year I drove 34,850
miles.

_____
_____
_____

_____
_____
_____

Photo 17: Jerry Newby, that's me. I'm a sports car enthusiast. I drive in road races. Last year I test-drove a new type racer at Daytona and clocked 147.6 mph.

Photo 18: You met me before, but you didn't meet my mother, **Alicia Deferes.** Here she is. Isn't she beautiful? Who would believe she's 19 years older than I am?

_____
_____
_____

_____
_____
_____

Quiz: Supply the Correct Name for Each Person You've Met

Pictures of the 18 people to whom you've just been introduced appear below. The order has been changed, of course, as part of your memory test. If necessary, repeat the quiz until you have each one correctly identified by name.

You have just learned how easy it is to remember faces and names. You should have recognized every person in the quiz.

Here are some additional pointers which will help to develop your ability to remember faces, names and facts about people.

How Advertising Men Cash in on the Techniques of Controlled Association

Some of the most talked about ads in the country are those which have been presented in such a way that the public has learned to instantly associate the object with the sales message.

How do the successful advertising men do this time and again?

First, they select a feature of the product to be advertised on TV or in the magazines or papers. They select a feature just as you have been selecting features of the people's faces whom you've just met.

Notice how the advertising men "exaggerate" those features to make them unforgettable.

The tonic bottle as big as a man in the ad; "Manners" the butler in the napkin ad (reversing the process by showing him as a tiny man); the toothpaste tube as big as a man; the puppet "Wildroot Charley"; the "Flintstones"; even "Smokey the Bear," the public service cartoon announcement, is a variation of controlled association.

Everywhere you look, whether on TV, in a magazine, a billboard or in your daily newspaper, you see countless examples of this technique. The use of ridiculous exaggerations to implant the feature, the quality or something else salient about the advertised product is a tried and proven technique. Remember the diagrams of your alleged digestion, headaches, muscle aches? You actually see those little hammers clanking in your head.

So remember, practice the *CASH DEPOSIT* formula of controlled association. Do as the advertising men do: work to remember everyone you meet by following the rules.

A Few Tips on How to Remember Unusual and Everyday Names

Zinserheimer may be an unusual name, but it isn't any more difficult to remember than the so-called colorful names such as "Green," "Brown," "Black," "White" and "Blue." You must remember the name as a concrete thing you can see. Never make the mistake of saying, "Green, that's easy. I won't forget it." You must see that person with a green nose. Or perhaps with green grass growing on his head.

Now let's examine the name Zinserheimer. Zin/ser/hei/mer. I remember it by visualizing a "zinc" suit of armor on a "sir" (knight) riding "high" in the saddle of a "mare." See how easy it is? Remember, pictures persist and you retain the ridiculous!

Look for the easy way to remember names and you'll be surprised at how swiftly you'll master this technique.

How to Sharpen Your Ability to Observe People Closely

It is surprising to learn that most people search for the tiny details and overlook the obvious. So remember, look for the obvious always. Select the most prominent feature of a person's face and focus your attention on it by using the forces of the *CASH DEPOSIT* formula.

To make you more aware of people's distinctive facial characteristics, you might do the following:

On Monday   Practice looking for big mouths. You will see all sorts of mouths. You will find hard mouths; mouths turned down at the corners; sensuous mouths; small mouths and mouths accentuated or exaggerated by lipstick or even mustaches. The result of this will be that you will notice mouths from this day on.

On Tuesday   Start looking at eyes. You will be astonished to find how many different types of eyes there are. Usually, we think there are straight eyes and slanted eyes, blue or grey or brown; but, there are lots of different eyes. Some are round, and there are almost square eyes. Look for baggy eyes, narrow-set or wide-set eyes. Do this and you will discover how many people can be identified by their eyes.

On Wednesday   Look at ears. The ear is a distinctive form of identification. Many law enforcement agencies are already using the ears as well as fingerprints for identification. Look for a cauliflower ear particularly. Although there aren't many to be found these days, you will see the

shell-shaped ear, the heavy ear, the triangular ear
. . . all sorts, sizes and shapes. Whatever you think
it is, that is what it is. If you think of it as heavy, it *is*.
heavy. If you think of it as pointedly triangular like
Satan's ears, that's what you should make it. Sharpen
your observation of ears, eyes and mouths, but pay
close attention to ears.

On Thursday   Look at people's hair, noticing mainly the hairlines
and the thickness or coarseness, thinness or firmness
of hair. You may come across an occasional wig. As
you observe hair, you will quickly learn whether to
call a man's hair receding, or at what point to call
him bald.

On Friday   Look for big noses. You will see a great variety of
noses in all shapes, sizes and thicknesses. Pug noses,
banana-shaped, ski-shaped, humped, aquiline. I would
like to point out that the word "banana" is more
concrete and descriptive than the word "concave,"
therefore, I prefer the use of "banana." The point is,
imagine that the nose is an "oddity" if it is unusually
shaped and use it as your "ID" for remembering the
face.

On Saturday   Practice total visualization. Look at a face, then look
away from it. Try to see the entire face with its most
important detail or details as a mental picture in your
memory. At first, you will be surprised at how much
detail you will have overlooked. Once you practice
looking at a face, then looking away from it, your
memory for faces will improve overnight!

On Sunday   Learn to associate the names of ten people with their
faces. Perhaps they are people you have seen before,
but of whom you are uncertain. Ask the usher at
church. Ask the golf club pro. Ask somebody who
those people are. Find out and make that association.

Another good thing to practice on Sunday is the
caricatures or cartoons in the funnies. Many of my

> students imagine the people they meet in caricature
> or cartoon form and even compare them, thus apply-
> ing the "silliness" rule of the *CASH DEPOSIT* for-
> mula.

As you acquire these habits of observing faces and remembering names and facts about people, you will quickly become the most popular person within your circle.

I am sure that you will agree you now have grasped the fundamental skills necessary to enable you to enjoy the great rewards that come your way as a result of your ability to remember faces and names.

At the beginning of this chapter I told you there was no single factor so important to personal success as the ability and the willingness to use what you have learned in this book. You must be willing to prac-tice these concepts or you will lose them.

It will profit you to go on, memorizing the names and faces of every-one you meet; but you will gain nothing if you let it go after having learned how and then fail to put this knowledge to use.

Don't be like the Mr. Know-it-all I've met occasionally who usually goes around after watching my memory demonstration saying: "I know how he does it. He does it by association." Don't be like this person. He knows all about it, but doesn't put it to practical use. And as a result, he'll say to me, "I might call you Mr. Nestle." He starts thinking of the reasons why he *can't* do it instead of settling down to practice what I have taught him.

How Joe and Tony Silva Win and Hold
Customers in Their Gas Station

Successful service station owners, Joe and Tony Silva have built a fine reputation in Stoughton, Massachusetts, and as a result enjoy a re-warding business. The secret of their success?

You've learned that in this chapter.

Not only do they know each of their customers by name, but they use these customer names constantly in their contacts with other cus-tomers, often bringing together old friends.

When you drive into their station, they make it their business to know your name. They greet you by name the next time you drive in. And nothing builds good will and prestige better than a businessman's ability to make his customers feel important. Calling a customer by name is the best way to accomplish this.

Once you put this rule into constant practice, you will find new opportunities everywhere you go to endear yourself to people, to build your career, to enhance your personal life and widen your circle of friends.

This rule works two ways. For instance, if you walk into a strange bank for some change and the teller's sign clearly gives his name, use it. "Good morning, Mr. Roundwood. Would you mind cashing this check for me?"

Even if he doesn't know you, the chances are he will endeavor to give you the service you want. And when you say, "Thank you, Mr. Roundwood," and say it as though you've known him all your life, you'll be flabbergasted the next time he meets you because he'll *remember you!*

The secret of the winning of friends is merely to practice the golden rule. But first you have to show interest in remembering their names. No one likes to feel that you don't think enough about him or his importance to have taken the trouble to remember his name.

I cannot overstress the importance of these factors when it comes to impressing others. You will do well to practice diligently the rules and cash in on them.

Remember, treat everyone as an important person.

You now have within your power the golden key that will open and reopen doors for you. You can now make yourself increasingly welcome everywhere you go. You can now not only make that wonderful first impression, but that sparkling second impression as well. Don't neglect the great potential of this new skill. Don't permit yourself to regress to those old slovenly habits of observation.

XI

The Secret
of Remembering
Groups of People

"Oh, I have roamed o'er many lands,
And many friends I've met;
Not one fair scene or kindly smile
Can this fond heart forget."
—Thomas Haynes Bayly,
O, Steer My Bark to Erin's Isle

You can remember the names of individuals in groups as easily as you can remember the name of anyone you meet singly.

Just as we often look at a long word and think, "I can't learn that," so it is when we see a group of 30 or more strangers and think, "There are far too many for me to remember."

So we fail to try and as a consequence we never learn that we can.

You already are convinced that you can remember one person at a time. You have already demonstrated this ability. And this is half the battle. Likewise, it is half the secret. The other half of the secret of remembering groups of people is this: YOU MUST MEET THEM ONE AT A TIME.

That's all there is to it!

The first thing to do is to tell yourself that you can do it. Don't shrink back and give yourself reasons why you can't. Instead, think of the reasons why you can. It's as simple as that.

123

How I Remember the Names of 100 or
More Persons in Less Than 45 Minutes

I often hear people saying this about me: "This fellow just went around shaking hands with everybody and then he called them each by name. And he didn't miss a name!"

Actually, it isn't as easy as all that. It does take some effort to be able to do it. And it requires constant practice. But if you follow my method, by the time you reach the end of this chapter you will be able to go right out and be introduced to at least 20 people in half an hour and successfully recall every name! After your first attempt, your speed will naturally increase.

The first rule I follow is this: I ALWAYS SET MY OWN PACE FOR BEING INTRODUCED.

I get rid of the solicitous host tactfully and then go around introducing myself, taking care to talk to *one person at a time.*

I apply the *CASH DEPOSIT* formula you have learned. After I have met two or three people, I pause to mentally recall their names. Next, I meet several more people, and once again pause to recollect the names of those whom I've just met.

In the event that a name escapes me because of the commotion or because I didn't get it clearly the first time, I go back and say, "I'm sorry, but I want to get your name right. How did you say it was spelled?" Sometimes I'll use something a little more indirect, but the point is that I make certain I have the name correct. Then I go on to meeting the next group of people. One at a time, *at my own pace.*

If I am at a banquet where it is important to know where each party is sitting in a group together, I group them in logical order, going around the room from left to right just as I look around inside my memory bank.

Everything nice and neat and orderly, at my own pace.

When you become adept at remembering names, it often will not be necessary for you to look back into your mind to refresh your recall. Self-assurance and self-confidence comes with practice, so in the beginning when you are first starting out, take your time and don't rush.

Remember: Set your own pace.

Start practicing this technique at your earliest opportunity. Try it the next time you go to a party. Try it at the PTA meeting, that political rally, or at a sales convention. The important thing is to jump in with both feet and get going. Plan to learn!

By all means make a concerted effort to begin learning the names and faces and facts about the people you know you will meet again and particularly those who are important to you!

How I Got Started on Learning Large Groups of People

In hopes that my own story will help spark you into action, here's how I got started.

I was 44 years old. I went to a Rotary Club meeting in Sharon, Mass., to give a talk on mutual funds. During the dinner, the program chairman happened to comment that the lieutenant governor of the state had recently spoken there and had memorized each man's name.

"Say, Bill," he turned and said. "Can you do that?"

At first I was taken aback. Such a thought had never before occurred to me. "I don't know," I said hesitantly. "Maybe if you told me their names. . . ."

Well, the program chairman told me their names and as he did so, I made a sketch on the table cloth of the five tables around each of which there were six chairs. Then I wrote in the names of each man in the proper order in which he was seated. I also made a note of each man's business.

By sheer dint of determination and repetition, looking at the name and the business and then at the man, one at a time, one table at a time, I memorized them all within a half-hour. Though I knew I'd done it, I still wasn't sure of myself.

Then the big test came.

When I got into my talk on funds, and explained how a fund drew its income from many sources, I suggested they could form something like a fund from their own membership. I said: "You men represent almost 30 different sources of income." Then I named each man and his specific business.

Right then I was floored! Then and there they jumped up and gave me a rousing applause. I had no idea in the world of knowing how unprecedented that was. But I did know I had hit on something.

The next week I met 47 people at the Stoughton Rotary Club. I kept on doing this the hard way, memorizing during the meal without meeting the men personally. Finally, I began to apply some shortcuts. I would memorize a club roster in advance. When I would attend the meeting and finally meet each man face to face, I could say, "Oh, yes. You're Fred. You run the supermarket. And you're Jack. You're in dry goods."

Though I continued to talk mainly about funds, I began to get a reputation for having a phenomenal memory. Before long I was invited to join the Stoughton Rotary Club. Later I was asked to provide a program.

That's when I made my first talk on how to memorize telephone numbers. Eventually, I polished my talk and started making the rounds of clubs where I had talked before to let them know I was still in the investment business. It has paid me handsomely.

This can happen to you just as soon as you start practicing what you've learned so far in this book.

Important Tips to Remember About Meeting Groups

Never allow anyone to prevent you from setting your own pace as you introduce yourself to strangers. Never let anyone throw you off the track, distract you, or attempt to monopolize your attention.

When you are pushed along and hurriedly introduced to many people too quickly to get the names, go back as soon as you can and say, "You know, I didn't hear your name." —or— "I met you too quickly to get your name right."

Then go along at your own pace.

The people you meet will love you for it. REMEMBER, YOU ARE THE STRANGER IN THEIR MIDST. THEY ARE MORE INTERESTED IN IMPRESSING YOU THAN YOU SHOULD BE IN IMPRESSING THEM. This is because while you are observing and memorizing their faces and names, they are flattered because you are paying them close attention and because you are interested in what they have to say.

When you do this, you build up their egos, inflate their personalities and tell them through the medium of your undivided attention: "I know you're important!"

How long has it been since you've felt this way? Didn't you love it? Of course. That's why this time-tested maxim never fails.

Again, I'd like to restate this most important fundamental: ALWAYS LET THE OTHER PERSON IMPRESS YOU.

Stop worrying about what he thinks of you. He is bound to have a good impression of you provided that you make the effort to receive a good impression of him!

What to Do Before Meeting a New Group for the First Time

By all means take time out to learn as much as you can about the people you are about to meet. If they are in allied businesses, or are associated in some way, be certain that you try to determine who's who beforehand.

Not to do this can be disastrous. I know of a well-known public speaker who publicly addressed an important high-ranking Navy officer (who happened to be in civilian clothes at the time) as a petty officer. His *faux pas* brought down a thunder of catcalls and he was forced to abruptly cut short his talk.

Always find out who the VIP's are beforehand and have them pointed out to you if a photograph is unobtainable. It pays.

At a fund raising dinner several years ago, a newcomer to the theatre was guest of honor along with a number of important personages and movie stars. In the audience was former president Harry S. Truman. Though the young actor had been informed that Mr. Truman would be among the guests, he didn't pay attention. Later, when mingling with the crowd, Mr. Truman greeted the young man and paid him a generous compliment. In reply the young actor remarked: "Say, I'll bet people kid you a lot."

Mr. Truman smiled roguishly and asked what he meant.

"I'll bet a lot of people take you for Harry Truman."

"What's wrong with that?" retorted the grinning former president of the United States.

"Nothing. Except that it's embarrassing."

By all means always take a few minutes out to learn something about the people you are going to meet, people you want to meet, or people you have met before, perhaps under more or less favorable circumstances.

Begin by thinking about the things an old acquaintance would like to hear about himself. Don't overdo it. Be sincere. Practice gradually. Apply appreciation in small quantities. The key point to keep in mind is to be natural. Act as if you've known each person, or at least known about him, all your life.

Why It Is Important Not to Get Groups
Within Groups Mixed Up

To stand before a group of Boy Scout leaders, for example, or a gathering of people from competitive organizations and to identify them improperly is one of the worst sins a public speaker can commit. Nothing is more humiliating to a person than to stand up to receive a reward or an honorable mention or merely to take a bow and then hear the speaker transfer him (in error, of course) to another group which also may be in attendance.

I once attended a sales convention of travel agents and saw what happened when a speaker improperly addressed his remarks to the group as a whole, referring to everyone present as "travel insurance agents." Though there were three men present who were insurance agents, the rest of the audience of 400 people were not. Such an error is unforgivable and is a result of sheer carelessness.

Salesmen and workers in every field of endeavor take pride in their jobs and in their affiliations. When one is an executive salesman, he doesn't like to be seated with the junior salesmen, much less being "grouped" or compared to those of lesser rank or importance.

A man's badge of importance these days is worn inside his chest. When you stab him with an insult—and to demote him verbally is to insult him—nothing damages that badge of importance as much. So always be careful to get his title right and rank him where he belongs. If he's one of the pawns, keep him away from King's Row.

How to Avoid Confusing Occupations
of Groups of People

Whenever I meet a large gathering of senior or junior executives or employees, I always try to avoid confusing their names by going over the list of names and titles beforehand. Then I take time to group them. Here's how I grouped the employees of a bank before which I recently lectured. I obtained this list beforehand and studied it.

Position	Name	How I Associated Name
Chairman of the Board	Edward J. Shatter	Mr. Shutter-board. Shatter, Chair.
President	Hamilton S. Foster	Ham is Foster father, president.

1st Vice President	Lee G. Graham	General Lee eating *one* graham cracker.
2nd Vice President	Herman Koch	Herman made a "kotch" at *2nd* base.
Cashier	Roger Richman	"Jolly" Roger rich-man is cashier.

As you see, I first grouped the officers in their order of rank or importance, taking care to link their titles to their names. This insured against my making them less important than they were.

Now here's how I group people of the same rank or class but of different affiliations or from competitive firms in attendance at the same meeting.

Affiliation	Name	How I Associated Name
Ryan Drugs	Ben Stone	Ben eating a stone between 2 rye bread slabs.
Finney Drug Co.	Fred Hendricks	Fried hen throwing bricks at finny fish.
Finney Drug Co.	Leo McManus	Leo the lion and McManus mouse feeding a finny fish to a man named Leo McManus.

That's all there is to it. When I later meet these same people, I have no difficulty whatsoever in keeping their names and affiliations straight.

As you have seen, I attempt to convert the names into symbols or images which are then concrete and clearly recallable. *Ryan* recalled "ryebread" to my mind. *Finney* reminded me of a "finny fish."

You would probably choose different pictures. This is as it should be. Remember, pictures persist and you will retain the ridiculous.

Remember, no matter what your occupation is, or what you do in life both socially and career-wise, it pays to follow the principles explained in this chapter if you want to remember groups or large gatherings of people.

The secret of this is simple. One half of the battle is to know that you *can*. The other half is to put into practice what you know by plunging headlong into the crowd and meeting people ONE AT A TIME.

Set your own pace. Ask him his name again. Get it right. Hear it spelled. Make some comment about how "interesting" that name is. Never say, "My, that's a funny name." To do this is to make a derisive remark about a man's most precious possession.

"My, that's an interesting name." or "My, you have an unusual name. Tell me, what is its derivation?"

When asked questions like the ones above, people burst with enthusiasm to tell you and to like you. And when they like you, they also make it a point to remember you. And when they remember you, they look forward to doing business with you!

Remember, when you are face to face with someone you've just met, watch his face and select some prominent feature. Say to yourself, "Mr. Nosegay, you *do* have a nose that's gay when I think of that big king-sized nose of yours painted in gay colors." See it now. Repeat it to yourself until you visualize Mr. Nosegay with his nose painted in stripes. Perhaps you might imagine some nosegay flowers growing from his nostrils. In any event, you must see these associations in your mind if you are to remember.

There is no difference in remembering groups of people or merely one person at a time. You meet them all, one by one, one person at a time. That's the secret of success in remembering faces, names and facts about people. That's the secret of success in remembering anything. You can only focus your undivided attention on one thing at a time. See it now, then go on to something else.

How to Remember a Roster of Names, Addresses and Facts About People

I once addressed a large organization and witnessed (before I was called upon to speak) the bestowing of awards on the top 25 persons. I didn't sit there idly while the ceremony was going on. I used every second filing away each name and each face and each comment about each name made by the corporation president in my memory bank.

Later, after I gave my demonstration, I closed by going through that list of names *backwards*. Here's how I did it:

> I saw Nancy Fisher sitting on a *nail* fishing for the new typewriter she had been awarded for being the best typist for the year. I saw that nail protruding from her distinctive dimpled chin. She was wearing *fancy* clothes-Nancy.
>
> I saw Joel Cardin dressed like *Nero* playing a fiddle by drawing a bow across that huge nose of his. I hung the gold watch he won in the middle of his grinning mouth and pictured on the dial of that watch a dozen minute hands, representing the reason

for the award. He had been the most helpful employee in the motor pool, often making the boss wish he had "more six-handed Joels."

I saw Aggie Burton dressed like *Naomi* shooting marbles (aggies) for a prize of Barton (Burton) candies. Aggie Burton wearing a biblical gown shooting herself right into trouble with marbles. A big box of candy was awarded her for "trouble-shooter" of the year.

Get the idea? Of course you do. And you can do it too because you've learned how. All I did was file away the information I heard about each person as the announcement was made, they took a bow and strode up to the speakers' platform to receive their awards.

Of course, I tied in my summation by demonstrating the importance of the awards these efficient and loyal employees had won. Needless to say, I astonished everyone by my uncanny ability (seemingly so to them) to recall not only the details about the awards and the recipients, but to recall them in perfect order *backwards.*

As you know, all I did was look into my memory bank, begin with *nail,* No. 25, recall the information in that storage compartment, then go back to *Nero* and so forth.

When you find it necessary to remember a list of names or facts about people, it often pays to take the time to memorize that list. You'll not only be the center of attraction when you do this, you will also win kudos and a reputation as a person who "knows" what he's talking about.

No matter if you're a school teacher, a strawboss, a club woman, a construction gang foreman, or a Boy Scout leader, the ability to remember not only groups of people but the entire roster of their names can serve you in more ways than one. The ability to make others feel important by recognizing them and by remembering their names and facts which are important to them *is* the direct route to personal success.

Above all, practice the concepts and rules. Practice with pictures in newspapers, magazines and in other periodicals. Look at the faces, decide upon the outstanding characteristics and fix them in your mind's eye. Next, look at the name. See it separately at first, then connect the two images. Stimulate your imagination by following the *CASH DE-POSIT* formula. Practice by going through the magazines, recalling the names without glancing at the cut lines beneath the photographs. You'll be amazed at how swiftly you'll learn to do this!

You won't have to do more than follow the simple steps in order to go on to developing the ability to remember the names of hundreds, yes, I said *hundreds,* of people.

No matter what you do in life, as long as you are in contact with people, as long as you have something to offer them and they have something to offer you, you cannot afford not to practice and perfect your ability to remember names, faces and facts about people!

REVIEW QUESTIONS

1. Can you remember the names of individuals in groups as easily as you are able to remember the name of anyone you meet singly?
2. What is the first thing you must do in order to remember the people you meet in gatherings?
3. Why should you set your own pace for being introduced?
4. Why should you not be concerned with making an impression on others?
5. Why is it important not to get groups within groups mixed up?
6. How should you comment upon a person's name? What should you say upon hearing an unusual or interesting name? Should you ever say, "My, that's a *funny* name!"? If not, why not?
7. Practice remembering a roll or roster of names which are important to you.

   Following are two exercises which should take you a total of 21 minutes to do. One is a list of the Presidents of the United States and another is a list of the 50 states and their capitals. You will find them enumerated only by the basic code words in your memory banks. This same method is used when you memorize lists of people. Take time out now to learn these two exercises. You'll be surprised at how handy this knowledge will be to you at some future date. By all means, time yourself. If you score a 100 percent recall after only 21 minutes you've mastered the techniques in this book competently. If it takes you longer, you need more practice. It should take you (after a little practice) 60 seconds to recite the names of the Presidents (forwards or backwards) and 90 seconds to recite the names of the 50 states and their capitals.

I used this method to memorize the names of the Presidents, the states where they were born, the states from which they were elected, and their wives' maiden names. This took me 46 minutes to memorize!

hat	1789—Washington	GiVe-uP	Montgomery, Alabama
hen	1797—Adams	CoPy-Key	Juneau, Alaska
ham	1801—Jefferson	FiST	Phoenix, Arizona
oar	1809—Madison	VoiCe-hoPe	Little Rock, Arkansas
whale	1817—Monroe	FighTiNG	Sacramento, California

shoe	1825—Adams	*FuNneL*	Denver, Colorado
key	1829—Jackson	whi*FfeN-Poof*	Hartford, Connecticut
wife	1837—Van Buren	hea*Vy-MuG*	Dover, Delaware
pie	1841—Harrison	*FoRT*	Tallahassee, Florida
toys	1841—Tyler*	*FRiDay*	Atlanta, Georgia
tot	1845—Polk	*ViRiLe*	Honolulu, Hawaii
twine	1849—Taylor	o*VeRPower*	Boise, Idaho
thumb	1850—Fillmore	*FLieS*	Springfield, Illinois
tire	1853—Pierce	*FLaMe*	Indianapolis, Indiana
till	1857—Buchanan	*FaiLiNG*	Des Moines, Iowa
dish	1861—Lincoln	o*FfSHooT*	Topeka, Kansas
duck	1865—Johnson	*ViGiL*	Frankfort, Kentucky
dove	1869—Grant	*Foe-CHoP*	Baton Rouge, Louisiana
tub	1877—Hayes	ha*VoCK-Guy*	Augusta, Maine
noose	1881—Garfield	*Foe-FaTe*	Annapolis, Maryland
knight	1881—Arthur	*ViViD*	Boston, Massachusetts
noon	1885—Cleveland	hea*Vy-FoiL*	Lansing, Michigan
Naomi	1889—Harrison	hal*F-FaB*	St. Paul, Minnesota
Nero	1893—Cleveland	hal*F-BooM*	Jackson, Mississippi
nail	1897—McKinley	*Foe-BaNG*	Jefferson City, Missouri
niche	1901—Roosevelt	*BuST*	Helena, Montana
nag	1909—Taft	*BuSy-Bee*	Lincoln, Nebraska
knife	1913—Wilson	e*PiDeMic*	Carson City, Nevada
knob	1921—Harding	*BouNDer*	Concord, New Hampshire
messiah	1923—Coolidge	*BeNuMb*	Trenton, New Jersey
meat	1929—Hoover	*PawNBroker*	Santa Fe, New Mexico
money	1933—Roosevelt	ha*Ppy-MaMa*	Albany, New York
mom	1945—Truman	*PaRaLyze*	Raleigh, North Carolina
mare	1953—Eisenhower	*PLuM*	Columbia, South Carolina
mail	1961—Kennedy	*BuDGeT*	Bismarck, North Dakota
match			Pierre, South Dakota
mike			Columbus, Ohio
muff			Oklahoma City, Oklahoma
map			Salem, Oregon
rose			Harrisburg, Pennsylvania
heart			Providence, Rhode Island
horn			Nashville, Tennessee
ram			Austin, Texas
warrior			Salt Lake City, Utah
reel			Montpelier, Vermont
rajah			Richmond, Virginia
rake			Charleston, West Virginia
wharf			Olympia, Washington
rope			Madison, Wisconsin
alehouse			Cheyenne, Wyoming

* Tyler succeeded to the presidency on death of President William Henry Harrison, April 4, 1841. *A Friday!*

XII

How to Use Your Memory as a Diary Planner

"Imagination, where it is truly creative, is a faculty, not a quality; its seat is in the higher reason, and it is efficient only as the servant of the will.

"—Imagination, as too often understood, is mere fantasy—the image-making power common to all who have the gift of dreams."
—J. R. LOWELL

The above words make you pause and think, don't they? And when we think, ideas take form, associate with other ideas in our minds and suddenly blossom into the flames of creativity. When we act upon these creative thoughts, we make them emerge as realities—as dreams come true. Ideas are the true seeds of creativity. Without them we cannot develop original or new and different ways to win the rewards of success.

More often than we will admit, we allow our ideas to elude us like stealthy thieves escaping into the night. When we offer no resistance to this wholesale pilferage of our creativity, we suffer with poverty—poverty of original thought, poverty of opportunity.

We each have experienced the excitement that comes when a bright new idea flashes in our minds. "Gee!" we marvel, "this *is* a great idea. I've got to try it. If it works, it should make me rich!"

But like the stealthy criminal, the idea escapes us before we have a chance to record it, enlarge upon it, develop it and put it into action. Before we realize it, usually within a few hours, but more often within a few minutes, the idea is gone forever. And so is the golden opportunity it had so fleetingly promised.

This need not be, however. Your memory power can be utilized as a diary upon which fleeting ideas and other important things you want to remember can be recorded. Here's how.

How to Control Ideas and Thoughts Before They Elude You and How to Record Them in Your Mind

I like to compare ideas to criminals. If I do nothing and let them escape, I am guilty not only of cheating myself, but I am also guilty of aiding and abetting a "criminal act." It is a "crime" to be robbed of money-making opportunities. I like to think of myself as a "crime-buster" doing something about arresting these sneaky culprits.

First, the elusive ideas have to be arrested before they can be controlled. For this task I've invented a mnemonic device which I call the *Hersey Idea Dragnet*. This is a diagram of it:

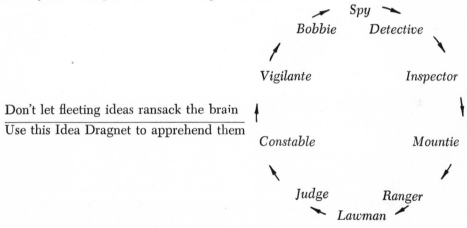

Don't let fleeting ideas ransack the brain
Use this Idea Dragnet to apprehend them

As you can see, the first consonant of each word arranged clockwise is a number. In my first dragnet I have 10 "policemen" who are ordered to track down the elusive idea and arrest him. Here's how it works.

Let's suppose I've just had an idea for a new mail order promotion brochure. I'm driving home so it is not convenient to write it down. Therefore I put my dragnet out after the idea before it escapes.

1. *Detective* takes custody of first clue. Brochure is 4-page offset.
2. *Inspector's* clue: Paper is 2-tone color which is striking.
3. *Mounty's* clue: Ink is in color which is a rich brown.
4. *Ranger's* clue: Front page of brochure is mock-up "dummy" like a daily newspaper with headline.
5. *Lawman's* clue: Paper text tells success stories about my students.
6. *Judge's* clue: Page 2. Photographs of my memory class in session.
7. *Constable's* clue: Self-addressed coupon inviting inquiries.
8. *Vigilante's* clue: Page 3. Text explaining the important features of having a good memory.
9. *Bobbie's* clue: Page 4. Testimonials from people who have benefited from my course.
10. *Spy's* clue: Success story of bank at which I trained its employees to remember faces and names.

Once I have my idea "culprit" surrounded by the dragnet, I arrest it. But what often happens is that I discover there are *two* ideas in one. I immediately "blow the whistle" and send out another dragnet. This time I call upon the armed forces.

1. Admiral
2. Ensign
3. Major
4. Airman
5. Lieutenant
6. General
7. Corporal
8. First Sergeant
9. Private
10. Seaman

I order the servicemen and officers to close-in. They do so efficiently. The idea is to make a tie-in mailing of the brochure corraled in the first dragnet with the bank's regular mailing to its commercial accounts. I could then benefit doubly and the bank would be the gainer because:

1. Admiral: The mailing cost would be partly subsidized by myself.
2. Ensign: The bank's success stories on page 4 would serve to "personalize" the bank's employees.
3. Major: If the promotion works, my brochure could be redesigned into a "house magazine."

4. Airman: The bank doesn't publish a "house magazine" so this may become an effective way to begin one at a negligible cost.
5. Lieutenant: If the bank agrees to make a mailing of the brochure, I could get hundreds of extra copies for a fraction of cost due to the bulk press run.
6. General: The brochure could be enlarged to carry more space about the services the bank has to offer.
7. Corporal: The bank could "sponsor" me in an honorarium fashion which would help "woo" new business from commercial firms their way.
8. First Sergeant: A memory "contest" could be held in the community, sponsored by the bank.
9. Private: The institution's employees could be invited to write testimonials telling how they use their memory power.
10. Seaman: The best letter of the month would receive an award of a dinner "on me"!

Of course, I associate these ideas by linking them according to the *CASH DEPOSIT* formula to the 10 "points" of the dragnet.

Now here are 10 more "idea dragnet" clue-catchers based on weapons:

1. Tear gas
2. Knife
3. Mortar
4. Revolver
5. Land mine
6. Shotgun
7. Carbine
8. Forty-five
9. Blackjack
10. Sword

And if this isn't enough, I call out the politicians:

1. Democrats
2. Independents
3. Mugwumps
4. Republicans
5. Liberals
6. Jack-in-office

7. Conservatives
8. Voters
9. Polls
10. Stay-at-home voters

Now, what happens after I've apprehended the elusive idea? Do I just leave it in the dragnet and forget about it? Absolutely not.

When I develop an idea in my mind, I impound the images by reviewing them several times. It doesn't matter if you store the idea in sequence in your memory bank, or if you keep it associated with the pegword lists I've just shown you. What does matter, however, is that you have a definite storage "place" for your ideas in which they may be held until you are ready to put them into action at a later time.

The use of a short list of key words for storage of ideas and other things you want to remember serves a variety of needs. You already have seen how the list of words that rhyme with numbers (one-gun, two-shoe, etc.) helps to memorize a financial statement. There are still other word lists which may be compiled.

Perhaps you may want to remember the birthdays and anniversaries of your relatives and friends. Here's how.

How to Remember Birthdays, Anniversaries and Other Important Dates

I picture my relatives with the date I want to remember. This is the simplest method of all. For instance, I have made a list of my grandparents on my father's side, my grandparents on my mother's side, four aunts and uncles on both parents' sides, and of course, my parents and in-laws. There are 16 people in all. I visualize them and associate the birth dates with their images. Here's how I do it. First, I give every month a number and begin the month words with "M" and make the *next* consonant represent the number of the month.

1–January, "Mu*d*"	7–July, "Muc*k*"
2–February, "Mi*n*e"	8–August, "Mo*v*ie"
3–March, "Mu*m*"	9–September, "Ma*p*"
4–April, "Mi*r*e"	10–October, "Mai*ds*"
5–May, "Mi*ll*"	11–November, "Mi*d-d*ay"
6–June, "Ma*sh*"	12–December, "Mu*tton*"

A birthday on the 23d of January might be associated as: "Mu*ddy* enemy."

A birthday on the 14th of February might be remembered as: "Mi*ne dear.*"

An anniversary on the 20th of March might be remembered as: "Mu*m noise.*"

An anniversary on the 7th of April might be remembered as: "Gooey *mire.*"

A birthday on the 15th of December might be remembered as: "*Mutton tallow.*" Get the idea? Not only is this fun, but once you've associated the date word-equivalents to the image of your friend or relative, you never will forget it!

The development of a mental diary "planner" is easy when you build your temporary memory banks with appropriate words to fit each situation. These are the first steps you must take before your mental diary will work for you.

For example, when I began to write this book, I compiled the following list of words beginning with "B" for book to use them for the temporary storage of ideas.

| 1. Bat | 2. Bone | 3. Bum | 4. Boar | 5. Bell |
| 6. Badge | 7. Bag | 8. Beef | 9. Babe | 10. Boots |

As an idea flashes in my mind, I surround it with the dragnet and arrest it. I take it into custody by making vigorous and ridiculously vivid associations with the dragnet words. This, then, is the first step to take before you can use your memory as a diary planner.

After your idea has been "prisoner," you retire the dragnet and keep it in readiness for the next time when you will activate it. As for the "imprisoned idea" which I have "sent up the river," it has been locked firmly by the chain of my mental diary.

Figuratively, the idea has been placed where it can be released on the day its "sentence" is up. For example, the idea I had for the brochure is scheduled to be set free on Friday when I have lunch with the bank president and the promotion director. But how do I remember it is to be released when Friday rolls around?

That's easy. Here's the explanation.

How to Develop a Perpetual Calendar
in Your Mental Diary Planning System

Thinking of your ideas as prisoners also makes you think of "shackles" or leg irons. Naturally this makes you think of a "chain gang." And men in a chain gang count the hours, days, weeks and months and years. At the day when their sentences are up *they let you know* the time has come for their liberation!

But no warden releases his prisoners merely on their say-so. He has a record book which he consults. At the beginning of each month he reviews all the sentences being served and schedules releases accordingly.

So it is in your mental diary. At the beginning of each month you merely "review" what must be done on the certain days of that month. Here's how I do it. I visualize this chain in my mind:

MUD – MINE – MUM – MIRE – MILL – MASH – MUCK – MOVIE – MAP – MAIDS – MID-DAY – MUTTON

Each time during the past weeks and months when I made an appointment or date, or wanted to remember a birthday or anniversary, I merely linked it with the mental chain of months. At the first of June (MASH) there were three things I wanted to remember to do during that month. I saw those things clearly in the chain gang of ideas linked to that picture word MASH. Here they are:

1. Collect $94.50 from Mr. McCoy on the 10th of June.
2. On the 15th return Mr. Wiley's certificate #32624.
3. On the 18th, have lunch with Mr. Tyler of 6210–81st Street and see if he has found the lost certificates Nos. 7500 and 482.

And here's how I've associated them with MASH:

1. I see myself in the *woods* with Mr. McCoy and we're sitting on some *barrels* of *mash*.

   woods = 10th . . . barrels = $94.50 . . . mash = June

2. I see myself and Mr. Wiley dressed as *outlaw moonshiners* guarding the *mash*.

   outlaw = 15th . . . moonshiners = 32624 certificate number
   . . . mash = June

3. I see Mr. Tyler and I calmly eating lunch atop a *vat* of *mash* while the *Revenue Agents* (led by Eliot Ness) are shooting at us.

vat = 18th . . . *mash* = June . . . *revenue agents* = 482
& 6210 lost securities.

Again you see the remarkable versatility of the number code and how it lends itself so appropriately to vividly memorable associations. That's all there is to it!

Now let's suppose you want to add the time of the appointment you are to keep or the weekday instead of the day of the month, here's what to do.

How to Keep Track of Time in Your Mental Diary

If you were in the service and had learned how to number the hours from 0100 to 2400, you can make your own list of words from the number dictionary at the back of this book. However you will find it difficult to come up with so many words beginning with the letter "H" which stands for hour. It is much simpler to have the words begin with a "T" for "time."

If you need to remember specific hours and minutes, you can use the time word code to signify the hour, then add to it a standard word to signify the minutes. Here are the words I use which begin with a "T" representing all the hours from 1 (A.M.) to 24 (midnight).

1. Tot	7. Tag	13. Toy dame	19. Tied up
2. Ton	8. Tough	14. Totter	20. Tines
3. Time	9. Top	15. Toddle	21. TNT
4. Tar	10. Tights	16. Toy dish	22. Tune-in
5. Tool	11. Tooted	17. Toy duck	23. Tan me
6. Tissue	12. Toytown	18. Teed-off	24. Tenor

Now here's how to remember precise times:

8:24 A.M. = tough Nero.	See tough Nero demonstrating how tough he is by hitting himself with the fiddle while standing in the flames.
12:49 A.M. = Toytown, Arabia.	See Disneyland in the middle of an Arabian City.
2:45 P.M. = totter reel.	See yourself tottering and reeling.

9:30 P.M. = TNT mouse.   See yourself trying to catch a mouse with a bundle of TNT. (Fuse lit, of course!)

The remarkable simplicity of this method enables you to do anything you want when it comes to remembering time schedules. This story illustrates the advantages you get when you adapt this method to suit your own requirements.

How Danny Morehead Was Promoted to Radio Station Manager due to His Phenomenal Ability to Remember Program Time Slots

Less than a week after he had completed my memory course, Danny, an assistant program director for an eastern broadcasting station, rushed into his boss's office. "I just realized that a mistake was made in the programming!" he cried. "If those two automobile commercials are played in the same quarter hour, we'll lose *both* accounts." He glanced at his watch. It was 8:43.

"But how'd *you* know that?" Danny's boss said a few minutes later after he gave the DeeJay orders to spread the announcements. "You weren't here yesterday. And the programs haven't been made up yet."

"I remember it from day before yesterday," Danny said.

"You *remember* it!" his boss replied. "But that's impossible. How could that be? Artie, you and I sat in this office and worked out the program for today. That was two days ago. And until last night, *I* had the only copy."

What happened next proved to be the most astonishing thing the radio station president was ever to witness. Danny called out every single commercial scheduled and the correct time it was to be aired for the next 12 hours, without a single mistake!

How did he accomplish this in such a short time? Danny had thoroughly applied himself to the practice of the technique you've just learned. His efforts were soon rewarded. Within four months he received a handsome raise in salary and was promoted to station manager. Not only that, but Danny also used the same memory power techniques explained in this book to master the difficult FCC technician tests to qualify as first phone for the job!

Here's how Danny used this method to memorize the program schedules.

First, he knew that his station always separated commercials which were in open opposition to each other in the same half- and/or quarter-hour segments. Not only was this common sense, but also it was an important principle which kept advertisers from becoming disgruntled. Therefore, he knew that no two firms in the same line were to appear together in the same quarter-hours, so he knew what to avoid. When he discovered the impending error-to-be his diary planner memory closed on it like a steel trap.

There are many other success stories just like Danny's which prove time and again that when one's memory power is unleashed in the right direction it is possible to rocket to success!

It doesn't matter what kind of work you do, whether you're a physician or a pharmacist, an attorney or a salesman, when you use the techniques you have learned in this book, and practice them daily, you too can develop a foolproof mental diary.

How to Remember Appointments and Schedules and Record Them in Your Mental Diary

Nothing is easier or more profitable than a daily plan which is followed. When you learn to work that plan, not only do you save wasted time and effort, but you also benefit from a well-ordered life. It's amazing how few people actually plan what they want to do in work or play, and it's even more amazing how some people accomplish anything at all.

We won't go into the merits of having a planned life and following it. Instead, we will discuss the few simple methods employed by the successful people who are successful because they get everything done that they plan.

It is astonishing how much more you accomplish when you don't forget to do anything. When you get more done during a workday, you are more valuable to yourself and to your family. For this reason it pays to follow a methodical schedule.

I always work out what I want to do with a pad and pencil, then I evaluate it in order to determine just what is the most profitable and most direct way to get things done. After that, I memorize the list. When this list is clear in my mind, I automatically schedule what I do without the time-consuming necessity of rooting through a briefcase or trying to decipher notes I had written previously.

The reason this works so well for me is because I have developed confidence in my ability to never forget. And because my mental diary planner is always in my mind, I think more about what I am doing and such devotion of thought is what makes successful achievement possible.

It is uncanny how many things you can think of to do when you have a well-planned mental schedule in mind. Everyone has heard the old saw, "plan your work and work your plan." Here's how I do it:

Every evening before I retire I check my idea dragnets for the things I am to do the following day. Then I lay out what I want to accomplish the next day. After that, I memorize the list and "sleep on it."

I have been doing this for years. It works for me and will also work for you when you remember to do the following things:

1. Memorize what you want to do. For this I use a daily list of basic words upon which I deposit my associations.
2. I use mental idea "notebooks" or dragnets to record the things I want to do during each day. I invent new lists of basic words once in a while to fit the various tasks to be done.
3. I keep my mental diary planner in mind and after completing each assignment I am able to recall the next thing to do and the next because they are clear in my mind.

Here's my daily list of permanent basic word "notebooks" upon which I note down the things to be done the following day.

Sunday: "WED" is the code word because "W" indicates "week" and "d" the first day. "WED" because most "weddings" occur on Sunday.

Monday: "WINE" is the code word because "W" again indicates "week" and "n" the second day. Many people have headaches from drinking too much "WINE" at weddings on "WED" day.

Tuesday: "WHAM!" That's when I really get up steam.

Wednesday: "WIRE" I'm a real hot "WIRE" by Wednesday.

Thursday: "WOOL" No time for "WOOL" gathering.

Friday: "WITCH" I use the broom of the "WITCH" to keep the cobwebs from my mind.

Saturday: "WICK" I make sure I'm not burning the candle's "WICK" at both ends.

Now you see how I have made pictures containing several elements to note down relationships for the day, hour, month and nature of the appointment.

Actually this is easier than it seems, but you can only find this out for yourself by practicing the "how to" rules I've just explained. It's like anything else. You can never know how simple a thing is to do until you learn the fundamentals and then put those fundamentals into action for your own profit.

You might not be able to remember all the details of a painting which hangs in a friend's home. However if you were the artist, you would probably remember most, if not every one of the details. This is because the painting is the child of your own creative imagination.

Try it and see.

Yes, try it and see. I've deliberately repeated try it and see because on every page of this book you cannot learn and then put into practice the principles of my memory system until you have tried it and seen!

By all means use your own imagination to coin new basic word lists to help you remember your own mental diary planner. You may already be thinking of other, more appropriate lists. Perhaps you are thinking of storing your ideas on the furnishings and fixtures of each room in your house. Or perhaps you are thinking of keeping them in your car like the automobile salesman does to remember his prices. One man I know always thinks of the months in different colors. You may use pictures which are unforgettably associated with certain months, as a firecracker exploding on the 4th of July or as a Christmas Tree for December, or perhaps as a candy heart for February.

Choose the techniques which enable you to cash in on the methods in this chapter at once. Use them to save yourself time, money and embarrassment. Use them to help build that reputation you want as a man or woman who gets things done. When you do this, your potential for successful and useful living will come to fruition.

REVIEW QUESTIONS

1. What are ideas?
2. What is the first thing to do before you can control ideas and thoughts before they elude you?
3. Why is it necessary to first capture an idea in your idea dragnet?
4. Why can't you merely leave your idea in the dragnet after you've nailed it?

5. Why must you move the idea to your mental diary planner after you review it later? Is this because you want to remember it for an indefinite period or because you don't want it to elude you again? Or both?

6. Why must you have a basic list of words to remember months? Why can't you develop a mental diary planner until after you construct temporary memory banks of apropos words?

7. Why is it necessary to have a perpetual calendar in your mental diary planning system?

8. How do you go about keeping track of time in your mental diary?

9. How can you cash in on your ability to remember appointments and times and dates?

10. Why is it necessary to have the following in this sequence before you can develop a foolproof mental diary?

    1. A mental idea dragnet.
    2. A chain gang of basic words signifying the months.
    3. A nomenclature of basic words for day of week by date.
    4. A list of words for the weekdays in mental notebook "form."
    5. A list of basic words for hours of the day.

11. Remember, *try it and see.*

XIII

One: How to Use
Your Memory for
Self-improvement

"Let not soft slumber close your eyes,
Before you've collected thrice
The train of action through the day!
Where have my feet chose out their way?
What have I learnt, where'er I've been?
From all I've heard, from all I've seen?
What have I more that's worth the knowing?
What have I done that's worth the doing?
What have I sought that I should shun?
What duty have I left undone?
Or into what new follies run?
These self-inquiries are the road
That lead to virtue and to God."
      —ISAAC WATTS, *Self-Examination*

Read over the poem *Self-Examination* and close your eyes to think over these thoughts for a few moments.

Self-improvement is contained and defined in this 17th century English theologian's poem. Those words were written 250 years ago; they still apply today.

I prefer to remember Isaac Watts' poem as his *"Chagrin Choir"* of self-examination. I have memorized this because I want to. Whenever I hear the words "Chagrin Choir" or the word "Jesus" I am reminded of this wonderful poem. The words "Chagrin Choir" have a double meaning to me. Isaac Watts was born in 1674, hence the word *"Chagrin"* which also means the state of being humbled. He was 74 when he died, hence the word *"Choir"* which also means that choirs still sing the hymns he

147

has written so long ago. I associate the word "Jesus" to signify the 600 poems and hymns Watts has written.

I mention this because I want to point out to you another way your memory power helps you improve your life. Whenever I hear the words "Watts," "Chagrin Choir" and "Jesus," I am reminded of this expressive poetry. Strange as it may seem, those lines have popped into my head just when I needed them most, often at the times when I needed to humble myself or to improve my manner of doing something.

Take time out now to commit these lines to your memory. It shouldn't take you more than six or seven minutes because there are only 13 lines. This is easily accomplished when you file away each line in the first 13 memory storage compartments in your mental bank.

Do it now.

Once you have thoroughly memorized this poem of self-examination, no matter what you want to do in the way of self-improvement you will remember to do! For instance, if I realize that I have a bad habit I want to break such as biting my nails or forgetting to take off my hat upon entering a restaurant, I remember it like this. I see lightning striking me every time I begin to bite my nails. Watts = electric power; electric power = lightning.

I remember the poem at once and, quick as lightning, the habit is broken! That's all there is to it. Pause now and think about the bad habits you want to break. Associate that habit with a lightning bolt and see it striking you whenever you catch yourself regressing.

How to Use Your Memory Power
to Overcome Absent-Mindedness

Absent-mindedness is the common affliction of the capable and conscientious alike. Everyone has experienced the frustrating and sometimes costly lapses of memory which come from too great concentration on one thing and not enough on another. In the main, most cases of absent-mindedness are not due to carelessness!

We tend to be absent-minded because we are not thinking about putting our keys down on the living room table when we do so and we aren't thinking about putting the cat in the refrigerator and the milk outside.

It is impossible to count the dollars, even the lives, which are lost each day because of absent-mindedness.

Recently a small airplane was lost and crash-landed in the Florida

Everglades because the pilot owner of the plane was absent-minded. He kept forgetting to have his compass adjusted.

Not too long ago an absent-minded boat skipper nearly lost his boat and his life because he forgot to check the weather reports before setting sail. If he had, he would have seen the gale warnings flying.

I once stopped in the lost and found department of a large New York hotel and asked the woman in charge, "What's the oddest article anyone has ever lost?"

She told me that a few years before someone had lost a glass eye. Seems impossible, doesn't it? But it's true.

She went on to tell me about a man who had even forgotten his wooden leg! The things most commonly left behind are men's pajamas and shirts. Women seldom forget pajamas or night clothing, but often leave their undies hanging in the bathroom.

The next morning I checked with her again. During the night a guest had forgotten a case of good Scotch and someone else had left five pairs of trousers hanging in a closet!

No doubt everyone has been absent-minded at one time or another, but, the point is, what can we do about it?

First, before we can conquer absent-mindedness we have to understand why we cannot remember where we placed our glasses or where we put the car keys or why we left that umbrella behind. Often, absent-mindedness indicates a tremendous ability to concentrate on one thing at a time. For example, when we are thinking about checking out of a hotel on time, catching a plane or train on time, we tend to forget the habitual things we do, such as removing our eyeglasses and putting them down on the dresser, etc. Therefore, because we are *unconscious* of the act of putting the glasses in our pockets or on that dresser, we cannot remember.

Try this cure and see!

How to Protect Yourself from Being Absent-Minded—Tie Mental Strings Around Your Mind

Suppose you want to store some candles in the attic. How will you remember them months later when you need them? How will you remember where they are? You must literally tie a string around your memory. Here's how: Picture those candles in the place where you store them *lighted*. See the flickering flames.

If you have been in the habit of losing your glasses or keys, next time and every time thereafter say to yourself, "I broke my glasses on the kitchen sink."—or—"I scratched the piano with my keys." The secret is that you must see those broken glasses on the piano or the sink or wherever you put them.

A businessman I know reminds himself of important things he wants to do simply by crumpling a dollar bill in his pocket. Whenever he reaches in for some parking meter change or a coin for a phone call, he remembers.

I know a surgeon who turns the face of his alarm clock to the wall whenever he wants to remember an operation he has to perform the first thing that day.

A housewife I know drops a pot-holder on the floor of her kitchen whenever she puts something in the oven. What housewife could forget that?

A more purposeful method is to place the oddity or thing you want to remember in the way of your thought pattern. The secret is to place it in such a way that you can't help but trip over it.

Whenever I want to remember to pick up my shirts from the laundry when I come back through Stoughton, I visualize those shirts stacked up so high that the underpass on the expressway at the Stoughton exit is blocked. I can just see my car smashing through that blockade with my good shirts flying every which way through the air. When I reach that exit later in the day, I see those shirts and remember to get then.

An accountant I know remembers everyone else's tax and financial affairs but has difficulty remembering his own. I helped him cure his habit by suggesting that the next time he sits down to dinner he can picture a tax form or a bill that's due in place of his plate. Who could forget filing a tax return if you had your dinner served on it?

Other methods may range from visualizing the thing you want to remember hanging from your key chain, pasted to your front door, suspended from the light fixture, plastered across the TV screen or in anyone of a thousand different and amusing ways. Try it and see.

What to Do When Your Mind Goes Blank
and You Lose Your Train of Thought

Everyone has at one time or another found himself unable to think of what he had just been discussing because of an interruption. Sometimes we are poised with a question to ask and just as we stand up to speak—blotto!

When this happens, as when giving a speech, avoid forcing your mind to race or grope desperately for the lost idea. Mentally review something you have just said previous to the blackout and see if that doesn't lead you into the missing thought. Naturally, if you are actually standing before an audience, you will avoid standing there looking foolish with your mouth flaps hanging open. The best thing to do is to be honest and admit it. Say, "I had a good thought, but for the moment it escapes me . . ." Then, repeat a few of the thoughts you had mentioned. "Let's see. We were talking about . . ." When you do this, your audience will like you for that human touch. They can identify sympathetically with you because the same thing has no doubt happened to them too!

Once I heard a man delivering a lecture that took one hour. Suddenly, he got stuck. After thinking a moment, he retraced his thoughts and picked up where he had left off before. Suddenly, the same thing happened again. This time he was unable to go on. Without hesitation he smiled at his audience and said: "This is ridiculous. I know this lecture thoroughly. I have given it many times as you all know. But I'm not going to let anything deprive me of sharing with you what I am prepared to give you." With that he reached into his pocket, took out a copy of the lecture, looked up his place and then continued.

As though of one mind the entire audience applauded this courageous and honest speaker.

Your victory over absent-mindedness is an important step in the direction of success with your memory power. Put these ideas to work for yourself now.

How to Use Your Memory Power to Help You Concentrate when Under Fire!

Concentration means the ability to focus attention in an *intense* manner on one subject, problem or object at a time. Today, the man who can fix his attention on a difficult problem while in the midst of the bedlam of modern-day distractions is a man who has the ability to forge ahead. He is undisturbed by outside influences. The more pressures brought to bear against him, the more effectively he functions as a decision-maker and a businessman. He has developed his ability to concentrate to such a degree that he can accomplish any task under fire, in the midst of jangling telephones, squawling babies, clanging machines or chattering women.

Most of us blame the lack of solitude or crowded working or living conditions for our inability to get jobs done; meaning, of course, work that requires concentration. Actually, this is the typical excuse of the procrastinator. He gives you the reasons why he can't do something; never the reasons why he can. This is why I'm not going to tell you to get away from it all in order to concentrate.

Here's how to concentrate in a methodical manner.

Build a Fence Around Yourself when
  Concentrating

As you know there are many degrees of attention. During sleep it is nil; when you are half-awake you are only half-aware, and so forth. When we build a fence around our mental faculties and then close its gate it is possible to shut out all outside distractions.

How to Fence Memory Power in While
Solving Problems and Learning or Reading

When roaring jets, shouting children, blaring TV sets and other sounds have been shut out of your conscious mind while you are concentrating, the faintest whisper will often distract you. This is because we attune ourselves to fix attention without following a specific plan of study or a systematized method of thought. In other words we can be disrupted during our attempts to concentrate because we are not practicing a definite concentration procedure.

The essence of concentration is attention and the essence of attention is sight. When you see by fixing your attention on an object, thought, or problem you are, to some degree, concentrating. If your brain is over-taxed from lack of sleep, you cannot focus your attention enough to concentrate deeply. Therefore, the first rule to observe is to make certain your brain has not gone too long without rest.

Secondly, it is possible to divide your attention. For instance, you can drive a car and carry on a conversation or listen to the radio. You can play some musical instrument and laugh and joke with your friends at the same time. But this does not, I repeat, this does *not* mean you *can concentrate* when your attention is divided. The second rule to follow is to be sure you can give the problem upon which you want to focus your mind your complete undivided attention.

In order to accomplish this you must develop a procedure which will compel you to concentrate deeply. To achieve this end I have developed a method which I have used successfully. By following this formula I have been able to lose myself in the deepest of thought during all kinds of distracting activities and loud noises.

The Hersey Memory Power-Fence, and How to Use It for Deep Concentration

When you visualize this formula and are able to focus your attention on each of the five procedures, neither a whisper nor a jarring blast will ever distract you again if you don't want to be disturbed. (*See following page.*)

What does this fence look like to you? Can you, with a stretch of your imagination, visualize it as a high-tension line or a fence which gives you the illusion of depth and perspective? If you can, you've got the idea.

Beginning with "FACTS," and descending deeper and deeper into the thought to the foreground where you eventually execute your decision or resolve your problem, are the five words which make up the formula.

Here are the images you must next associate with these five "fence" words:

1. **FACTS** = See yourself in a room inside your memory bank. You are seated at a long polished library table. Around you within reach of your hands are shelves. The shelves are laden down with books of facts. Before you is this diagram on an imaginary piece of paper:

    FACTS
    ALL THE FACTS
    CONCENTRATION
    THOUGHT
    SUM UP

2. **EVALUATION** = You will now see yourself placing all the facts before you on the huge table. You then will concentrate on them, think about them and

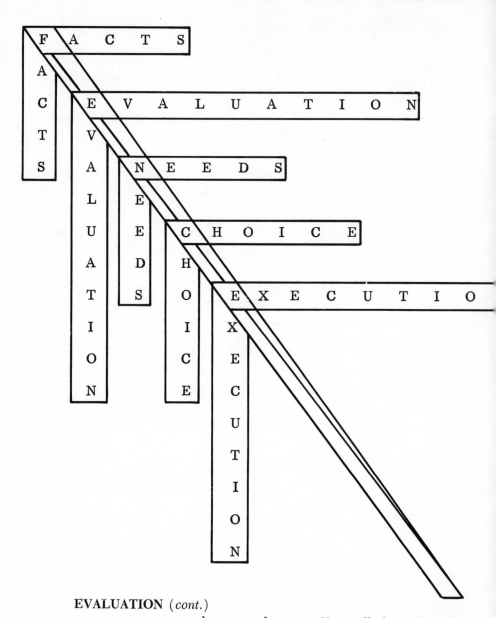

EVALUATION (*cont.*)

then sum them up. You will then place the sums of these facts before you for evaluation. You are concentrating on each step, each picket in the fence around you. Before you is this formula on the paper:

EVALUATION (*cont.*)

> EVALUATION
> VIEW ALL VIEWPOINTS
> ACCEPT ONLY LOGIC
> LOOK FOR LOOPHOLES
> UMPIRE PROS & CONS
> ADAPT THE RIGHT SIDE
> TALLY THE BENEFITS
> INQUIRE: "IS IT WORTH IT?"
> OPTIONS YOU CAN TAKE
> NO OR YES

3. NEEDS = Consider each point in the evaluation process. Then consider these needs:

> NEEDS
> EDUCATION
> EDGE OVER OTHERS
> DRAW DIVIDENDS
> SECURITY IN FUTURE

4. CHOICE = Consider next each of the NEEDS, then *review* the first three steps going over each point which you have placed on the pickets of the fence around you. Then make your

> CHOICE
> HAVE AN OPTION
> OBLIGATION TO SELF
> IS IT THE BEST?
> COMPARE AGAIN
> ELECT ONE CHOICE

5. EXECUTION = Now that you have gone over each step so far and have reached a final decision, put your plan into action by following the formula below:

> EXECUTION
> X IT OUT—IF YOU'RE NOT SURE!
> EVACUATE FOR ACTION
> COOL OFF NEXT
> UNLEASH YOUR ENERGY
> THINGS MUST NOW HUM

EXECUTION (*cont.*)

INCREASED EFFORT
ON THE GO OR BUST!
NEVER QUIT

Amazingly simple, isn't it? Because of its simplicity, this formula can prove to be one of the most dynamic mnemonic aids to success you've ever mastered, once you put it into action. Here's a living example of how it works.

How Ted Marsh Learned the Memory-Fence Formula and Used It to Make a Fortune

Ted Marsh still wasn't sure after learning the memory-fence formula. He wasn't sure he would continue to remember the memory system, and he wasn't sure of exactly how he would ever learn to make decisions.

This was Ted's main problem. He had been unsure of himself most of his adult life, since the time when he had first left school and went into business for himself, repairing TV sets. A short time after he had established his business he made the mistake of overexpanding, going overboard on advertising and hiring more servicemen than the trade could support.

At age 25, he was bankrupt. For the next 10 years, he halfheartedly worked as a TV technician for someone else. Though never content with his humdrum job, he plodded along in the traces, hardly dreaming of the day when he might re-enter business for himself.

Ted's wife happened to work for an organization where I was conducting a training course. When she saw the self-confidence and the new zest in herself and everyone around her after the course was given, she asked if she could enroll her husband in my next class. Then she explained why. "My husband is so afraid of making a mistake again that he can't decide on anything. I believe that if anyone can help him, you can. Your memory course will help him remember the reasons why he went bankrupt. Perhaps then he'll stop blaming himself and become the man I was once so proud of!"

This sounded like a tall order, too much to expect, but by the time Ted completed my course he and I had become friends. He wouldn't admit, however, that he had mastered the system. Over coffee after my last class he made a chance remark that he had an opportunity to buy out his employer who was retiring because of poor health. "Gosh, Bill," he said, "I don't know what to do."

"Oh, come on," I chided him. "How about my memory power-fence formula you learned night before last? Have you put it to the test?"

He nodded.

"Well, get busy then."

"But I can't," he protested. "This is different. In order to buy the business, I'll have to take out a second mortgage on my house. I couldn't do that and . . ."

I cut him off with an impatient gesture. "Try it now, Ted. Use the formula and let it help you make a decision. If it's no, forget it. If it's yes, and if you believe in yourself and your ability, do it now!"

Ted went home, drew a chair up to the kitchen table and concentrated on the imaginary piece of paper. At first he couldn't see the facts on it. He tried, but he couldn't project his thinking. He just couldn't give the opportunity his undivided attention.

Then, he thought of the words "all the facts." About me, he wondered, or about the old man's business? No, first I have to start with myself. What are the facts about myself? I failed because I was an undercapitalized eager-beaver with grandiose ideas. I failed because I overexpanded too quickly. I failed because I was too young and too inexperienced at the time. Now I know better. Now I can see how it was with me then. I can see myself as I was then, and now.

The opportunity? It's good. Real good. A chance like this doesn't come every day. There won't be any good will to buy, just the fixtures, tools, stock and the service truck. I can take over the lease.

Now I've got to *concentrate*. Let me think about it now. Teddy thought to himself, concentrating deeper and deeper, wrapped in thought. He went on to consider every aspect of the business. Then he summed up what he had to offer and what the business had to offer him.

He placed all the facts before him on the imaginary table in his mind. When he had them completely organized in his thoughts, he began to see that one of the reasons why he had been so irresolute since his business failure was because he hadn't remembered or thought about the reasons he had gone broke. He could see them each clearly at long last. With the power of his memory he saw things for the first time which he had never before been able to recognize.

Then he began to evaluate, first examining all the viewpoints. He took into consideration his side of it and the customers' side of it when he asked himself why should the same customers continue as before when it became known that his employer had sold out? For the first time, due to the method of the formula, Ted discovered that he wasn't viewing the optimistic viewpoint: Why shouldn't people continue to call the firm for service?

He began to grow more confident and sure of himself. He kept himself hobbled somewhat, as though afraid to become enthusiastic for fear that this might cloud his reasoning. He began to look only for the logic and it made sense. As a skilled TV technician, he knew what he was doing. He knew the trade from both sides, the workbench and the counter. He had every right and reason in the world to go through with it.

Loopholes were his next consideration. Was this really on the up and up? Were there any hidden loopholes which his employer had failed to reveal? Would he be fully protected?

Ted then began to judge the pros and cons. At first he had to umpire them, because the pros and cons were clashing in conflict. Before long he recognized and then began to adapt the right side of the argument. It was *right* for him, but what next did he have to consider?

Tally the benefits. He realized that he had everything to gain and only a second mortgage on his house to pay. He could pay it off out of the profits.

But is it worth it? He considered that point also. Of course it was. He had been working in the place long enough to know the business was profitable. The price was reasonable and he wasn't paying for "blue sky."

He next considered the options he could take. By continuing to work as he had been with his wife answering the phone, he wouldn't have to hire an extra man right away. He could make the service calls and work late repairing the sets. Instead of living so far from the shop, they could move nearby where the wife wouldn't have so far to go to prepare dinner and to be at home when the children came from school. There were other options too. He could elect to increase his drawing or decrease it accordingly. He could eliminate some of the advertising which he knew to be ineffective and save money there.

Yes. It certainly appeared to be worth it and worthwhile. Could the business supply what he wanted out of life? Yes. Could it answer the need for independence he had always felt? Yes. Could he earn enough to supply his family needs? Yes. Would he be able to provide for his family's education? And would he be able to benefit from the experience he had learned because of the bankruptcy? Would he have an edge over others now that he would be a businessman instead of merely a working man all his life? How could he draw dividends and what kind and in about what would they be? He knew that he could reinvest his profits to buy inventory and perhaps a few TV sets he could sell. Other dividends would be his personal happiness in owning his own business. He would feel like a new man again.

Moreover, the business would provide his future security. If he followed his plan he would someday be able to retire with a comfortable nest egg. In deep concentration now, Ted considered each of his needs and then went on to decide what choice he was going to make. He had an option to accept the deal or reject it. If he rejected it, he would never be able to live with himself. He admitted he had an obligation to himself to accept a new challenge in life. But is this the best thing for him? Is it really? He thought about that and his answer was an emphatic, decided yes. But following the fence formula still, he compared all the facts once more, reviewing them in his mind, adding them up and finally coming to one conclusion. He elected one choice. He'd do it!

Okay, now he was going to carry out his plans. Am I sure? He thought about this for a time. He didn't have to X it out because he was certain. Now, clear off the big table and plan with the decks cleared for action on what his next step would be. But first, contemplate the overall picture by cooling off. Am I being swayed by my hopes instead of my reason? Is my enthusiasm obscuring my viewpoint? No, was the answer.

Okay again. Now it's okay to unleash my energy. He planned on ways and means he would make things hum. How increased effort on his part would increase business once he took it over. From now on, he decided, he would be on the go, or bust. But he wouldn't think about going busted. And finally, he would never quit. He would maintain an optimistic viewpoint. First thing in the morning he would make the deal with his boss. Right now, he would call him and tell him he had decided to accept the offer.

"Ted. Ted!" his wife had been calling him. "What's wrong with you?"

He blinked and looked up. She had been sitting opposite him, pouring coffee. He had been wrapped in his thoughts so deeply that he hadn't been aware of her presence. He smiled, reached for her hand and told her the good news.

Ted Marsh succeeded. Within two years after going into business for himself, after making his careful decision, he expanded his operation cautiously, opening two branches in neighborhood shopping centers. At the end of the second year he invested his surplus in land. Today that land is worth $325,000! And the future is brighter than ever.

About a year after Ted had gone into business for himself, I happened to bump into him one morning. He greeted me like a long-lost brother. "You know, Bill," he said. "I would never have made the decision to go in business for myself if it hadn't been for that memory power-fence formula. You know, without it I might never have been able to reach that decision. I wouldn't have been able to think of all the points to be considered. As you know, in this world nobody makes decisions for you. You have to make them for yourself. I was able to remember the mistakes I had made and look at all viewpoints. I wanted you to know. Thanks. Thanks a million."

The moral of this story is this. Without memory power to help you reach decisions, learn from earlier mistakes, learn new ways of doing things, success is often unobtainable. It doesn't matter what you do in life, you too will benefit when you learn how to concentrate deeply and carefully weigh all the decisions before being decisive; and consider all the considerations; and evaluate all the facts before taking action. No matter if you are a student, housewife, doctor, businessman, salesman, or blue collar worker, when you apply the step-by-step technique of the "fence" formula, you cannot fail to make the decision that's right for you!

This same technique may be applied profitably whenever you want to take time out for careful concentration. The man who develops the knack of thinking is the man who gets somewhere in today's world!

Be that man now!

REVIEW QUESTIONS

1. Have you memorized the poem *Self-Examination?*
2. What does this represent to you? Isaac Watts, Chagrin Choir, Jesus.
3. How many ways can you use your memory power to overcome absent-mindedness?

_____   _____   _____

_____   _____   _____

4. What is the best thing to do when your mind goes "blank" temporarily?
5. Sit down and see if you can visualize the entire Memory Power-Fence formula. If you cannot, go back and review it, taking time out to make each image sharply vivid.
6. How will the formula help you make decisions, concentrate, learn and learn from the things you read?

XIV

Two: How to Use Your Memory for Self-improvement

—"Many a man fails to become a thinker for the sole reason that his memory is too good."
—NIETZSCHE, *Maxims*

Yes, many of us do fail to improve ourselves and get what we want out of life because our memories are *too good*. We remember the hard work and effort it takes to achieve our goals and we give up, saying: "It's too much trouble"—or—"I'll never do that. It's too much work."

Instead of keeping the fruits of our labors in mind, we tend to remember only the effort. Many a man fails to become a success in life because his memory of the hard work he'll have to do first is too good.

For this reason, more than for any other, we fail to break bad habits, form new habits, win raises and praises, or go on to bigger and better things in life. This need not be. The memory power-fence formula you have just learned in Part One (Chapter XIII) enables you to use your memory to improve yourself. Just do this: *Surround your goals or the things you want with the fence!*

How Eddie Kraft Used the Fence Formula to Begin a Career of Law at Age 51!

All his life Eddie Kraft had wanted to be an attorney. He even had gone as far as to enter law school on several different occasions, but

161

somehow he kept losing sight of his goal and kept dropping out of school after one or two night semesters. He would drop out because he lost sight of his goal and remained conscious of the effort and hard work it took.

"Now I'm too old to go back to school," Eddie told me. "I'm too old to put your memory power-fence formula to work."

"How much is too old?" I asked him.

"You know something, Bill?" he replied after a few moments. "I don't know."

"Then why not put the fence formula to work and try it and see? You can quit what you're doing and go to school for the next two years full-time. Just keep in mind that you *can* become a lawyer—and a good one too—in two years. Put your goal in the middle of that memory power fence and keep it there until you build the gate. You can do it if you want to."

A few days later Eddie did just that. At the time of the writing of this book, Eddie was finally admitted to the bar of his home state! He was able to achieve this seemingly impossible goal because he learned how to isolate it and fence it in. Here's how he did it:

First, he considered all the facts.

Next, he *evaluated* all the points to be considered. After that he thought about the *needs,* and then his *choice.* Finally, he decided upon a definite plan of *execution* which he carried out. However, he was able to carry out his program of study solely because he was able to keep in mind, to keep fenced in, that dream of being a lawyer!

Yes, no matter what your dream or goal in life, you can win it provided you thoughtfully apply the memory power-fence formula. It doesn't matter if you are merely keen on learning a new skill or learning how to ski; if you are interested in breaking a habit or getting a new job; you will get what you want when you apply the memory power-fence formula.

How the Memory Power-Fence Formula Helps You Reach Decisions and Break Bad habits

As you recall, learning is an associative process. We learn by associating new ideas or facts with others we have learned. The memory power-fence formula helps you solve problems and reach decisions because it is a memory guidepost which points out the way. For example, with this mnemonic aid we can learn the short-cuts for multiplication, addition, division and other mental feats in arithmetic.

How to Use Your Memory as a
Calculating Machine

Suppose you want to multiply 5 times 174,342, how would you do it? If you are like most individuals, you would use the conventional method: 5 times 2 equals ten, write down the zero and carry the 1, 5 times 4 and write down the 1 you carried and carry the 2, etc.

The way to accomplish this mentally is to double the 5, multiply by 10 because it is twice 5, then divide the result by 2; 5 is half of 10, we remember, therefore we can visualize the answer in a moment when we compute: $174,342 \times 10 = 1,743,420$, and 1,743,420 divided by $2 = 871,710$.

Multiplying 174,342 by 15 is just as easy when you *think* that if 10 times a number is added to 5 times that number the total equals 15 times the number. For example, $174,342 \times 10 = 1,743,420$ then add the result, 871,710 (which is half of 1,743,420). $1,743,420 + 871,710 = 2,615,130$.

When multiplying fractions the same rule applies. For instance, when multiplying $12\frac{1}{2}$, think of it as being either 10 *plus* one fourth of 10, or 1/8th of 100. Therefore, a product of $12\frac{1}{2}$ times a number is equivalent to the product of 100 times that number, divided by 8.

We will not go into details here because space does not permit. However, any good book on high-speed math will be full of examples. The point is, think of the means and ways you can use to solve problems in your mind without pencil and paper.

You use your memory to "double" and then "divide" in half the problems in order to compute them. The principle is this: It is easier to multiply by one digit than by two. The secret is to convert the two-digit multipliers into single units. For instance, to compute 16 times $57\frac{1}{2}$, divide 16 in half and double $57\frac{1}{2}$. You can compute 8 times 115 in a fraction of the time it would normally take to do this on paper!

Still another way to use your memory in multiplication is to employ the "successive" method of multiplying by the power of 2.

To multiply 86 by 4, for example, it is unnecessary to use the conventional method, multiplying 4×6 and 4×8, carrying the numbers and so forth. When the numbers are "carried" the chances for error increase. Therefore, because 4 is "twice" the 2 factor, the answer may be derived by mentally adding 86 plus 86 which equals 172 plus 172 = the answer, 344. You won't lose track of your successive additions if you do it systematically.

The number code will enable you to carry this procedure much further into long and complicated mental computations. But this requires practice and a willingness to "fence" in your mental arithmetic problems. Division can be as simple as multiplication too when the same principles are applied. Work out a few problems in your head and think about them. You'll be amazed at how swiftly you'll learn this knack.

How to Use Your Memory as an Adding Machine

The one single factor which makes addition difficult, particularly the addition of long series of digits, is the time-wasting practice of injecting "and." 8 and 9 and 5 are 22 and 11 and 10, etc. Instead of this, merely think, "8, 9, 5, 22, 11," and so forth. Further, it is *incorrect* to say "five hundred and ninety-five." Five-hundred ninety-five *is* correct.

Another factor which makes addition difficult is the "carrying" of numerals. The way to eliminate this and speed up the process is to add from left to right instead of right to left! When adding 5237 and 356 in our minds it is better to add, first the 300, then 50, and finally 6. This narrows the process down to three simple steps which produce the partial totals like this:

$$
\begin{array}{lll}
5237 & 5537 & 5587 \\
+\,300 & +\,50 & +\;\,6 \\
\hline
5537 \quad \text{then} & 5587 \quad \text{then} & 5593
\end{array}
$$

The addition of numbers which end in 7, 8, or 9 is speeded up when we increase the value of the last digit to 10, complete the process of addition, then subtract from the answer the value by which the original number was increased.

When adding two, three or more columns of figures at the same time, here is another way to do it mentally. Just take in the digits in the hundred's columns, say "4800," the ten's columns, say "33," the unit's columns, "21":

```
                711
                643
                995
                980
                312
        4800    432
          33    865
          21    213
        ────    ────
        5151    5151
```

See how deceptively simple it is? And there's no need for pencil, paper or carrying! Test yourself on these problems:

```
883   654   991   223   908   786   311
123   765   110   342   897   607   345
623   876   873   310   156   188   443
      231   910   876   643   903   810
            450   564   314   988   650
                  545   222   442   895
                        316   331   320
                              404   709
                                    224
```

In subtraction, we are more apt to make errors than in addition because it requires more concentration. Let's suppose we want to subtract 72¢ from 91¢ mentally. The easy way to do this is to make both figures (or one figure) nearest to a round sum. Hence, we would think of 71¢ from 91¢ = 20¢ minus 1¢ = 19¢. Or, 72¢ minus 90¢ = 18¢ plus 1¢ = 19¢.

In subtracting 780 from 996, again we would find it easier to increase the number to be subtracted to the nearest 100. We could make 780 into 800 and arrive at an answer of 196 plus 20 = 216, or we could add 4 to 996, make it 1,000 and subtract 780 from it giving us an answer of 220 minus 4 = 216.

There are two ways to check subtraction. One is by addition of the answer with the lesser amount (subtrahend) to see if the figures total the larger amount (minuend). The other way is by casting out 9's. To prove that 996 minus 780 equals 216, we follow this procedure:

```
 996   9 + 9 + 6 = 24   Casting out the 9's leaves 6.
-780   7 + 8 + 0 = 15   Casting out the 9's leaves 6.
────                                                ─
 216   2 + 1 + 6 =  9   Casting out the 9's leaves 0.
```

More About Mental Calculation

There are many other methods of using mental shortcuts to solve arithmetic problems. Another method is the "double-double" technique of division. In this you merely double the figures. For instance, if you want to divide 38 by 7½ we could do so easily by dividing 76 by 15. The division of 450 by 4½ is easily accomplished when you divide 900 by 9. See how easy it is?

Remember, no matter what you do, no matter what your job is, there are easy ways to do your mental calculating when you fence the problem in and arrive at a solution by using plain common sense. It doesn't matter if you are computing your commissions, figuring costs and selling prices, breaking figures down to decimals and fractions. This formula will work for you if you learn the ways and means and then practice those methods. The number code will help you to retain the results.

How Claire Welles Was Promoted
to Department Head When She Learned
How to Use Memory Power
for Mental Calculation

Claire Welles had worked in the accounting office of a large woolen mill for six years without getting any place. When her roommate invited her to attend my memory classes one night, little did Claire realize that within six weeks from that date she would win a promotion to department head of the accounting office as a result of what she was to learn!

Claire attended the class as we were discussing the pros and cons of how to put memory power to work. She heard others point out how they had used their new memory power to isolate and solve everyday problems.

Claire thought about this. She was always computing costs the long way, the conventional way. A salesman would call in for a quotation and she would have to compute the cost of goods per yard in fractions. Because she was slow she was usually the last one to be asked for information. Then she thought about this. Suddenly it dawned on her. There were quick ways she could calculate the percentage rates, profit ratios, and decimal fractions. She sat down with a book on basic math and worked up a series of formulas which would help her cope with the everyday problems. Within a month she was able to compute discounts, percentages and decimal fractions without using a pencil! All she did was list the figures which were common to her office and then commit them to the bank of her memory.

She was then able to compute the costs of mill-end closeouts simply by using her head! Here's a typical answer which she was able to supply at a moment's notice.

> *Question:* Our Crawford pattern closeout is being sold for $736.00 at a discount of 30%. How much is the total order?
>
> *Claire's computation:* 3 times 73,600 = 22,080 $220.80 is the savings to the customer.
> $220.80 less $736.00 equals $515.20 total cost.

> *Question:* Customer B is entitled to 52½% discount. How much does he get off his previous invoice of $785.00?
>
> *Claire's computation:* 50% of $785 (½ of $785) = $392.50
> 2½% (½ of $39.25)   =   19.62
> 52½% of $785.00 . . . . . . $412.12

When her supervisor saw how quickly she could compute problems which others in her department (including the department head) had to work on paper or on calculators, she was noticed. At the first opportune moment, she was promoted. It goes without saying that the ability to use your head as a mental calculating machine is the first step in the right direction—toward success! Take time out to devise new and better ways to use your memory power to do the everyday tasks your job requires. As soon as you do, everyone around you will take notice.

How to Use Your Memory Power to Break Bad Habits

The easiest way to break a bad habit is to develop a new good habit to replace it. A man I know had an obnoxious habit of chewing on a pencil. I showed him how he could break that habit by using the pencil to form new numerical-equivalent words. Within a few days he had acquired the habit of making up number words. Every time he caught himself chewing on his pencil, he went to work. Today he has command of nearly 5,000 words which have numerical equivalents.

Another man I know had a bad habit of falling asleep every time he picked up a book or newspaper. I showed him the easy way to break this one. I call it the *force* habit of reading. Here's how it works.

*F*ast reading, not lazy reading is remembered.
*O*rderly minds learn faster than disorderly minds.
*R*acing thoughts stimulate your thinking processes.
*C*oncentration is better when you read rapidly.
*E*xtra benefits are derived when you read fast.

When he applied the *force* formula and learned to read fast, he never fell asleep again. Think over the thoughts expressed by the above formula. Put them to work. Learn to scan as you read and you'll be amazed at how much more you'll retain and how wide awake you'll become! My speed jumped from 375 words per minute to 1500 words per minute with 90 percent comprehension when I put these steps to work.

How Paying Attention Helps
Self-Improvement

I once listened to an excellent talk on business communications by the head of a national advertising agency. After the talk was over, I had occasion to sit opposite him at the banquet table. Because I had paid attention and had deliberately tried to retain most of what he had said, I was able to talk intelligently to him. I was particularly interested in his impressions of life behind the Iron Curtain.

He was delighted that I was able to ask intelligent questions which led him on to amplify his remarks. After that, I was able to share the substance of his talk with others who knew the speaker. I had nailed down 47 ideas, many of which I have profitably used later. But the moral of this story developed a little later. The speaker remembered *me*. And so did several of his friends with whom I had discussed his interesting talk. As a result, they invited me to lecture one of their groups at a handsome fee.

The ability to concentrate by listening, paying attention and forcing yourself to grasp ideas pays off in more ways than one.

Remember, it pays to pay attention. And when you remember what you learn and then remember to put it to good use, that's the only short-cut to self-improvement there is! Break the bad habit of inattention. Enhance your reputation by making mental notes on every conversation.

My father-in-law was a student of business who prided himself on his thoroughness. He had made an extensive study of the theory of values as developed by the late Professor Perry of Harvard. One day my father-in-law was telling me about some aspects of the theory. He listed 10 of Perry's points. When he finished, I took up each point and questioned him further. He was astonished that I could recall these points after one verbal exposure.

On several occasions I have listened to prospects as they spoke about the good stocks they owned. As they talked, I memorized the lists. I awaited my chance and then displayed proof of my interest by asking questions like: "Tell me, what did you pay for American Tel and Tel?"

I then complimented them on their judgment and, as soon as I could, made a written record for my files so I can have this data at my fingertips the next time I make a call on them, perhaps months later. Often, I review and memorize these lists and look up current prices. If they haven't been doing well, I know where to start conversations that hit home. Several times I have made substantial mutual fund sales because my memory has enabled me to let them discover their own weaknesses.

How to Use Your Memory as a Life- and Time-Saving Device

With today's high-speed superhighways, one needs all the mental powers at one's command in order to get directions straight and not commit any dangerous highway blunders. A wrong turn or a sudden stop in the middle of a superhighway has caused more than one tragic accident. Here's how I prevent this from happening to me. In order to be certain of my directions from my home to New York City, I have memorized these time-saving directions

Route 123 to 114
Right on 114 to 116

> I know Route 123, so the first key point I must not forget is "right on route 114." The word for 114 is "daughter." I picture my daughter standing at the turn-off, pointing with her outstretched arm to the right.

Left on 116 to U.S. 6

> The next key turn is "left on 116." I composed the words "Tie Dutch" from this. I visualized my daughter tying a Dutchman

to the direction post. With his one free arm he is waving me to
the left. U.S. 6 is next. The word for "six" is "hedge." I picture
U.S. 6 as a hedge extending westward across Rhode Island and
continuing into the Connecticut Pike. Once on the pike I'm out
of trouble until I want to find that exit. I've missed it in the past
and had to drive many miles out of my way. That was before
I put my memory system to work.

Connecticut Pike to Exit 13 of N.Y. Thruway

The code word for "Exit 13" is "team." I visualize a football
team right across the Thruway just as I leave Connecticut.

Cross Westchester Parkway to Second Entrance on Hutchinson River
Parkway just beyond Merritt Parkway Sign

The next one is tricky. I could go either way on the Hutchinson
Parkway. I picture a client of mine named Hutchinson standing
at the second exit waving me up to it.

Go for George Washington Bridge

This is my next clue. It is well marked, so I'm out of trouble by
now except for getting off the Thruway.

Follow Hudson River to 56th Street Exit

I see myself following the Hudson River to the 56th Street exit
where Henry Hudson is standing there with a "lash" to make
sure I make the turn! From that point on I'm on familiar ground.

This is the sort of system it pays to use on every long trip through
unfamiliar territory. Memorize the key point for each leg of your journey
and fix it in your mind. Try to determine all stops in advance. Plan where
you are going, when and where you will stop and every trip will be
more rewarding and time-saving.

Another lifesaving idea applies particularly to people like myself
who travel extensively. I have made up a list of police numbers, including
those of State Police in the areas I cover. I have committed these to my
memory. And though I haven't had occasion to use them, one of my students not too long ago was able to save a man's life because he had taken
the trouble to know the number of the local State Police barracks.

As he was driving over a lonely stretch of road he came across a
wrecked car in which a man was pinned. He saw he could do nothing
for him so he back-tracked to a highway phone, dialed the number and
the State Police arrived just in time to save the man's life. Had a long
delay occurred during which time the operator had to find the correct

police department for that remote area, the man might have bled to death.

There are many other applications of your memory in lifesaving situations. New ways of applying artificial respiration, antidotes for poisons, overdoses of sleeping pills, etc., are mighty handy things to know in emergencies. Who knows, the bit of lifesaving data you might take the trouble to learn next time you hear it might very well turn out to save your own life!

The purpose of this and the preceding chapters has been to prod your thoughts into action. The action you take in using your memory as a self-improvement aid will pay off in rich dividends before you realize it. The point is, do it now! You have the know-how, do it now! Try it and see.

Review Questions

1. How many ways can you list which will enable you to improve yourself with your memory power?

   _____

   _____

2. List the bad habits you can break with the aid of your memory power:

   _____   _____

   _____   _____

3. How can you adapt the memory power-fence formula to improve yourself?

   _____

   _____

4. Review what you have learned in the section explaining mental arithmetic.

5. How many ways can you improve your mental calculation? List some short-cuts that you can apply.

   _____   _____

   _____   _____

6. Can you explain the force formula that helps you stay awake while reading? Explain how it helps you. What do you gain by applying the technique?

   _____

   _____

7. How many ways can you list which will enable you to use your memory as a life and time-saving device?

   _____

   _____

XV

How to Use Your Memory for Greater Profit on the Job

"Make all you can, save all you can, give all you can."

—J. WESLEY

If you are an office worker, you can use your memory power to gain recognition, increase your pay check and prestige and build a future. You can achieve all this and more when you use the common sense suggestions in this chapter. If your work brings you into contact with people outside your firm as well as within it, by all means develop the easily acquired skill for remembering names, faces, and facts about people. Develop an "ear" for telephone voices. Listen, hear the personalities of the voices on the phone and respond accordingly.

It is possible to make a tremendous and unforgettable impression on everyone you meet, simply by following the techniques shown in this book. These people are important to your progress, and subsequently, your pay check. The more effective you are in your contact with others, the brighter will your personal future become as a result. Many clerical workers feel they have little chance to create a profitable impression. This is a mistaken belief. The big secret is in recognizing and remembering people.

Today, a good deal of potential business is lost by firms in all fields because a minor clerk or the receptionist failed to recognize an important client or customer. If you make it a point to treat every prospect and customer with the utmost courtesy, you cannot help but be successful, because this courtesy is contagious. Compliments about you will eventually reach the top echelons and before you know it, you'll be on your way upstairs too.

One young lady who had a fondness for people remembered the name of a little old lady who occasionally visited the non-profit charitable institution in which she worked. She always made the little old lady feel important and at home. When the aged visitor died a few years later, she left a half-million dollar gift to that institution—all because she had been remembered!

I could go on citing success stories. But the point has already been made. *You owe it to yourself to take pride in your job and to take an interest in what you do.* The more you can remember about the people you contact and the more you can remember about the details and the routine of your job, the more valuable you are to your employer. As a result, your stock goes up.

Most clerical work is involved with recording and classifying information. This involves knowledge of accounting, codes, file codes, numbers of customers' accounts, etc. The clerk who greets the man who comes in to pay his bill by his name and not his number, "Here is good old reliable No. 33689790-H," is the clerk who does a sales job for his firm. No one likes to lose his identity in a number. Through the number code you have learned, you are able to translate these meaningless numbers into meaningful words which help you recognize these important customers.

For instance, a former student of mine, a teller in a bank, is able to remember her customers not by number, but by association with their numbers. Thus, when a customer forgets an account book, the name recalls the number and everyone is pleased all around. She knows that Mr. Morse's account number is 974. The number code reminds her of the word "baker" which she has formerly associated with Mr. Morse, seeing him dressed as a baker. She is then able to expedite the posting of his payment without long delays and time-wasting references.

Many businesses and banks are called daily to check on the credit ratings of their customers. The requests are always by name. If you are a clerical worker who answers these inquiries, you know how much more efficiently you can reply when you have taken the time and the trouble to associate the names with the account numbers.

Another time-saving (and therefore money-saving) application covers the allocation of expenditures in bookkeeping. In one case I know of, there are more than 400 separate accounts to which various types of income and expenses are posted. Almost all clerks know the frequently used accounts, but how many know those which are little used? Yes, is the clerk who gets the praises and the raises who is the one who remembers all the obscure data. The more thoroughly you learn the details of your work, the more secure will be your future.

Order clerks need to remember customers' account numbers, addresses, voucher numbers and other data. When their memory power is called upon to accomplish these tasks, work is speeded, expenses and overtime costs minimized and working conditions are pleasanter. The clerk who consistently gets his job done more speedily and efficiently is the person who doesn't remain a clerk long. He's destined for bigger and better jobs.

Memory power can be called upon to improve one's handwriting, one's ability to operate office machines ranging from adders to xerographers, or merely one's ability to spell accurately. The secret is in the willingness to learn the right way to do something, then using memory power to master the fundamentals.

How Your Memory Power Can Help You
Improve Your Handwriting

There are two reasons why most of us suffer from sloppy handwriting habits. We may have "forgotten," or don't know how to write legibly and properly, or we don't take the time.

If your job demands neatness and legibility in handwriting, by all means use your memory power to re-learn the rules of penmanship. Take out a few quarter-hours to practice penmanship. Any good library book on the subject will help you improve your handwriting as much as 100 per cent if you will only take the trouble. More people in clerical positions are fired from their jobs every day because they cannot write properly than for any other reason! Don't let this happen to you. Learn the rules over again, commit them to memory and practice.

How Your Memory Power Can Help You
Improve Your Spelling

The person with the ability to spell words accurately is one who has a good *visual* memory. He knows we "read" one English language and "speak" another English language. In other words he doesn't make the mistake of spelling words the way they sound rather than the way they read.

How to Keep Your Spelling Ability
Up to Date

Were you one of those pupils who did very well in spelling in school but have become less sure-footed about it as the years have passed? Then you share a condition many of us have to face. When we are trying to pass a course, when our vocabularies and interests are more limited and our efforts relatively more concentrated, we do fairly well with spelling and other subjects. However, if our work does not lead us into writing things out, or if our reading doesn't require great new effort, we may become careless with our spelling. If a businessman has a careless stenographer, he may find himself unwittingly letting misspelled words go out that will reflect discredit on his abilities.

I am including two lists of words in this chapter: "100 Business Words Most Frequently Misspelled" and "100 Words Most Commonly Misspelled by Educated People." If you find that you are misspelling words on the second list, welcome to the ranks of educated people. Now what can you do about it?

Basically, the problem boils down to the fact that we spell by ear more and more as we grow older. More of what we learn comes through sound than through the printed page and so we start to spell words as they sound rather than as they look. To remedy this we have to put our vision back to work. I'm going to show you how visualization can keep you out of spelling trouble.

Here are several types of errors in spelling and the remedy for each:

1. One wrong letter inserted. Example, seperate instead of separate. Remedy: write the word "separate" out five times but when you get to the "a," stop and print it as a capital letter like this, sepArate, sepArate, sepArate, sepArate, sepArate. Now you have replaced the careless use of an "e" by the vivid visualization on the capital "A." You are back visualizing, seeing things as they are plus a little flip of exaggeration to make the point penetrate. Look over the lists and see if any of your misspellings fall in that group. If they do, why not correct them now before we go on to the next common error? Go ahead, get that pencil and paper. The book will wait.

2. Adding an unnecessary letter to the end of a word. Example, de-velop*e*. Remedy: write the word out incorrectly. Yes, I mean it. Write it wrong but when you finish, take your pencil and make a big cross-out mark through that extra "e." Like this: develop¢, develop¢, develop¢, develop¢, develop¢. Again you have made the error visual, and just like the cross bones on the bottle of poison, you have a visual warning.

3. Using one of a kind when two are due. Example, aco*mo*date instead of accommodate. Remedy: write it out five times. Print the pairs of letters and underscore them. Like this aCCoMModate, aCCoMModate, aCCoMModate, aCCoMModate, aCCoMModate.

4. Forgetting to link a silent letter to another. Example, spelling jugment without the "d." Remedy: write it out and draw a circle linking "d" and "g" judgment, judgment, judgment, judgment, judgment.

These visualizing exercises will correct most of your errors. There is, however, one little rhyme that will help you with the troublesome deci-sion as to whether "i" or "e" comes first in words like deceive. You may remember this from school days: *i* before *e* except after *c* or when sounded as *a* in neighbor and weigh. Now all you have to watch out for are the exceptions of "seize" and "leisure."

May I remind you to practice this now. Have someone test your ability to spell the words on the two lists that follow. Then systematically start correcting your errors with the suggested techniques. Who knows, you may be able to upgrade your secretary's spelling!

Never underrate the value of the ability to spell correctly. A mis-spelled letter of application will not win you an appointment or a job. A misspelled business letter will not win new business. A misspelled sales report or office memo "tags" you as a careless, untrustworthy, in-efficient worker.

Here are the three reasons for spelling failures.

1. We usually spell from 25 to 100 everyday words incorrectly and keep on *repeating* these errors instead of taking steps to correct them.
   Solution: List your spelling errors and practice spelling the words correctly.

2. We do not know the meanings of many words we spell incorrectly. We do not know the correct way these words should "read."

A
accessible
accommodate
accrued
acquitted
across
allege
allotted
all right
apparel
athletics
audible
auxiliary

B
benefited
besiege
bookkeeper

C
calendar
Cincinnati
cite (quotation)
collateral
concession
consensus
counterfeit

D
develop
dictionary
disappear
disappoint
discipline
dissatisfied
dissimilar

E
eligible
embarrass
enervate
equipped
especially
exhilarate
existence
exorbitant
extension

G
grammar

H
harass
height
hypocrisy

I
illegible
incredible
inoculate
intercede
irresistible

L
laboratory
legitimate
license
loneliness

M
mail chute
maintenance
management
mileage
misspell
momentous
mucilage

N
Niagara
ninth
noticeable

O
occasion
occurred
occurrence
ofttimes
omission
omitted
optimistic

P
pamphlet
penitentiary

personnel
persuade
precede
preferring
prejudice
principal
procedure
profession
pronunciation

Q
questionnaire

R
recommend
referring
repetition
restaurant

S
seize
sentinel
separate
sergeant
serviceable
site (a place)
strictly
superintendent
supersede

T
tragedy
transient
typing

U
unmanageable

W
welfare
whose

Y
yield

Investigations have shown that 95 percent of the spelling errors that educated people make occur in just 100 words. Not only do we all misspell the same words, but we misspell them in about the same way.

1.
all right
coolly
supersede
exceed
proceed
succeed
precede (all others)
procedure
stationery
stationary

2.
recommend
separate
comparative
ecstasy
analyze
paralyze
repetition
irritable
inimitable
absence

3.
superintendent
conscience
anoint
ridiculous
despair
surprise
inoculate
definitely
privilege
incidentally

4.
predictable
dissipate
discriminate

description
balloon
occurrence
truly
assistant
grammar
parallel

5.
drunkenness
suddenness
embarrassment
weird
pronunciation
noticeable
development
vicious
insistent
argument

6.
embarrassing
judgment
indispensable
disappear
disappoint
corroborate
sacrilegious
tranquillity
exhilaration
newsstand

7.
license
irresistible
persistent
dilemma
perseverance
until (but till)
tyrannize

vacillate
accommodate
oscillate

8.
dilettante
changeable
accessible
forty
desirable
panicky
seize
leisure
receive
achieve

9.
holiday
existence
pursue
pastime
possesses
professor
category
rhythmical
vacuum
benefited

10.
committee
grievous
plebeian
tariff
sheriff
connoisseur
necessary
sergeant
misspelling
conscious

> *Solution:* List the words you do not know. At a convenient time look them up, study them, write them.

3. We tend to spell words the way they "sound" rather than the way they "read." Consequently we do not divide the words into parts. As a rule, we misspell only a syllable or a letter or two within the word instead of the entire word.

> *Solution:* Listen for the "meanings" instead of the phonetic pronunciation of words. Learn to divide the words into parts. Learn the rules of spelling.

Now here is my simplified method. I call this the *BETTER SPELL-ING* formula. Note how easy it is to mnemonize. Now get busy and learn it. After you finish committing these rules to your memory, I guarantee that you will improve greatly within a few minutes without tedious hours of study and practice!

The Hersey Better Spelling Formula

B–E–T–T–E–R S–P–E–L–L–I–N–G contains all the rules you need to know in order to master the skill of correct spelling. Commit this formula to memory now. I have deliberately abbreviated it to make the mastery of this formula easy. Once you know these rules thoroughly you *will* spell as accurately as a walking dictionary!

*B*isect words into prefixes and suffixes.	Prefixes such as *trans, in, un* and others do not change the spelling of the root.
	in + breed = inbreed un + equal = unequal
*E*xtract the roots.	A word without a prefix or suffix. *Spell* is the root. *Mis*spell is the root with a prefix and spell*able* is with the suffix.
*T*ransformation of the spelling of roots does *not* occur when prefixes are added.	Re + compense = recompense Re + commend = recommend, not re*c*commend. *Uni* + lateral = unilateral
*T*wo consonants are retained by an added suffix beginning with the same final letter of root.	Casual + ly = casually Commit + tal = committal Commit + tee = committee
E after *i*, except when after *c*, or when pronounced like *a*, as in weigh or sleigh.	Another rule is to "never be*LIE*ve a *lie.*" Seige is wrong—*siege* is correct. Seize is right—note the "c" sound.

Reject and drop the *e* whenever it is silent and comes before a suffix beginning with a vowel.

side = *siding*   size = *sizing*. When the *e* is needed to prevent misunderstanding it is retained; i.e., *mileage,* etc.

Suffixes beginning with a consonant always keep the silent *e* when it appears before the suffix.

Particularly notice the suffix *ceed* and also super*sede* should not be confused.

Endings of words in which the *y* follows a vowel doesn't alter the spelling of the root.

i.e., nine = *ninety*. Exceptions are judgement *or* judgment and others which vary according to usage.

Cede means to yield. *Ceed* means to go before or on; i.e.: *accede* = to yield. *proceed* = originate or go on.

ay, ey, oy, uy as in *laying, buoyant* etc. Exceptions: Words ending in a *y* preceded by a consonant changes the *y* to *i*. defy = *defiance*.

Lone or single syllable words ending with one consonant preceded by a vowel *doubles* itself by adding another consonant.

Last consonants in words of more than one syllable preceded by a single vowel double the final consonant before suffix.

Chip = *chipping*   chop = *chopping*. Exception: Don't double consonant for word ending in silent *e*. i.e., hope = *hoping*.

Commit = *committed*   spit = *spitting*

Ible, able & *ble*. The form *ible* is suffixed to words going back in origin to Latin verbs as in *ere,* and *ire.* (i.e., *contemptible*) The form *ble* is used (*tremble,* etc.) when root contains an *o* or *uous* formation. *Ible* is used when the root is *not* a whole or complete word (with some exceptions). *Ible* is used when the root ends in *-miss* (*remissible*) or in *-ns* (*comprehensible*) and when root ends in soft *c* (*ce*) or *g* (*ge*). *E* is sometimes used after the *c* or *g* with the suffix *able* instead. (*changeable—peaceable*)

Able is used with words of French origin, (i.e., *fashionable*) and also after silent *e* as in Rule S. *Able* is used when the root is a complete word with or without the final *e* as in *admire-admirable*. *Able* is also used when the *y* in the root is changed to *i*; if it ends in a hard *c* or *g*; and when *a* is in the word's derivatives.

Never use *ence* when the root has a hard *c* or *g* sound or if the root has an *a* in it. Instead, use *ance,*

i.e., *eminence* vs. *remittance, significance, excellent*. Same rule applies for *-ant* and *-ent* suffixes.

Greek, French, Spanish or Latin words sometimes keep the plural of their original languages; i.e., *index* or *indexes* or *indices, curricula* or *curriculum* etc.

The easy rule about the rest of the plural forms of spelling can be remembered when you think of P-L-U-R-A-L-S and add these rules to it:

Plural nouns do not have an apostrophe except when they are possessive and where the apostrophe comes after the regular plural form. i.e., *Adams'* apple owned by *one* man named Adams. (Singular possessive) *Adamses'* apples owned by *two* or more men named Adams. (Plural possessive) Subjective and objective plural are *Adamses.*

Letters, numerals, and abbreviations add an apostrophe *'s* to indicate the plural number. *B's, C's, 9's, J. P.'s, BPOE's,* etc.

Usually only nouns which indicate the singular case have a singular *s* added to the root to form the plurality. *apple + s = apples, etc.*

Rich words get *rich-es* of *es* to show their plurality by adding *es.* Nouns which end in *ch, sh, j, s, x,* or *z* are "enriched" by the addition of *es.* i.e., *witches, wishes, sexes.* Exceptions are *ox-x-en = oxen. fish* and other words identical in both singular and plural.

All nouns ending in *y* which comes after a consonant (i.e., *candy, candies*) are changed from the *y* to *ies.* All nouns ending in *y* which come *after* a *vowel* and not a consonant (i.e., *buoy, buoys*) keep the *y.* All names or proper nouns ending in *y* are pluralized by the addition of *s* only. The *y* is retained. i.e., *Johnny, Johnny's, Johnnys', Johnnys,* etc.

Lasso, *potato, tomato* and all other nouns ending in *o* which comes *after* a consonant, form the plural by adding *es.* i.e., *lassoes, potatoes, tomatoes,* etc. Words as *duo, woo* and others ending in *o* which comes *after* a vowel are pluralized by adding the *s* only. i.e., *woos, duos,* etc.

Some nouns which end in *f, ff,* or *fe,* are pluralized by changing the *f* to a *v.* i.e., *knife–knives; wife–wives,* etc.

These remarkably simple rules: B–E–T–T–E–R S–P–E–L–L–I–N–G and P–L–U–R–A–L–S contain all the elements you need to know in order to spell correctly without using a dictionary!

Of course, there are exceptions to these rules. But when you remember to apply the secrets of the memory system you have learned in this book, and then to remember it is the sound that does not count in written language, your ability to become a master speller will be proven from now on. If you will note the easy image-producing rules beginning with each letter of the formula, B–E–T–T–E–R S–P–E–L–L–I–N–G and commit them to your memory just as you have with the other formulae you have memorized, you will find it's amazingly easy. You might also note how the "sounds" as the *ch, sh, j, g,* etc., are also linked. Perhaps you might wish to remember some of the rules applying to these as number equivalents and use them to help you remember the rules.

How Ernest Ritter Won a Promotion
to Editor When He Learned These Rules

Ernest Ritter was entering his sixth consecutive year as a reporter for a small weekly newspaper when he decided to throw in the towel. He made this decision when the publisher informed him someone else was going to get the job of an editor who was retiring. "I'm sorry, Ernie. You're a good reporter and you have a nose for news. But your spelling is atrocious. If you only knew how to spell, you'd have this job."

When I met Ernie a few days later, he laughingly told me that he wanted to improve his memory because he wanted to learn a new trade.

After he had explained, I quietly asked: "Why not learn how to spell?"

"Are you kidding?" he cried. "Do you want me to memorize every page in the dictionary or something?"

Once I explained how easy it was, I asked him to phone the publisher to find out if he could get that editorship provided his spelling improved.

Though he didn't take me seriously, Ernie picked up the phone. When he hung up a few minutes later, he was grinning from ear to ear. "Know what he told me? He said it was impossible. But he went on to say that if my spelling should by some miracle improve, not only would I get that job, but I'd also get a raise!"

Well, that miracle did happen. When Ernie mastered the rules which you have just learned, his spelling improved 100 per cent. Within a month he was behind that editor's desk.

As you have seen from this story of what happened to Ernest Ritter, it is possible to get somewhere when you know how to spell.

Yes, your memory really can enable you to learn heretofore "impossible" skills overnight when you follow the step-by-step procedures in this book. No matter what you do, what type of job you have, it pays enormous dividends when you spell correctly.

Still another way to use your memory on the job for profit is to use it to develop an effective vocabulary. If you are a salesman, you certainly know how it feels to find yourself at a loss for words when it comes to describing the product or service you sell. How many times have you groped for the right phrase or expression and could only come up with a weak, "Isn't this lovely?" "Isn't this beautiful?" and lost the sale because you didn't have the right words at your fingertips? How many times have you admired someone who spoke with the eloquence of a powerful orator, and wished you too could also master such a wide vocabulary?

But what about that so-called wide vocabulary? How many words did the speaker use that you did not know? Chances are, you knew every word he used. Yes, you know those words too, but you just don't use them. And that's the reason you don't have a wide vocabulary.

Nothing is more boring than to listen to a speaker who makes what he says monotonous by repeating the same words over and over when other more effective and descriptive words would have made his talk interesting.

How to Increase Your Vocabulary of Spoken Words

First, think of all the words you use over and over again. Make a list of them.

Next, leaf through the pages of a pocket-sized dictionary and make a list of the words you do know but rarely, if ever, use.

Do not try to do this in one day. Spend a few days on this project and make it your business to employ at least three new words every day in your normal conversation. When you do this, within 20 days your conversation will take on a new sparkle and zing! People will begin to listen to you as they never have before. Do it now. If you do, you may also benefit in the same way as one of my former students did. This is what happened to him.

Nat Reiner was well liked by the customers and friends to whom he delivered milk each morning in a small eastern college town. However, when it came to spending time soliciting new customers, Nat fell down miserably. No matter how hard he tried to increase his route (and subsequently increase his weekly take-home pay) he just couldn't seem to make himself talk to non-customers in his territory.

Though Nat had taken my memory course some months before and had used his new knowledge to remember names and facts about his customers, an ability which enabled him to build loyal friendships among his following, and though he had saved effort and time by memorizing each stop on his way instead of wasting time fumbling through his route book as he made his rounds, he still had not been able to increase his earnings. Something was amiss and he didn't know what it was.

"I can't figure it out, Bill," he told me one afternoon when I happened to bump into him at a gas station. "Now that I have more time on my hands, I still can't seem to talk to new prospects. I'm kind of tongue-tied. I guess your memory training ain't good for canvassing and pitching people."

That remark was a challenge to me. "Why are you tongue-tied, Nat?" I asked pointedly.

He blinked and shrugged. "Beats me. Maybe it's because I don't have such a good education. Had to quit school in the tenth grade to help the folks you know. Maybe it's because of that. Maybe that's the reason I get all balled-up when I try to pitch those college professors and their wives."

I immediately countered: "What kind of an excuse is that?"

He was momentarily startled. A few seconds later he grinned. "Know something, Bill? I never looked at it like that. The reason I get all balled-up and tongue-tied is my own fault, ain't it?"

I laughingly made a wry face at his redundant language. I nodded and suggested we take a few minutes to talk about it over coffee.

That conversation which lasted less than a half-hour was responsible for an amazing transformation which took place in Nat Reiner's life. I told him pointedly: "Every day from this minute on, do this. Replace three words in your vocabulary with three new words which you haven't used before. For example, you've used the words: *balled-up, ain't,* and *maybe,* a total of *too-many* times. More than once are *too-many.* Next time you catch yourself about to say *balled-up,* use the word *confused* instead. Next time you catch yourself about to say *ain't,* use the more correct word, *isn't.* Or *are not,* or the contraction, *aren't,* instead.

"When you find yourself about to say *maybe,* stop and use the word *perhaps.* Another important thing to remember is this: there is no such thing as making a *pitch* in your industry. Milkmen don't *pitch* bottles, nor do they hurl *tar* at their customers. Quite the contrary. You perform a vital job. You deliver a *service.* You represent—*not work for*—your dairy because you like working there. And the reason why you enjoy your occupation is because you have the best quality product, isn't that correct?"

Nat smiled thinly, nodding. He began to see a clear picture of what I was focusing on. "I get it," he said. "You want me to use—to change my language by using three new words everyday?"

"Yes. But notice, I did not tell you to learn words you don't know.

Merely begin using the words you do know but do not use in your everyday conversation. Once you grow accustomed to using a variety of words, instead of the same worn-out ones, you'll be able to hold your own with any college professor! Here's the secret, Nat. We use a small and limited or cramped vocabulary because we haven't learned the habit of using the words we know in our daily conversation. Therefore, when we are face to face with someone who makes us conscious of our poor vocabulary choice, we become stifled mentally. Get the idea? In other words, when you learn to use the words you do know, your vocabulary will increase by more than half. You won't use words you do not know because this will make your conversation seem affected or stilted. However, by only improving your speech at the rate of three words per day, your entire vocabulary will be exactly doubled within 150 days!"

Nat was puzzled.

I explained. "As of now you probably use about 450 words in your daily conversation. You are no doubt familiar with 10 times that many. But let's not concern ourselves with that. All you need remember is this: add three words *you know* each day to replace three words you use and know too well—so well that you use them without being aware of them!"

Nat took me to task. He spent several hours reconstructing his conversation and compiled a list of expressions, phrases and words he habitually used. He then listed synonyms for those words and phrases and began forming the habit of using them at the rate of eight new words a day!

Within a month and a half, not only had his vocabulary doubled, but also his list of new customers. Suddenly he had begun to discover that he could hold his own in conversation with his highly educated prospects.

Almost three months later, Nat had succeeded in adding so many new customers to his route that it had to be split with another man in order to be serviced properly. Moreover, exactly 15 months from the day when we met by chance in that gas station, Nat was promoted to the position of supervisor over all the routes in three counties served by the dairy, at a salary three times that which he had been earning before!

Yes, anything is possible when you put the recipe for success into action. Just as an increased and enhanced vocabulary hitched Nat Reiner's milk wagon to the star of success, so can your conversational power be rebuilt to make you successful!

Start now. No matter what you do, a sparkling conversational ability and an adroit choice of words will enable you to get what you want out of life. You can have this too, if you begin now. Begin using three new (unused) words daily. And if you begin right now, exactly one year from this moment, you will have increased your speaking power and vocabulary by 1,095 words!

Think of it like this. If each word is worth $5, by next year at this time you will be cashing in on these new words at the rate of $5,475 a year!

Give yourself that $5,475 raise next year by starting *now*.

How an Effective Vocabulary Wins Friends

"Whatcha know?"

"Ehhhh, grmpthfth."

"Me too. Lousy, cruddy life, ain't it?"

"Grmpthfth."

"What else's doing?"

"Ehk. Grmph."

"Sure is rough."

What you have just read is a verbatim report of a conversation I heard this morning on the subway! Obviously, it was a discussion between two acquaintances.

Now ask yourself what you say when you meet and greet others? Do you use these expressions? "Do you look terrific!" "Gee, Bill, am I glad to see you!" "Gosh, was I surprised when I heard your good news. Congratulations!"

It is obvious, isn't it? The use of expletives which are trite and negative serves to tag the user as a dull person. However, the use of complimentary remarks intoned as exclamations or enthusiastic greetings, when delivered *sincerely*, identify the user as "a wonderful guy." The man who hears your words and sees that smile of delight in your eyes when you greet him is the man who often says, "I'd give that guy the shirt off my back!"

Think about this for a moment. Have you ever said this same thing about another person? Of course you have. Now, consider this. Why did you? Obvious, of course. You were impressed by him because of his manner and more importantly, because of his radiant and vivid language; because of his warm and friendly words; because of his ability to impress you with his choice of words; because of his ability to hold your interest in what he had to say to you through his varied vocabulary which did not bore you.

How an Effective Vocabulary Breaks Bad Language Habits

One of the worst language habits is that of employing trite, worn-out words and phrases which have lost their meaning through overwork. Today the world is changing. The words which were household "by- or buy-words" yesterday are no longer meaningful today. The words of greeting we used yesterday are no longer appropriate or meaningful today.

The worst language habit there is, is being vapid, corny, hackneyed, or dependent on profanity.

Do you want to buy from the clerk who drags his feet in your direction and asks: "May I help you?"

Does the sign hanging on the door of the food market which you see when you leave, "Thank you, call again," mean anything to you? You don't even see it at all, do you? Would you ever forget it if the checkout operator said, "Thank you. I know you'll enjoy these groceries!"

"What's new?"
"Lovely day, isn't it?"
"How's the boy?"
"How ya doing?"
"Just pennies a day."
". . . your friendly serviceman."
"Service with a smile."

And how about this one which indicates a lazy sales department—"What you don't see, ask for." So who asks when they see such a sign?

And still another meaningless slogan, "Bargain Sale!" or "Clearance Sale Days!" Overworked? You bet. Why? Because businessmen are too lazy to think up new signs and neglect taking down the old ones from their store windows.

"How are you feeling?" is an expression of concern which dates back to the age of superstition when it was important to know if your friend was safe to be with. (You had to know if evil spirits were possessing him or not.)

"Take it easy."

"So long."

"See ya around."

Hearing those three makes you want to see that person again, and you are left with a memorable impression of your meeting, aren't you?

The salesman who spends time and energy and often many dollars in travel expenses to visit a prospect or customer wastes his effort when he puts his prospect in a poor frame of mind by mopping his brow and saying: "Hot as hell, ain't it?" And what customer feels like buying when he's reminded of the terrible weather? Or the business slump? Or the world situation? Or of the salesman's poor state of health? Or of the terrible state of everything in general?

Enough said? Now let's explore some ways to develop an effective manner of speaking that overcomes these bad language habits. Here are the rules I follow. These are easy to remember when you recall that it pays to:

B–E   C–H–A–R–M–I–N–G

*B*e positive, not negative in what you say.

*E*ffective speech is in how you make the commonplace seem new.

*C*reate novel ways of expressing yourself.

*H*ave something original and interesting to say.

*A*lways have a good word or compliment for the other fellow.

*R*eadily talk about the things he wants to hear.

*M*ean what you say. Be sincere and interested in him.

*I*mpress him with your memory of facts about him.

*N*ew words and expressions should be used every day.

*G*oodbyes must be verbal remembrances.

As you know, the most direct way to break a bad habit is to form a new *good* habit to replace it. When you follow the B–E   C–H–A–R–M–I–N–G formula you will develop the good habit of being charming with an effective vocabulary.

How to Be Positive, Not Negative in What You Say, When Using Effective Language

"Isn't it a great day?" is most certainly a positive statement. This is effective speech. It is certainly more adequate than the negative, "Isn't it a terrible day?"

The secret of positive, effective speech is in your choice of simple words to express in everyday language the positive or optimistic thoughts you wish to impress upon others. Effective speech leaves good effects because it is accomplished by conversation which exudes or radiates optimism naturally.

How Effective Speech Makes
Commonplace Expressions Obsolete
by Using New "Twists"

The clerk who greets his customers with a snappy, "Good morning!" and then smilingly adds, "You folks certainly look happy today," is speaking effectively. Instead of using the hackneyed, "Lovely day, isn't it?" he greets newcomers with a mood-setter which puts them in a "buying" mood.

"Gosh, do *you* look great!" is an effective way of putting a new twist in the trite, "How ya feeling?"

"I heard you just broke another sales record!" is still another greeting that brings a smile to the other fellow's face. He doesn't frown and become glum as he does when he runs into the "Business is terrible, ain't it?" happiness-killer.

"We'll deliver this to your home in our especially equipped van. The delivery men will then set up the furniture and place it where you want it. You don't pay them a cent for their labor. This is just another of the many ways we stand behind the quality of our merchandise." Certainly this is effective when used to replace the time-weakened expressions: "Service with a smile. Free delivery. All merchandise strictly guaranteed," etc.

As you see, it doesn't take much thought to put those new twists in the commonplace expressions which are overworked. No matter what type of work you do or what your job is, you can invigorate your speech if you try.

How to Create Novel Ways
of Expressing Yourself

Whenever I make a phone call to a business establishment and hear the operator say, "Good morning, this is Mosely's," I reply, "I'm glad to hear it." I then pause while this sinks in, especially if Mr. Mosely is in!

This makes an interesting variation in the operator's day and insures that you will be thinking positively and smiling when you start talking.

Like most salesmen, I'm sick and tired of people saying, "It's a lousy day, isn't it?" Every time it rains or storms this can be discouraging if you let it get you. My usual reply is, "Oh, no. There's nothing wrong but the weather. It's still a good day to save money and make more money." Any salesman can turn this gloomy gripe into an opening for his sales talk.

Anyone can do likewise. Just use your memory power. Develop new expressions from old ones. Dickens once wrote: "Words are the dress of thoughts." We can express this same thought creatively by changing it to state: Words are the clothes your ideas wear. If your ideas are to be put to work, dress them in work clothes according to the task they must do. Use the right words and your ideas will be properly dressed to make money for you.

Get the idea? Of course you do. Start now. Plan how you can create new and novel ways of self-expression. Remember to do this daily.

How to Have Something Original and Interesting to Say at All Times by Planning Ahead

Each day have a definite series of thoughts in mind which will enable you to do the following without talking about the "weather."

Plan a different expression every day with which you will:

a. Greet the people you see daily.
b. Greet people you bump into unexpectedly.
c. Thank others for their favors.
d. Compliment others and express admiration for them.
e. Converse intelligently.

Once you acquire the habit of planning something original and interesting to say before you begin the new day, each day will become an enrichment for you. It doesn't matter which path of life you travel. You will benefit enormously and you will see startling results within several weeks. By using this method, after only 30 days you will have an interesting and original repertoire of attention-arresting greetings, comments and tidbits. Start on this project now.

How to Always Have a Good Word or Compliment for the Other Fellow

When you follow the plan in "c" and "d" above you will always have the right compliment on the tip of your tongue. Do this now. It's one of the most important rules to remember. When you follow it religiously, it guarantees that you will be instantly liked and admired by others. Go back and review the rules.

How to Always Be Ready to Talk About Things the Other Fellow Wants to Hear

You have learned how to remember names, faces and facts about people. You cannot help but remembering facts which you have associated with their faces and names. This, then, is the secret: Get the other fellow to talk. If you have remembered he has a French poodle, get him to talk about it. He'll soon give you more facts which you can store "on his face" which you will be able to talk about next time you see him. If he has an interesting name, do comment upon how unforgettable it is. Remember, unless you are a hermit who lives alone on a mountaintop, in order to be interesting to other people, you *must* always be ready to talk about the other fellow's favorite topic. The favorite topic? Not you, but *himself!*

How to Mean What You Say by Showing How You Are Sincerely Interested in Him

The fact that you are able to remember facts about the other fellow indicates your interest in him and in his importance. This shows you appreciate him. And one of the foremost basic human ego needs is the desire to be appreciated and admired by others. When you take the trouble to get his name spelled correctly and are among the few who pay him the compliment of pronouncing it correctly, you mean what you say. He tabs you as that sort of person: a person who is sincere and well meaning. He must like you because you like him. You belong to the same club: his mutual admiration society. Pay your membership dues to his club every time you meet him and before you know it, he'll nominate you for president!

Once you acquire, by constant practice, the knack of doing this, you'll never make an enemy. Everyone will love you for the warm, stimulating, sincere person that you are.

How to Use New Words and Expressions Socially and in Your Work

During the time you set aside daily to compose interesting greetings and things to talk about, spend a few moments with a dictionary. Select three words you do not use, then memorize them, pronounce each word three times and spell it three times. After that, think of how you might bring them into your normal conversation.

How to Make Your Goodbyes Become Unforgettable Remembrances

It happens every day. You meet a friend or associate or relative and exclaim: "You'll never guess who I ran into today."

This doesn't happen every day: "You'll never guess who I ran into *yesterday.*"

And this is rare: "Guess who I saw *last month?*"

This is common: "Whatever happened to him?"

If you want to really be remembered next month, and if you don't want others to ask: "Whatever happened to him?" you will commit this rule to your memory bank right now:

Always make the other fellow feel that meeting him was the greatest, most important thing that happened to you that day! This is the secret of how to turn your farewells into verbal remembrances. He'll talk about you to everyone he meets when you use your memory power to practice this law. You'll never be forgotten by the other fellow when you take these simple steps:

1. Remember to let him talk about himself. Ask questions and remember what he says.
2. If he has given you advice, accept it eagerly and make him feel you appreciate it sincerely.
3. Never give him advice unless he asks for it; give only when you are certain he really wants it and isn't using the "advice approach" as a fishing hook to snag compliments for himself; don't give when you can't be certain of your advice.

4. Make your visit short. Don't run the risk of wearing out your welcome. Don't remind him of how busy you are; instead comment upon how busy *he* is and leave before you "take up any more of his time."

5. Finally, upon making your exit, use your memory to review the following:

    a. Tell him how much he's cheered your day.

    b. Tell him his advice solved your problems.

    c. Apologize for your inability to give him advice but bolster his confidence by telling him you're sure he knows the right thing to do.

    d. Sum up the reasons why you must see him again, and git!

One of my friends never says, "goodbye." He says, "Remember, good is always by!"

Wesley's succinct words at the beginning of this chapter have set the theme clearly. "Make all you can, save all you can, give all you can."

I like to think of this as: "Make every memory count, save and savor all the knowledge you can about facts and people, and give all you can." You must be ready, willing and eager (not able, because you already are able) to give! You well know that you must give more always than you receive. I did not learn this only from this biblical quotation: "Cast thy bread upon the waters, for thou shalt find it after many days." (ECCL. 11:1)

I learned it from conscious daily effort which I have expended down through the years without thinking about what I was to get in return. Each time I learned something new or did a favor for someone, I did not stop to ask myself: "What am I going to get out of this?" Instead, I worked hard in every way I could, taking pleasure in everything I did. So it must be with you if you are to use your memory power profitably in business and in society.

You have learned the secrets of how to make an unforgettable impression upon others. But I am certain you are not that vainglorious to think that you will use your newly developed memory power solely to impress others. No, you will use it in every manner you can to improve yourself and to use it as a tool with which to provide the better things in life for your loved ones.

There are hundreds of ways in which these concepts may be applied to aid you. The secretary who is not content to sit back and watch the clock, but instead employs her memory power to learn more about her employer's business is a girl who gets more out of her career because she puts more into it.

The clerk who uses his memory wisely to make the store manager's job less burdensome is the person who is using his memory power to groom himself for bigger and better things; perhaps even the manager's job when the manager is promoted because the clerk had helped make that promotion possible.

Yes, I could go on and on about the countless ways and means the knowledge you have learned may be used to improve your station in life. But I will leave that up to you. From this point on, you must rely upon your own ingenuity to adapt the techniques of my memory system to fit your needs. Begin now.

Remember this: "Whatsoever a man soweth, that shall he also reap." (GAL. 6:7) But also remember this: "He that regardeth the clouds shall not reap." (ECCL. 11:4)

REVIEW QUESTIONS

1. How can your memory power help your penmanship?
2. List the three reasons why we fail to spell accurately.

_____   _____   _____

3. Review the Hersey *BETTER SPELLING* formula.
4. What procedure has been recommended to help you increase your vocabulary?
5. How will a better vocabulary enable you to improve?
6. Review the Hersey *BE CHARMING* formula.

XVI

Everyday Uses of
Your Memory Power

Annette Pritchard's dream came true last spring because she cashed in on the principles explained in this book. Her dream of a lifetime? To spend an April in Paris. Why had she been unable to go there for so long? Because her husband's untimely death made it necessary for her to go to work as a secretary in order to bring up her three young daughters. Here's how it happened.

While waiting in line at the post office to mail some registered letters for her boss, a prominent attorney, she happened to see a letter fall from an elderly gentleman's pocket. When she picked it up, she glanced at the name and address. Suddenly, an association flashed on in her memory bank. "Ralph Jonas, missing in the whale's mouth."

Annette handed the letter to him and as he turned around she remembered the face on the yellowed photograph in their office files. Though the picture had been taken nearly 40 years before, the facial characteristics were unchanged. There was no mistake about it.

"Are you Ralph Jonas, sir?" she asked politely.

The old man blinked and nodded at her dumbly. As though staggered, he moved out of the line and blinked again. "Are you a policewoman?"

Annette laughed. She told him who she was and why she'd asked. "Our firm is trustee for the Jonas family estate. If you're the same Ralph Jonas who vanished in May of 1931, you're a rich man!"

Yes, it turned out that Ralph Jonas *was* the missing heir. Because of a family argument which grew out of his choice of a wife, Ralph Jonas had packed up and left home. As the years rolled by, he eventually lost contact with his family. He wasn't eager to find them because he had taken some money (though it was rightfully his) from his guardian.

For her alertness, Annette received a handsome reward, part of which she's using toward her daughters' college education and the rest of which she is planning to use for another trip abroad.

Aside from the everyday uses of a trained memory, there are many other ways people from all walks of life profit from their abilities to remember. A man from Canada has successfully used his memory of maps and terrain to stake mining claims. A housewife from New York earns an average of $100 weekly by appearing on quiz shows. Still another man uses his memory to give public exhibitions of his ability to remember the entire contents of a mail order catalogue.

How to Use Your Memory Power to Become a Super-Secretary

A well-known secretarial service was started on a shoestring by a young lady whose boss dismissed her with these words: "Betty, I'm going to do you a favor. You're worth far more than what I'm able to pay you. You do more work in one day than any other girl who ever worked for me did in five. I'm letting you go, but hiring you back on a part-time basis, instead. Perhaps you can find other businessmen who will be glad to hire you on this same arrangement. I'll recommend you highly. And of course," he smiled, "you will earn twice what I can afford to pay you full-time."

Well, Betty thought at first this was just the old brush-off. But when she reported for work the next morning to clean out her desk, her boss arrived a few minutes later with two men. He introduced them and they agreed to hire her for two days a week each. It really wasn't the heave-ho after all!

Before long Betty began to get requests from other businessmen who heard of her astonishing ability as a super-secretary. She knew of two other girls who also had had memory training and put them to work for her too. With a little over $400, she rented and outfitted an office. She advertised by sending postal cards to businessmen in the surrounding area, offering typing, mimeographing, dictaphone, mail and phone service and even medical, legal, and engineering secretarial services.

Today Betty's service uses a staff of 56 girls, each of whom have been taught the same memory techniques you have learned in this book. What are the secrets of Betty's success and how does she use them so profitably? Here's how. These are the rules each one of her girls have thoroughly memorized. They are quoted from her handbook of instructions:

You already are a competent secretary. You know the basic skills: typing, shorthand, filing, record keeping, but you are now one of Betty's Girls and you will soon receive the high pay and the recognition of being affiliated with our organization of "super-secretaries." But first, you must use the memory system you have learned in order to achieve this status rapidly and to maintain it perfectly.

1. REMEMBER THE NAMES AND FACES OF EVERYONE YOU MEET IN BUSINESS

The most certain way for you to guarantee that visitors, clients employees and others will say something complimentary to our many client-bosses is to remember them, who they are, and their affiliations.

Remember to use their names. Greet them by name, address them by name and say goodbye to them by name. Follow the *BE CHARM-ING* formula Mr. Hersey has taught you. When you do this you will be a charming Betty Girl!

Practice this rule diligently and soon you'll never forget the face or name or facts about anyone you meet.

2. MEMORIZE THE BOSS'S SCHEDULE IN ADVANCE

For those of you who arrange appointments and schedules for our clients, it's wise to remember their diaries at least a month in advance. Of course, you keep his appointment book posted up to date. But check every day to be sure you know of that day's appointments. Be sure to memorize the more distant dates. You can save him a lot of time and trouble when you remind him he has to be in town that certain week three months hence.

Men are so accustomed to this routine that they accept it as standard. You are not a standard secretary. You are a super-secretary. When this happens in an office, you can bet the girl is just average:

The boss is on the phone. Someone at the other end of the line says: "Suppose we get together on this at lunch next Thursday." The boss buzzes his secretary. She appears with poised notebook and pen. He asks: "Mary, do I have a luncheon date for next Thursday?"

There is a costly delay while Mary retreats to her office, looks in his date book, and comes back. "No, Mr. Big, it's open."

This is time wasted for the girl who wants to impress her boss and for the busy executive whose time is figured at from $12 an hour up!

When you reply to his question at once, without checking a notebook, and are able to do this time and again, the boss knows you are an indispensable employee. Consequently your job is secure, you get the credit—and the raises.

3. MEMORIZE YOUR TICKLER FILE EACH DAY

When you are able to walk into his office without the file folder under your arm and calmly reel off the day's appointments and schedules, nothing makes a deeper impression on an employer.

It is important to remember your daily chores as well as your boss's "must-do's" also. Without the habit of planning your work, you may slip up by neglecting priorities and your work will lack organization. This is the keynote: have a daily tickler file memorized with the tasks and follow-ups sorted in the order of their importance. When you acquire this habit your workdays will be more efficient and rewardingly pleasant.

4. DEVELOP THE HABIT OF MEMORIZING ALL PHONE NUMBERS YOU MAY BE ASKED TO CALL

Remember, it takes an average of 30 seconds to look up a phone number and an additional 20 to 30 seconds to get the party on the line. Add this up 30 times a day and you see how much time and motion you lose when you fail to practice this rule.

One way to make an unusually favorable impression is to give him hair-trigger results every time your boss asks you to get a number for him. This is the best kind of job insurance there is. Once he becomes accustomed to this super-service, no other secretary can ever replace you in his admiration and esteem.

5. DEVELOP THE HABIT OF MEMORIZING TELEPHONE VOICES

This habit is priceless. Nothing is more irksome to an important client of your employer's than to be subjected to a "quiz" each time he calls. On the other hand, when he is instantly recognized and greeted by name *before* he states it, he's a pleased client.

Remember to concentrate on accent, intonation, enunciation and pronunciation while listening to and memorizing the voices of your boss's contacts. Pay close attention to their speech mannerisms and recognizable greetings. Develop an ear for speed and pitch of their voices. It is far easier to memorize a voice than a face because you can concentrate on only one dimension of the personality.

6. MAKE AN ALL-OUT EFFORT TO MASTER NOMENCLATURE SYSTEMS AND
FILING METHODS FIRST

A place for everything and everything in its place. As soon as you
are placed on a new job, use the forces of your memory power and
deposit everything in your memory banks.

An easy way to create a mental file of your folders is to memorize
the list with numerical-equivalent words beginning with "F." You will
find them in the number dictionary at the back of this book in the
"800" series. Of course, you may have some of the words starting with
the alternate for "F" which is "V" (filing isn't such a vile job when
you master this technique after all). Associate the headings for each
file folder with the key words you have preselected.

If you will run through this list in your mind, you will be amazed
at how many ideas need attention. When you remind your boss of
these, he soon grows completely dependent upon you and your ability to lighten his load.

7. USE THE MEMORY CODE TO REMEMBER KEY FIGURES

If you are employed by an advertising agency and there is the
slightest chance that you will be asked for the current space rates of
a magazine for a client you know who occasionally uses that medium,
by all means memorize them. If you are a legal secretary, by all means
memorize the standard forms for briefs, contracts and documents.
Know the numbered statutes. If you are a medical secretary, save
time by memorizing those file numbers of X-rays and other records.
If you are a secretary working for a retailer, know wholesale and retail prices, delivery costs, discounts, and markups pertaining to your
field.

If you are employed by a sales firm, make it your business to
memorize those important sales figures, the previous records and the
projections. If you are in accounting, know the procedures of computing and memorize the formats of profit and loss statements, financial
statements, work sheets and tax forms. Memorize all key addresses
and names, account headings and the like.

For all secretaries it is extremely important to know your boss's
wedding anniversary, his wife's and his children's birthdates, their
ages, sizes, tastes, and hobbies. These are vital if you are to personalize
yourself. Do suggest the important things to remember at all times.
Your boss will appreciate it. Remember the days and the dates holi-
days fall upon.

8. KNOW YOUR BOSS'S RECORD AND PROFESSIONAL BACKGROUND BACKWARDS
AND FORWARDS

The secretary who can instantly recall what year and month her
boss served as volunteer chairman of a community drive; when he attended a certain convention or executive seminar; the date he was invited to Washington to consult with foreign businessmen; or when
he won the golf tournament and what score he had—is a secretary who
is invaluable because she will not only extoll her boss's importance
and save him trouble and embarrassment, but will also save herself
hours of research.

9. USE YOUR MEMORY TO REMEMBER PLANS AND CHECK LISTS FOR SPECIAL
OCCASIONS

The girl who memorizes the plans for a sales meeting or a convention is indispensable to the busy executive. She never forgets the
little things so often overlooked because she has made a mental note
of everything that needs to be done, and then follows through by seeing that it is done. Table favors, place cards, invitations, engraved
awards and the like are always delivered on time because she has
seen to it that every little item was taken care of in an orderly manner.

Peggy Norton Rollason, public relations executive with Ray Jo-
sephs Associates of New York, a free lance writer who began her
career as a secretary, believes in this important rule firmly. As an example of her thoroughness, here is how she remembers in advance.

For instance, if your boss has to make a speech, take these steps
to help you both through the big event:

1. List date, time, place, occasion, sponsoring organization, contact and phone numbers.

2. Help research your boss's subject, title, length and time of
speech. Check his spot on the program and list other speakers and
their topics if possible to avoid conflicts.

3. Note date his photo and background sheet must be sent to
sponsoring organization for advance publicity.

4. Working backwards from S-Day, plan dates when first draft,
second and final revision must be ready.

5. Make a note of the styles and types of visual aids, charts,
pamphlets he will need and where to get them.

6. Send copies of the speech to the public relations department.
If your company has none, your boss may want to send out the releases himself.

7. Have list of newspapers, radio stations, TV stations, business
and trade publications who should receive release, speech and photo.

8. Set date when releases and covering letters must be in mail to media.

9. Notify your clipping service of which publications to watch for releases.

10. Arrange for tear-sheets from papers and magazines for your boss's scrapbook and other uses.

11. If necessary, secure reservations for travel and hotel accommodations early. Have alternate travel arrangements, train, bus, car rentals, time tables, etc., ready in the event that flying weather is bad.

12. Prepare special folder for your boss to take along, containing all pertinent correspondence, copies of speech, press releases, photos, data sheets, and don't forget "tickler" memos and business cards. If his wife's birthday is coming up during his trip, by all means remind him to phone her or have you send a gift.

You will do well to memorize this check list and keep it in your mind by reviewing it until every phase has been covered and he is on his way. You *can* be a super-secretary or an administrative assistant and your paycheck will tell the tale when you use your memory to take care of each detail. It's up to you.

How to Use Your Memory to Build a Professional Following of Clients

Bernie Winer, a pharmacist who lives in a Southern city, is part owner of a drugstore because he cashed in on his memory to build a personal following which amounts to more than 2000 customers! When Bernie learned the number code, he originally mastered it for one reason. He wanted to keep a running inventory—in his mind—of his stock of drugs. This was easy. Within a few weeks he could enumerate how many pills were remaining in hundreds of bottles.

Then one day during a rather busy season while he was alone behind the drug counter because the owner had gone fishing, Bernie was overwhelmed with confusion. As though it had been declared "lost prescription day," eight customers in a row came in to have their prescriptions refilled carrying their empty jars and bottles. For some strange reason the druggist who owned the store had never bothered to file the prescriptions numerically. Nor had he bothered to file them alphabetically.

After that hectic day, Bernie went to work numbering each prescription and marking a corresponding number on each medicine bottle label. He was determined never to be caught like that again. Though his boss could locate each prescription (which were filed in the cubby holes of a battered roll top desk), Bernie had always had to ask him to locate them.

Finally, after two months, all the prescriptions were numbered. As he did so, Bernie began to associate the numbers with the faces and names of his customers. Suddenly, because of his uncanny ability to remember each customer, and give instant service, everyone began to ask for Bernie and no longer asked to see the store owner.

Customer after customer came in, often without their prescription bottles or filed prescription numbers, and found themselves gaping in awe. Why? Because Bernie not only remembered them by name, but he also had the amazing ability to remember each five-digit reference number with unflagging accuracy! When Bernie was offered a better-paying position by a competitor, his boss suddenly saw the handwriting on the wall. If Bernie went, so would all of his customers. It was as simple as that. So, he made Bernie a partner in the business.

Today, Bernie Winer is a successful druggist because of his memory power. He enjoys the loyal friendships and dogged confidences which his vast following demonstrate dozens of times each day. "No, I only wanna see Bernie the Doc," one of those loyal customers says each time he comes into the store. "Doc Bernie, he knows all about me. He's even got my prescription number in his head so's he can give me his personal service!"

The professional man in any field can learn from this true success story. True professionalism can be enhanced through personalization of oneself with one's clients. When a client is made to feel that important and that well-remembered by the businessman behind the desk, the broker behind the counter, the doctor in the treatment room or the druggist behind the apothecary jar, he remembers to tell all of his friends, and more importantly, remembers to come back again, again and again.

A fishing boat captain I know has a mental chart of reefs and shoals. His memory serves him faithfully when running before the weather or locating his position, finding the best fishing spots above sunken hulks where fish congregate, or keeping track of his position while a sportsman has a game fish on the hook. After any of these maneuvers he is able to sail for home without plotting a new course on a chart. He is one of the most successful boat captains in the business because of his prodigious memory. Any man who is able to accomplish such a feat without consulting charts is a man whom fishing parties trust and admire.

Whatever you do in life, it pays to have a profound knowledge of the waters over which you move. When you think of Carlyle's words which are on the first page of this chapter, "Everywhere in life, the true question is not what we gain, but what we do," and then practice this sage advice faithfully, the everyday uses of your memory power will increase enormously. Your life will take on new and more profound meaning. The subsequent rewards you will then gain will bring you happiness and success.

Review Questions

1. How many ways can you list in which you can use your memory to win rewards?

_____

_____

_____

2. How can you benefit from the section on how to be a super-secretary? (If you are a housewife, a salesman, a professional man, a merchant or a white or blue collar worker, how can you benefit from being your own super-secretary?)

_____

_____

_____

3. List here the things you do every day which you can memorize. Think about the time you can save by memorizing not only your daily list of things to do, but also the step-by-step procedures you must take. Then consider how you might benefit by memorizing road maps, recipes, formulas, proper business forms, mechanical plans and so forth.

_____

_____

_____

XVII

How to Be a Hero
to Your Children

"Read my little fable:
He that runs may read.
Most can raise the flowers now,
For all have got the seed."
  —TENNYSON, *The Flowers*

Yes, you can raise the flowers now because you have the seeds of memory know-how.

Now here's how to start sowing. Go back to school. The classroom is in your mind. You are the teacher, principal and student. Perhaps you don't have the time to study. If you don't, make it your business to find the time. A way to do this might be to acquire the habit of spending time with the children, perhaps helping them with their homework.

In any event, you must let your thoughts linger awhile on these seemingly nonsensical ideas. Let the expressions on this page stimulate the uncontrolled associations into action. Now let's go!

How to Be a Hero to the Children
By Helping with Their Homework

Just as I was about to give a course to a group of salesmen, one man stood up grinning and said: "Just a second, Mr. Hersey. We aren't school kids, you know. Our minds are kind of weathered. I sure hope you're going to make this easy for us to get by using the 'kiss technique.'"

"Well," I said, glancing around at the men seated before me, "I never kissed men before, just girls. And I don't intend to begin now."

Everyone howled. But not my questioner. He let me have it. Knowing I was only joshing him, he explained.

Keep
It
Simple
Stupid

This is not only good advice, but it illustrates an old and sound memory technique. The first letter of words or names are employed to form acrostics, or key words which serve as aids for remembering the whole. You have already learned this in the CASH DEPOSIT formula, the BETTER SPELLING formula, the BE CHARMING acrostic method and others.

Another application is to make sentences out of the words beginning with the first letters of the things you want to remember. For instance, you all remember the lines on the musical staff as "E G B D F" by the sentence, "Every Good Boy Does Fine." (The staff spaces, of course, spell "FACE.") Today's hep youngster might come up with something more modern or original, such as the boy in Boston who said, "Empty Garbage Before Daddio Flips."

Now here's how our grandfathers learned the piano keys. Read this poetic lesson and see if you can apply the acrostic method to help you remember.

> All the G and A keys
>> Are between the black *threes*
> And 'tween the *twos* are all the D's;
>> Then on the *right* side of the threes
> Will be found the B's and C's;
>> But on the *left* side of the threes
> Are all the F's and all the E's.

If you have used the rhyming form to remember this verse, fine. You now know how rapidly you can memorize anything after reading it once!

Let's look at a few other acrostics from various fields of education. In biology, many students remember the elements in protoplasm by the sentence, "*See Hopkins Cafe, mighty good*":

C   Carbon

H   Hydrogen
O   Oxygen
P   Phosphorous
K   Potassium
I   Iodine
N   Nitrogen
S   Sulphur

Ca   Calcium
–Fe   Iron

Mg   Magnesium

In the study of government, students often have to remember the names of the departments in the Cabinet. Here is the sentence to remember them, "SLIP TAD, CHEW JAG":

S   State
L   Labor
I   Interior
P   Post Office

T   Treasury
A   Agriculture
D   Defense

C   Commerce
–HEW Health, Education and Welfare

JAG   Justice (Attorney General)

In geography, the Canadian provinces may be remembered by the acrostic BAS, MOQ, 3 N's and a P. An ingenious young friend of mine thought this one up. "BAS(S) is for the bass they catch. MOQ is for the moccasins they wear. And when they are told N(O), N(O), N(O), they P(OUT). So we have:

B   British Columbia
A   Alberta
S   Saskatchewan

M   Manitoba
O   Ontario
Q   Quebec

N   Newfoundland
N   Nova Scotia
N   New Brunswick

P   Prince Edward Island

The reasons why acrostics are so helpful: First, they clue you to the words you want to remember; second, they give you an infallible check list of initials which let you know when you have *covered* all the points and *concluded* with everything *complete* and *concise*. CCCC. See?

The acrostic enables us to use other letters which you can easily remember are not significant. But you will only know this when and if you take time out to invent your own acrostic.

For instance, in PHILLIPIANS 4:8, there occurs an inspiring list of things which are beneficial to remember.

> . . . whatsoever things are true, whatsoever things are honest, what-
> soever things are just, whatsoever things are pure, whatsoever things are
> lovely, whatsoever things are of good report; if there be virtue and if
> there be any praise, think on these things.

When I tried to remember this verbatim, I found it difficult. Then one morning I decided to try remembering them by listing the initial of each major point in sequence.

T   True
H   Honest

J   Just
P   Pure

L   Lovely
G   Good Report

Because the initial letters seemed to spell nothing of significance, I decided to insert vowels just as we do in the number code to compose words. Here's what I came up with: THE JAY PLUG (THe Jay PLuG)

It is obvious there is nothing to connect this sequence of words to the inspirational Scripture message, but it holds the information in the library of my mind where I can get to it.

Still another variation is the use of the number code to invent phrases to help you remember tables. Here is how I remember the metric tables. I found this necessary when I had to purchase some metric wrenches and couldn't find them. I merely bought some American wrenches in the larger size and had them machined down to the exact size I wanted.

10 millimeters (mm) = 1 centimeter (cm) = 0.3937 in. I remembered this as 0¢ worth of SWAMP MUCK per inch. (Swamp muck is worthless!)

10 centimeters (cm) = 1 decimeter (dm) = 3.937 in. I remembered this as 1¢ worth of WAMPUM WIG per inch.

10 decimenters = 1 meter (m) = 39.37 in. I remembered this as 10¢ worth of HEMP HAMMOCK per inch.

And to remember this: 1 kilometer (km) = 0.62137 of a mile, I remembered that "a good cook will walk a mile for SAGE NUTMEG spices"!

Yes, it is surprising how many ways there are to develop mnemonic devices to help you remember. How many bookkeepers or accountants do you know who can tell you how many zeros there are in a *nonillion?* Here's a simple method to remember this:

There are 9 zeros in a BILLION. Think of suBway bill (SuBway = 9, 9-zeros).

12 zeros in a TRILLION. Think of housToN trill.

15 zeros in a QUADRILLION. Think of a quadlegged sTooL.

18 zeros in a QUINTRILLION. Think of sTeVe quinn.

21 zeros in a SEXTILLION. Think of sex saNiTy.

24 zeros in a SEPTILLION. Think of seNioR goes to school in september.

27 zeros in a OCTILLION. Think of sNaKes writhe like octopuses.

30 zeros in a NONILLION. Think of saMSon (no hair).

33 zeros in a DECILLION. Think of swiM hoMe, desi!

The above are easily remembered when you connect them like this:

"I rode on a subway with bill all the way to houston where we listened to an operatic TRILL sung by a soprano standing on a QUADLEGGED STOOL. We met STEVE QUINN who gave us a lecture on SEX SANITY after the SENIORS left the theatre to go to school in SEPTEMBER. We saw a triple feature about SNAKES and OCTOPUSES, another movie about SAMSON with NO HAIR, and a film entitled: SWIM HOME, DESI, Lucy's waiting!

This brings us to another device for retaining things in mind. It is called the code or invented word. In physics, such a word is VIBGYOR. This stands for the initial letters of the colors in the spectrum from the shortest progressively to the longest wave length:

V   Violet
I   Indigo
B   Blue
G   Green
Y   Yellow
O   Orange
R   Red

Another way to remember that red has the longest wave length and violet the shortest is to remember "V for V-neck short-sleeved shirts" and "R for long red underwear" or "long stemmed red roses."

Sometimes one abbreviation enables you to remember another. The initials *BPOE* are familiar to everyone because it stands for *"The Benevolent Protective Order of Elks."* But many a sailor has used these initials to remember the color and positions of black can buoys along waterways and harbor entrances like this:

B   Black
P   Port
O   On
E   Entering the harbor

The red can buoys are on the starboard side of the channel when entering a harbor. They are remembered by many as RRR:

R   Red
R   Right
R   Returning home

Many landlubbers are taught which end of a vessel is which like this:

PORT wine warms the heart which is on the left looking forward just as your heart is on the left side of your chest. *Port-side lights are red like wine.*

STARBOARD is easily remembered when you think of green stars on the right aboard the vessel. *Starboard lights are green stars.*

BOW is the forward section of a vessel and can be remembered like the lullaby you'll think of if you stand on the BOW in bad weather. "When the BOW breaks, the cradle will fall, etc."

ABAFT is toward the stern. And you're "daft" if you go abaft without looking.

CLOSE-HAULED is when you "haul the vessel as close to the wind as she will go."

CRUTCH is the crutch you use to support the *spanker-boom* to keep it from spanking you when the sail is not set. You need a CRUTCH when there isn't any wind in your sails!

THWARTS. When you sit on the seats going across a boat to row it you can get warts. *Thwarts* are the seats going from port to starboard. ATHWARTS means the direction across the boat. THWARTS-ATHWARTS = warts.

I used these techniques to learn vast amounts of information for an appearance on the nationally televised program "To Tell The Truth." I impersonated Captain Ellsworth Coggins, captain of the replica of the ship *Bounty*, which was built specially for the motion picture, *Mutiny on the Bounty.*

Though I knew nothing about the sea or sailing ships, the *Bounty* or the film when I started, I learned all I needed to know within 24 hours. I learned every detail of the ship, its rigging, its dimensions, the dimensions of the original ship, its crew, navigation course, cities it had visited, the entire cast of the picture, the entire production staff, latitudes and longitudes, ship stores, sea lore, ranks in the British Navy as compared with the U. S. Navy and literally hundreds of other facts. I started on this at Tuesday at one P.M. and the show was taped the following evening.

The real captain, incidentally, got only one vote out of four.

The extent to which these imaginative ideas may be used are unlimited. For example, did you know that the derivative of a code word widely used in our language "hooch" (for alcoholic drinks) is simply the formula for alcohol spelled backwards? "HCOOH."

It is remarkable how ingenious many of these ideas are.

Recently, I was discussing some of these techniques with the circulation manager of a newspaper. "That reminds me!" he laughed, "it's like a word I made up,

"Miss Beempentergeverzer"

which enabled me 30 years ago to remember the prefixes to the inseparable verbs in German. Here are how they break down: *mis be emp ent er ge ver zer.*

In Latin, some students prefer to remember the riddle, "Why are the third and fourth conjugations like an old maid?"

Answer: "Because there are no 'bo's (beaux) in the future."

Not too long ago, my son had to remember the following six claims for special assistance to the farmer:

1. Low income tax status.
2. Farm progress promotes soil conservation.
3. Farmers are often victims of the weather.
4. Farmers are vulnerable to business fluctuations.
5. Other industries have special assistance, like tariffs.
6. We would like to preserve the American farm as a way of life.

To do this he used a chain of associations. He connected picture-links representing point one with a picture standing for point two. He then associated an image for point three to the picture of point two, and so on. This is the way he saw it and remembered. Of course, you would make different pictures.

He saw a farmer with his pockets empty and turned out. He was contour plowing (representing soil conservation). Suddenly, a cloudburst washed out the terraced furrows, dissolving the lines of the washout into a business graph spiral that coiled downwards. Across the field the farmer saw representatives of other industries laughing at him and driving by in Cadillacs bought with tariff money. Finally, he pictured the farmer rejecting them and turning back to his farm, determined to continue that way of life no matter what. He saw his farmhouse with a huge American flag above it waving in the breeze.

As you see, it is easy to connect thoughts into connecting links, which, when chained together, enable you to remember the entire thing without missing a point. Try this now. Go back and review this chapter quickly, forming one image after another and then linking them together. Once you do this you will be able to recall everything you want without over-looking a single point!

How to Use the Number Code
to Remember Dates and Mathematical
Constants and Statistics

MaD RaDiSH is the constant for *pi* (3.1416). The constant for *e*—2.718281828 can become NeCK TouGH NaVy, TouGH NaVy. Notice how the last four digits are a repetition of the preceding four.

If you want to remember the melting point of metals in degrees centigrade, here is one way to do this:

Iron melts at 1535.   TaLl MiLl   A blast furnace is in a tall steel mill.

Lead melts at 327.   MoNKey   Picture yourself pouring lead into a mold to make a lead monkey.

Silver melts at 1950. Tea BaLlS   Most tea balls are made of sterling silver.

Now here is a list of numbers and their square roots. It is important to notice that it isn't necessary to remember the whole number to the left of the decimal point since our common sense tells us what it must be.

Number	Square Root	Picture
2	1.414	RiDeR. Picture *two* riders in a race.
3	1.732	KiMoNo. See a wrestler wearing a *kimono* in a tag team match with 3 others.
5	2.236	eNMeSH. There are five fingers on your hand. See it *enmesh*ed in a glove made of screening.
6	2.449	RaRe Bee. Six suggests a six-sided hexagon, and the cells in a bee hive are hexagonal. Picture the queen bee which is a *rare bee* in the center of the bee hive.
7	2.645	SHRiLl. Seven suggests a craps game. See a policeman blowing a *shrill* whistle and pinching the players.
8	2.828	heaVy kNiFe. Eight suggests the word "ate." See yourself eating with a *heavy knife.* Tsk, Tsk. Such manners!
10	3.162	TouCH Nose. See yourself *touching* everyone's *noses.* Ignore the final "s" sound.

Now here are some more examples of things you might want to remember. How would you apply them? Consult the number dictionary at the back of this book and start having fun! How would you remember the following?

Mt. Fujiama in Japan is 12,365 feet _____

6 feet is 1 fathom _____

1 nautical mile = 6080.20 ft. (U.S.N.) _____

8 furlongs = 1760 yards or 5280 feet or 1 mile _____

40 rods = 1 furlong _____

144 square inches = 1 square foot _____

4 quarts = 1 gallon or 231 cubic inches _____

90 degrees = 1 quadrant _____

4 quadrants = 360 degrees or 1 circle _____

There are 1,335 Ben Franklin 10¢ Stores _____

There are 42,703 auto dealers (new) in the U. S. _____

There are 42,717 rated furniture stores _____

There are 26,450 jewelry stores _____

17,360 American lumber yards sell Hardware & Building Supplies _____

There are 50,029 listed drug stores _____

There are 2,566 pet shops _____

Remember, form words which make sense to you and then use these to link together each image. It doesn't matter what system you employ to recall each thing you want to remember. What does matter is that it is easy for you. Memorize facts and figures pertaining to your interests or business and you will always have them at the tip of your tongue when needed.

Remember to do this every day of every month each year. By the way, that reminds me:

> "Thirty days hath September
> April, June and November
> All the rest have thirty-one
> Except February, eight and score
> Till leap year gives it one day more."

XVIII

How to Remember Speeches, Sales Talks, Presentations, Jokes and Anecdotes

"As a vessel is known by the sound whether it be cracked or not; so men are proved by their speeches, whether they be wise or foolish."
—DEMOSTHENES

MONOTONOUS words = 32,120 words the average individual speaks during a seven-day week. Think about that for a moment. During that meeting you attended last month, how many monotonous words were uttered? Yes, you have to admit it, you thought of a number of things you could have said, but didn't—after the meeting was over. Instead, you merely added to the pointless monotony.

This need not be when you remember to take steps to be prepared to say what you want to say when your chance comes to say it. In all, there are only four basic steps to follow which will enable you to become a dynamic speaker who never forgets or stumbles. Here they are. I call this my T–A–L–K formula.

T   Think-out and plan what you want to say.
A   Apply your memory power.
L   Link your thoughts to be expressed.
K   Know your audience.

Believe it or not, that's all there is to the art of remembering speeches, sales talks, presentations, jokes and anecdotes. Or for re-membering anything you want to say.

Of course, we are not dealing with the basic fundamentals of speak-ing such as enunciation, articulation, gestures, stage presence, and so forth. Any good book on public speaking will cover those points. Here we are only concerned with the application of my memory system and how it helps you to display and cash in on your hidden memory power.

How to Think Out and Plan in Advance
What You Want to Say

Tremendous advantages await the man who is always able to cover each essential sales point in a presentation. The same holds true for the public speaker; the club member who only occasionally is called upon to make an address or commemoration; the business executive; the poli-tician and the professional man.

It is important to reiterate this point: First, before you can expect to receive, you must *give*. Yes, you must give thought and planning to what you are to say before you can ever expect to achieve the rewards for which you are aiming.

Every day, businessmen, advertising agencies and men from all fields and professions send representatives out to deliver their carefully con-ceived presentations, sales messages and appeals. And every day the majority of them fail because the man telling the story doesn't tell the whole story. In other words, all that careful preparation and costly planning is wasted because someone did not remember all the salient points.

The major reason why we do not buy that product or service, or vote for that particular candidate, or give our consent to one appeal or another is that we do not thoroughly understand all the benefits or the points to be considered. Those loquacious talkers fail to sell us because they talk too much about the wrong things and too little about the right things—the important things in which we are interested. We do not buy what they sell not because of what is said, but rather because of what they have forgotten to tell us!

To avoid forgetting the main points of what you want to say, it first is necessary to think out what you are to accomplish. Here's how I planned and developed a speech I was called on to deliver on the subject of "How to Commemorate Others."

First, I considered these points which I wanted to take up; if you notice, I have linked each point to a key word to enable me not to over-look any single thought.

	Speech Key Word	Thought
1.	hat	inspiration distilled from lives
2.	hen	know useful, inspiring, service
3.	ham	passed on, stone or bust with two dates
4.	hare	dedicate building to memory
5.	hill	from lives left facts born and died
6.	hedge	few qualities were preserved, plaque
7.	hook	opportunity members church, lodge, etc.
8.	hive	preserve footprints dedication
9.	hoop	successive generations
10.	hot-house	Lincoln Memorial

By connecting these key words or "cue" words to the thoughts, I was then able to develop my entire speech within several hours. You have already learned how to use your memory banks to store thoughts, so it isn't necessary to go into great detail again. I'm confident you will see how it is possible to deliver a speech verbatim when you work this exercise. In the paragraphs below are the thoughts within the framework of the speech I subsequently gave. Underscore those thoughts and notice how it is impossible to omit any of them or to mix them up.

There is a vast amount of inspiration to be distilled from the lives of others. We all know people past and present whose lives have been use-ful, inspiring, and of great service to their fellow man.

Yet, too often when they have passed on, we put up a stone with two dates, or a bust with a name and dates, or we dedicate a building to their memory.

From these lives which were of such value as to demand commemora-tion by those whose lives their deeds affected, we leave to posterity only two facts common to every other mortal: they were born and they died.

In relatively few cases, some of the qualities that made the person outstanding are preserved on a plaque.

The opportunity and responsibility may come to you as a member of a church, a lodge, a veterans or service club, or in some other capacity to help preserve the footprints of dedication, service and inspiration which have passed your way, just as it has come to me on this day.

One of the great memorials in our country, if not the world, is the Lincoln Memorial in Washington, D.C. . . . It is great not because of its architecture. The Taj Mahal is more famous for that. It is great not because of its impressive statue and the appreciative inscription above it. It is great to visitors from all countries because we have not simply enshrined there the name of Lincoln; we have there also his immortal Gettysburg Address, and the stirring and challenging words of his Second Inaugural Address. His thoughts are there for us to share. His words that spoke the challenge and offered the solution remain a purposeful, productive, and inspiring memorial to each succeeding generation. The fact that it was not dedicated until fifty-seven years after his death confirms the carelessness with which we fail to make available the distilled essence of great lives to succeeding generations.

You don't have to build a Lincoln Memorial to preserve for others the lessons of lives that you yourself may have been benefited by.

In the Back Bay of Boston, where he who walks may read, there is a simple monument. On it you can read the inspiring story of a young immigrant who came to America and made good. This is the inscription.

Patrick Andrew Collins
1844—1905
Born in Ireland and always her lover.
American by early training and varied employment.
Upholsterer from 15—23.
Harvard Bachelor of Laws at 27.
From 1871 Lawyer.
1868—72 Member of the Mass. Legislature
1883—89 Member of Congress
1893—97 Consul General in London
1902—05 Mayor of Boston
A talented, honest, generous, serviceable man.

The symbolism of the two bronze women on either side of this stone may be obscure, but here is a message in keeping with the Biblical injunction, "Write the vision and make it plain upon tables that he may run that readeth it."

If you can discern and draw upon the highest qualities of others, if you can spark and maintain your inspiration from the flame of theirs, you will be a more valuable person. If you are not doing this, you are short-changing yourself. It has been said that those who fail to learn from history are compelled to repeat its mistakes.

We certainly should never forget and we should adequately commemorate the contributions made by the men and women who served in our country's defense. Whether they went willingly or unwillingly, whether they were gentlemen or bums, whether they survived or lost their lives in a simple home base accident or in storming enemy strongholds, they all paid a price that their nation and its ideals might live. Abraham Lincoln set the goal for us at Gettysburg: *"That from these honored dead we take increased devotion to that high cause for which they gave the last full measure of devotion, that we here highly resolve that these dead shall not have died in vain, and that government of the people, by the people, and for the people shall not perish from the earth."*

Servicemen of a later period may lack a Lincoln to highlight their sacrifice and contribution, but every legion post, every veterans' group can do something that will leave a message of simple dignity and significant import in addition to the mere name of a serviceman on public view in squares and parks of our nation. The message of one such inscription might well be duplicated widely. It is on a bronze plaque at eye level on a small post office in Weymouth, Massachusetts. It reads:

> This building is dedicated to the memory of
> *John Thomas Gunn*
> United States Marine Corps
> Who died in the service of his country at
> Espiritu Santo New Hebrides 20 April 1944
> *"He stands in the unbroken line of patriots who have dared to die that freedom might live and grow and increase its blessings. Freedom lives and through it he lives in a way that humbles the undertakings of most men."*
>
> Franklin D. Roosevelt
> President of the United
> States of America.

It is not necessary to rear marble or bronze and spend hundreds or thousands of dollars. A simple message set in type, even typed in large textbook type, together with a picture can be prepared and laminated to a wood background with a plastic process that will survive unnumbered glassed frames. Such a plaque is ideal for interior use and would seldom cost over $20. The one that introduced me to the possibilities was made for the dedication of a room in the church in Danbury, Connecticut, where my father served his last pastorate. Perhaps the expression of the thoughts in it may help you to arrive at a suitable inscription when you have the occasion to prepare one.

"Pause for a moment to consider the occasions and people who have hallowed this room. To each of us there is a different memory although to some of us there are many similar ones—the Sunday school services—the young people's meetings—the choir rehearsals—the social times—the good fellowship of friends and workers who have developed faith, strengthened resolution, and inspired sacrificial service.

"*We dedicate this room to the memory of the Reverend Harry Adams Hersey. Why? There are already many who never knew him personally. In time to come there will be no one. What sort of a man was he that we consider him worthy of remembrance? What were the qualities in his life which compelled his associates to want his name to be remembered?*

"*He was kind, and this kindness extended not only to his own parishioners but to the stranger hospitalized far from home and to the entire world through his active support of organized efforts to improve the lot of mankind everywhere.*

"*He was courageous: He left a successful business at the age of twenty-five, made up his high school work and went on through seven years of college to become a minister. He was a genial crusader for worthwhile and at times unpopular causes. He spoke out vigorously for the God-given rights of every individual of whatever race or religion. He devoted years of freeing mankind from the enslaving effects of alcohol and tobacco. He never flinched in the face of organized bigotry or the pressure of commercial interests. He was indeed 'Mr. Valiant for Truth.'*

"*He encouraged young people. He made it possible for many to want and to obtain higher education. He opened the doors through which they could pass on to higher attainments. He worked diligently to improve education at all levels.*

"*He was optimistic. He knew that good does in the long run triumph over evil. He had great confidence in the millions of people whose actions never make headlines, and he instilled this confidence in others.*

"*These qualities were not his exclusive possession. They are the qualities which have compelled admiration wherever and by whomever expressed. They are the qualities that can help us all to lead a fuller, more useful and more satisfying life.*

"*Father of mankind, we honor a man who loved all men and served them to the best of his ability, without stint or restriction. We thank Thee for him. May his spirit permeate this place and inspire others to serve their fellowmen.*

"*To the memory of Harry Adams Hersey and to truth, love, and service, we dedicate this room.*"

How to Apply Your Memory Power in Public

On your own two feet you are able to look the world squarely in the eye and say what you have to say. You are able to do this because you are not worrying about repeating your prepared talk word for word. You are able to do this because you are certain of your ability to recall each *thought* you want to express.

The main thing to remember about using your memory is this: The more you exercise it, the stronger it becomes. Once you are accustomed to relying on your memory bank to deliver the stored thoughts with push-button speed, you will be using your memory power in public speaking. And you will be using it effectively.

But you need to remember more if you are to display your extraordinary intellectual powers and your persuasive ability. That is where the other forces of your mind are called upon. The first of these is *enthusiasm*. The second is thoroughly explained in the BE CHARMING formula you learned in an earlier chapter. *Enthusiasm* plus the BE CHARMING formula adds up to success because enthusiasm is the mood exuded by a speaker that captivates and sways audiences.

When you are able to concentrate fully on the thoughts you are expressing and when you are able to voice them naturally and with spontaneity, you are then capable of getting "excited" about what you are saying.

Just remember. Get with it, brother! Let your dynamic words infect your listeners with the contagion of your excitement. That's the "how" of the "A" in the TALK formula. The rest is just common sense.

How to Link the Thoughts You Want to Express

When giving a sales presentation, as in a speech, it often becomes necessary to repeat a point you have made earlier, then resume where you have either been interrupted or had to leave off.

Here is how a furniture salesman representing a manufacturer of cedar hope chests associates the key points of his sales talk which he uses to sell a retailer:

Key Word	Sales Point	Association
hat	Most profit, new customer-getter	Brides and bridegrooms entering store carry lots of cash in tall silk hats and wedding dress trains.
hen	Line is nationally known and accepted	A hen dragging a string of hope chests up to the United States Capitol Building.
ham	Pre-marriage good will	A couple carving a big ham for a group of hungry people in order to get good will.

Key Word	Sales Point	Association
hare	Additional pyramid sales	A hare jumping over a pyramid.
hill	Widest price appeal	A hill with wide prices painted on it.
hedge	Seldom repossessed	The bride fighting with a repossessor to keep the chest on her side of a hedge.
hook	Builds your good name	My business card hanging from a hook.
hive	Greater profits	I visualize the prophet Isaiah getting great gobs of honey from a bee hive.
hoop	Nationally advertised	Children all over the nation rolling hoops with advertising copy on them.
heads	The Key to Complete Room outfit sales	I'm balancing roomfuls of furniture atop my head with a key in my mouth.

Assuming that the furniture salesman was interrupted just as he was halfway through point No. 5 (hill), the linkage of the thought could be easily picked up simply by back tracking, then briefly reviewing what had been said.

This is extremely important in selling. Often, when a prospect has been called away to wait on a customer or answer a phone he loses track of what the salesman has just told him. His train of thought must be set into motion again. The only way to do this successfully is to review what you have said, in a brief manner, then pick up the threads by recalling the hen and the role she plays in the controlled association, the ham, the hare, and the hill. "As I was saying," the salesman goes on, "our product has the widest price range in order to appeal to your installment buyers as well as to your cash customers. In fact. . . ."

No matter how long your presentation or speech may be, link the thoughts you want to put across in a logical sequence, then deposit them into your memory storage compartments. In selling anything, whether it is yourself to a new prospective employer, or a broom to a savage who lives in a cave, you cannot close a sale until you have made your prospect want to buy. The only way he will want to buy from you is to listen to everything you have to say. You must build the foundation for the close.

He must have enough information to make him have confidence in you and in your product or service.

This method in the "L" for link in the TALK formula, when diligently applied with the first two steps, will work selling miracles for you.

How to Know Your Audience

You have planned what you want to say, you have applied your memory power, and you have linked the thoughts you want to express in a logical sequence. This leaves you free for the other things for which a dynamic speaker must be prepared.

Those audiences before you are those other "things."

To know them, remember this simple acrostic formula:

KNOW—HOW—AWAKENS
S N   A P
O   K
W   E
S E E

KNOW-HOW AWAKENS AUDIENCES
SNAP KEEPS THEM AWAKE
OK TO BE DIFFERENT
WE, NOT THE I, I, I
SEE THAT THEY SEE THE POINT

How you apply these simple rules is up to you. Basically, you know your subject. When you apply your memory power effectively and display your ability to quote statistics, facts and figures without resorting to notes, this kind of know-how awakens audiences. They blink in disbelief at your expertness.

When you use snap to keep them awake, they give you their undivided attention. Your remarks are not anticipated. You are not telling them things they already know or have heard before. Being original and entertaining is to use snappy ideas. Be yourself in your own way. Talk as you would if you were with an old friend. Let your style be natural and enthusiastic. When it is, your personality will shine through and snap will be added to the power of your words.

It's perfectly okay to be different. By all means use jokes and analogies to liven your material and give variety to long periods of lecture-type talk. In the event you see that you are boring your audience, wake them up with an unexpected joke or anecdote that will illustrate your point, return to your topic by briefly reviewing what you said before, then go on. If you discover that your prepared talk is not going over, drop the subject by asking the audience questions and play it from the batter's box. Their questions will lead you back on the right track.

Always use *we* and not I. This rule doesn't need explanation. The man who uses too many I's gives the impression he loves to hear himself boast.

Finally, see that your audience is getting the point. Are they nodding in agreement, or are their nods accompanied by snores? You must watch for signs of understanding or misunderstanding and act accordingly.

How to Personalize Your Talk by Using Know-How to Awaken Them with a Joke

During your preparation of material, you should always include a few jokes and stories which may be tied in fittingly with the audience's background, occupation or interests. For instance, after listening to the spirited harangue of an employer at a sales meeting, you might take your cue from what he has said to break up the tension of the audience when you stand up to talk next.

By taking another joke you have heard and changing it slightly you can make it sparklingly humorous and original. Your lead-in could be:

> "Well, gentlemen, I've seen history being made tonight. This is the first time I've ever seen a sales organization pull in its belt so the salesmen can let out theirs. But seriously . . ."

or

> "See? The weatherman was finally right. The cooler weather he promised back in July, finally made it!"

or

> (If the meeting room is overcrowded) "300 people jammed into one little room like this. No wonder this reminds me of Sunday brunch at Hyannis Port!"

or

> (If the banquet rates are high) "$50 a plate! I wouldn't give my dentist $50 a plate . . . if I had to spend $50 for a dinner, I wouldn't be able to eat the food. I'd have it bronzed like baby shoes . . ."

As you can see from the nature of the above stories, these jokes cannot be told unless you truly know your audience! You should know beforehand how far you can go. You should know if the man you are kidding can take it or not, and you should know most importantly if your jokes are in character. You are not a comedian. You are there as an expert or a personality. Therefore, you must never tell jokes which are out of character as some of the ones you've just read certainly may be before certain groups of individuals.

You may personalize your talk by using your know-how to awaken them with a joke that fits the occasion. But do use good taste. Some of these are all right in a night club, but not at a business gathering. A comment such as this is in better taste. It is excellent as a lead-in to your topic and an audience warmer-upper: "My little girl was only five, but at that early age she showed a marked knowledge of the Bible. For instance, when I had to give her a teaspoon of medicine one day, I called out to her:

"Open your mouth, honey, and shut your eyes. I've something to give you that'll make you healthy, wealthy and wise."

"Oh, Daddy!" she cried waving a finger at me. "That's just what the serpent said to Eve!"

"Yes," your remarks go on, "everyone knows you can't be fooled when you have your eyes open. How else can you see what's going on?

"But getting to my topic on *observation*, it's important that you . . . etc."

Once you have carefully built a storehouse of jokes which may be adapted as lead-ins or analogies, personalize them by making yourself the brunt of the joke. Or perhaps by characterizing yourself and the thing for which you are known. "It goes without saying, gentlemen, that one can't be too cautious these days. Last month when I was down in Texas to speak before a group of businessmen, they wound up selling me several oil wells.

"What an investment I thought I had! Yep, they produce 500 barrels a week. No oil, though. Just barrels."

Yes, it is amusing when you use an appropriate story for any occasion and then use it to make fun of yourself, to personalize yourself and to wake up the audience. If you're unsure of your audience, you cannot go wrong poking fun at yourself.

Here's one I often tell about the days before I became a memory expert. One of my worst faults was my absent-mindedness, forgetting to mail letters and so forth. At breakfast one Saturday morning, my wife said to me, "Did you have any mail this morning, dear?"

"Only some advertisements," I replied over the rim of my coffee cup.

She didn't answer at first. She buttered a slice of toast in that special way wives have of intimating that something's going to explode and exerted an effort avoiding my gaze. "By the way, honey," she asked, her voice dripping with sweetness, "those letters I gave you yesterday. Did you mail them?"

"Of course I did!" I cried. (How else was I going to defend myself?)

"Well," she said with that innocent smile of hers, "that's funny. I can't understand why you didn't get a letter this morning. One of those I gave you to mail yesterday was addressed to *you!*"

As I have numerous anecdotes and jokes in my memory, I remember them easily by filing them in my memory bank compartments under "J" for jokes. You will find this list in the number dictionary section under 600 beginning with:

Jesus	600
Jesuit	601
Jason	602
Juicy-ham	603
Juicer	604
Jessel	605
Juicy-hash	606
Juicy-chew	607
Joseph	608
Jasper	609
Judas	610

The anecdotes which I have remembered are of course associated with each image or key word. I have not referred to them in my explanation for the simple reason that what I do is take each story out of my memory bank and reconnect it with the topic of my speech subject.

Now here's how I connect each thought in my topic to the analogy I want to use to illustrate it. I simply remember the anecdote with the thought image to be included in the talk. You can use this memory system if you want to avoid using the same stories before a group twice. However most successful speakers have found that as long as the story is good and well told, the very people who have heard it before will enjoy it most.

Never ask if they have heard it. Go ahead and tell it if it has a useful point.

Here are my picture words for talk "thoughts." This is a list which I use when composing a speech whenever I am at home in my study. Instead of using code words, I use the objects in the room in this consecutive sequence:

1. desk
2. desk lamp
3. desk ash tray
4. phone
5. pen set
6. blotter
7. desk chair
8. lounge chair
9. end table
10. bookcase

When I want to remember the anecdote to illustrate my comments on the Lincoln Memorial, for example, I visualize myself sitting at my desk in the Lincoln Memorial below the magnificent statue of Abraham Lincoln.

When I want to remember the anecdote to illustrate the importance of observation, I see myself using my desk lamp as an observation beacon. You see, *desk* is the first thought, *desk lamp* the second, etc.

And there you have it. That's all there is to memorization of sales talks, presentations, jokes and anecdotes. Whatever you do, whether it is speaking before a political rally or enormous convention, or merely making a presentation before a prospect, remember the simple rules explained in this chapter. Practice them and put them to work methodically. When you acquire the habit of doing this, more and more people will sit up and listen when you take the floor.

REVIEW QUESTIONS

1. Explain the T–A–L–K formula. List here what each letter means to you.

T _____

A _____

L _____

K _____

2. Explain the acrostic formula:

KNOW — HOW — AWAKENS

	S	N	A	P		
		O	K			
		W	E			
			S	E	E	

3. Practice memorizing some reading matter, business letters, or other things which are important for you. Connect the cue words you select with an orderly list of key words.
4. Begin to build a mental file of anecdotes, analogies and jokes.
5. Plan your next talk according to this formula. If you are a salesman who uses a regular sales talk, go over it first on paper or in your mind. Select each key point and associate it. Now practice going over those points backwards and forwards, or picking up at any given step along the way.
6. Develop the habit of using the different numerical series of words in the number dictionary to help you remember different talks, speeches, jokes and so forth.

XIX

How to Have Fun
With Memory Power

*"I am a great friend to public amusements; for
they keep people from vice."*
—Samuel Johnson in Boswell's
Life of Johnson

This chapter is for relaxation, entertainment, fun and the development of mental muscle through playing games with your friends. This will give you a few pointers on the performance of a memory demonstration which you can use at parties, conventions, or anywhere you go. Moreover, you will learn several other interesting applications of your memory power.

How to Memorize the Contents
of a Magazine

You can amaze audiences with your ability to remember the contents of a magazine page for page. Imagine what happens when you are given a magazine which you read through *once*, then tear apart, handing out the pages to each person in attendance who then ask you to tell them what's on each page!

Not only will this give you the money-making ability to apply the same technique and skill to learning the contents of trade journals, catalogues, location of material within reams of specifications of a construction project, but you will also learn to master entire textbooks! Strangely enough, you already know *how* to do this because you have mastered the techniques of the memory bank system and the number code.

The memorization of the contents of a current picture magazine is a fairly standard demonstration in memory entertainment. The principles are simple. It involves using your standard list for the page numbers: hat for 1, hen for 2, ham for 3, etc., and then associating these basic words with the picture on the page you want to remember.

Here is an example of how to remember several pages. I am illustrating this to show you how to cover a wide range of varying subjects.

You will notice that in many cases I use the key word to trigger one pictorial association which in turn may lead to another. When I review the pages, I try to see them, each one in its entirety, as a picture. This will be clearer as we go through this together. Let's go!

Page	Code Word	Content of Page	Association of Code Word, Content
1	Hat	Bride and bridegroom on cake. New Wife. New home. New needs for insurance.	I put a tall silk *hat* on the bridegroom but had it come down over his eyes.
2	Hen	Root beer ad, table of contents.	A *hen* drinking root beer and scratching out the table of contents with her foot.
3	Ham	Voltage regulator: ad for regular car maintenance.	Pictured *ham* being cooked in a garage. Cooking controlled by voltage regulator.
4	Hair	Mobil home living. Man in living room of trailer with fishing tackle. Wife on sofa.	She's tearing her *hair* because he brought the fishing gear into her mobil home living room.
5	Hill	Relief for hot itchy feet. Letters to the editor. Cartoon of bell ringer. Ad for padlocks.	The bell ringer is climbing a *hill*. His feet are red hot. He stops to write a letter telling the editor to padlock the concern who says their preparation will cool his feet.
6	Hedge	Blurred car "One nice thing about an air-cooled engine."	Picture the car whizzing along top of *hedge*, air blowing through its engine.

Page	Code Word	Content of Page	Association of Code Word, Content
7	Hook	You never run out of air— no radiator, hose, water pump.	Picture a *hook*. On it are hooked the radiator, hose, pump, and a big balloon full of air.
8	Hive	People buy this liquor by the case. Couple in board walk buggy, being handed a case.	Picture the bottles studded into a *hive* instead of a regular case.
9	Hoop	A freckled face girl drinking a Cola drink.	She's rolling a big *hoop*, hitting it with the bottle of Cola.
10	Toes	Continuation of Cola ad. "The difference comes through." Picture of six-pack of bottles.	Wading in the Cola and seeing it come up through her *toes*. She carries the six-pack.

Have someone try you out right now on a magazine. You'll become a source of amazement to them as soon as you *demonstrate* what you can do.

How to Have an Entertaining Memory for Playing Cards and Tricks

In this demonstration you memorize an entire deck of cards in order! Here's how you can amaze your friends by calling the name of any card in a deck from 1-52 when asked. First, you must have a set of code words, one for each card. These words must be easy to remember. To set up the code, we consider the four suits: clubs, diamonds, hearts, spades.

For clubs we will start each code word with the consonant sound of hard "C." The ace will be "1" of each suit, the jack, "11"; queen "12"; king "13." Next, we make up words for the clubs with consonant sounds which represent the number of the card in the suit. For diamonds we use the words beginning with "D"; hearts, "H"; and for spades, "S."

Here is the list I use. You may use other words if you wish. However, try to avoid words on your standard list of 1–100.

Clubs	Diamonds	Hearts	Spades
1. Cut	1. Date	1. Hut	1. Suit
2. Coon	2. Den	2. Honey	2. Sun
3. Comb	3. Dam	3. Home	3. Seam
4. Cur	4. Door	4. Hare	4. Sewer

Clubs	Diamonds	Hearts	Spades
5. Coil	5. Doll	5. Hail	5. Sail
6. Cash	6. Ditch	6. Hootch	6. Sash
7. Cake	7. Duck	7. Hack	7. Sack
8. Coffee	8. Dove	8. Hoof	8. Safe
9. Cup	9. Dope	9. Hip	9. Soap
10. Caddies	10. Duds	10. Heads	10. Suds
11. Cadet	11. Dotted	11. Hooded	11. Statue
12. Cotton	12. Deaden	12. Heathen	12. Stein
13. Coy dame	13. Diadem	13. High dam	13. Steam

Practice these associations by going through a deck of cards repeatedly until you are able to quickly come up with the right code word the moment you spot the card. As soon as you are familiar with the code words, you are ready for the "baffling" demonstration.

As the cards are turned over, make pictorial associations between the first word on the standard list and the code word for the first card. For example, if the first card is the four of diamonds, code word "door," picture a big *hat* hanging on a *door*. Second card is queen of clubs, code word "cotton." Picture a *hen* picking up *cotton* with her beak, lots of it.

You will soon find that you can do this stunt in less than 10 minutes for an entire deck. However, I would suggest that you only do half a deck when entertaining your friends. It will prove your point and won't be too boring.

If you want to use this as a conversation piece, memorize the deck in order. Put a rubber band around it and carry it with you. Ask someone to name a number between one and 52. Suppose he says "thirty-three." You toss him the deck of cards and tell him to count carefully down to the 33rd card, and he will find it to be, let's say, the 10 of spades. This is a fast demonstration because you've done your memorizing in advance. Be sure to tell him the name of the card before he gets the elastic off the deck. Be sure he doesn't disturb the order of the deck. I've met a lot of interesting strangers just by studying a deck of cards during breakfast or lunch.

Another demonstration that is really much easier is possibly even more spectacular. I call it the missing card demonstration.

To do this, you have four hands dealt as for bridge. Ask the people receiving the cards *not* to arrange them by suits. Then ask each one of the first three to call off the cards in his hand as they come, pausing only to let you memorize the cards. When three have finished, you state that you will now name the remaining cards in the fourth hand by suits and in order within each suit. This sounds terrific, and it is. But to you it is simple. Even simpler than memorizing the deck in order. Here's how to do it.

As each person calls off his cards, think immediately of the code word for the card and make a vigorous, ridiculous or violent association between that word and *yourself*.

For instance, suppose the first five cards are:

four of spades	sewer
seven of diamonds	duck
eight of hearts	hoof
queen of clubs	cotton
king of spades	steam

When you hear the four of spades called, you think of "sewer" and immediately picture *yourself* stuck in a *sewer*.

When you hear the seven of diamonds, you think of "duck." *I* shot a great big *duck*.

When you hear the queen of clubs, you think of "cotton." *My* ears are stuffed with *cotton*.

When you hear king of spades, you think of "steam." *I'm* cooking in a *steam* bath.

You keep doing this and when the three hands have been called off, you simply start going through the code words for clubs in your mind. When you strike one that you have *not* made a recent personal association with, that is the card in the fourth hand! When you finish clubs, move on mentally through the list for diamonds, hearts, and spades. It's easy. It will amaze your friends, and it takes only a few minutes. As a matter of economy of time, you may want to use a deck without face cards. Forty cards prove your point as well as 52. When doing a demonstration for a large audience, I have someone chart the cards on a blackboard so that all can see what I'm trying to find in the fourth hand.

There is just a touch of irony here. People come up to me and say, "you'd be a tough man to play poker with," and I have to remind them that they are confusing memory with judgment. It's one thing to know where the cards are, and something else to know what to do about it. But then this is for entertainment and mental exercise.

Strangely enough, most people lose at poker because they do *not* know how to play their hands. The man who cannot decide whether or not to hold an ace as a "kicker" more often than not *fails* to improve his hand because he doesn't know that the mathematical odds are against him when he holds the ace with a pair in draw poker.

The odds against bettering a hand when a "kicker" is held with three of a kind are 11 to 1. As you see, the average poker player doesn't know the odds are against him. For this reason alone, most players usually lose.

I'm not going to call this part of your "money-making memory." Instead, I'm going to show you how to win more and lose less by using your memory power to *learn* those odds.

How to Use Your Memory Power to Win at Poker

If you are in a poker game trying to draw one card to an "outside" straight (for instance, if you have a 4, 5, 6, 7 sequence) and are trying to get a 3 or 8 to make a straight, what would you do if you were caught between two heavy bettors who were raising and re-raising?

Would you keep throwing your money into the pot, throwing good money after bad just to stay in to draw to that straight? Of course you wouldn't if you knew that the odds were 6 to 1 *against* your catching an 8 or a 3!

And did you know that a professional gambler never draws to an "inside" straight because he knows the odds against filling it in are 12 to 1?

It has been proven mathematically with this table that there are 1,302,540 different poker hands of less than 1 pair combinations. This means that of the 2,598,960 possible poker hands, more than half of your chances to draw a pair or better are on the other side against you. You go in with one pair, putting your money into the pot without realizing there are 198,180 hands which are higher than your one pair!

Once you know the odds, you can win at poker *more* than you are now winning if you play occasionally. Here's how to win by learning the statistics:

POKER HAND PROBABILITIES AND ODDS

What you must know in order to win
1. The values of the hands
2. How many cards to draw to various combinations
3. What sort of hand may be expected to win a pot must be learned
4. The odds against winning with a particular hand
5. How to figure the odds offered by the "pot"

As you see, I am not going into the fine points, the rules, etc. Nor am I going to tell you how to win. Instead, I'm going to give you the known tables of statistics and then show you how to memorize them. The rest will be up to you.

THE TABLES OF POKER HAND PROBABILITIES

52-card deck with nothing wild

Poker Hand	Possible Number of Hands	Odds Against Making	Code Words To Remember These Odds
Royal Flush	4	649,789 to 1	Weary wager hope, give-up
Straight flush	36	72,192 to 1	Much agony thigh-bone
Four of a Kind	624	4,164 to 1	Junior award shower
Full house	3,744	693 to 1	Haymaker hurrah! Chop him
Flush	5,108	508 to 1	Loot Savoy, haul safe
Straight	10,200	254 to 1	Hideous noses win holler
Three of a Kind	54,912	46 to 1	Oily rubbed wine hair wash
Two Pairs	123,552	20 to 1	Den homely lion highness
One Pair	1,098,240	4 to 3	Odds hope, few winners war home
No Pair or "Busts"	1,302,540	even	Tums inhalers, head to toe

Total possible combinations: 2,598,960 = Noah lop-off bushes

53-card deck with 1 joker   *52-card deck deuces wild*

Poker Hand	Possible Number of Hands	Code Words	Possible Number of Hands	Code Words
5 of a Kind	13	Doom	672	Chicken
Royal Flush	24	Nero	484	River
Straight Flush	180	Thieves	4,072	Roscoe knee
Four of a Kind	3,120	Madness	30,816	Misfit shoe
Full House	6,552	Jail hellion	12,672	Town shaken
Flush	7,804	Key officer	13,204	Demon Czar
Straight	20,532	Nice lemon	66,236	Asia Chinamen wash
Three of a Kind	137,280	Tomahawk knives	355,056	Mole-hill slush
Two Pairs	123,552	Den homely lion	95,040	Highball sewers
One Pair	1,268,088	Heathen chiefs heavy wife	1,222,048	Dine noon serve
No Pair or "Busts"	1,302,540	Tums inhalers	798,660	Cab of judges

Total Combinations: 2,869,685 = Navy ship shovel —or— Naive shabby wishful   2,598,960 = Noah lop-off bushes

The above tables show you the chances you have of being dealt such combinations in the first five cards you get in a poker hand. The odds *against* making any particular hand may be reached by subtracting the number of combinations from the total combinations and then dividing the larger number by the smaller number.

For example, you can compute the odds against being dealt a straight in your original 5 cards (with a 52-card deck, nothing wild) like this:

1. Deduct the number of possible combinations from the total:

$$2,598,960$$
$$-10,200$$
$$\overline{2,588,760}$$

2. Divide the subtrahend into the answer:

253.8 to 1 are the odds.

$$10,200\overline{)2,588,760}$$

Now here's how to remember these statistics. First, make a visual association of a royal flush. Perhaps you might see a picture of a king flushing a drain with a plumber's friend while the other members of the royal family are telling him it's a *weary wager hope, give up!*

If you bet into a raiser and a re-raiser in a game with a wild joker with only one pair in your hand, you'll wind up on the menu of the *heathen chief's heavy wife* who'll sit down to *dine* at *noon* while the other card players *serve* you! (Carve you up too!)

Now here's another way to figure the odds of improving your hand.

Let's assume you have four hearts and want to draw one heart to fill the flush. Common sense tells you the odds are 4 to 1 against you because you have one chance in 5 of getting the proper suit. You don't have to use the table to figure this.

Now here's how to remember some of these statistics. To remember that the odds are 7 to 3 against you improving your hand by drawing three cards, to improve that one pair you have, remember this: "I'll bet the *K*ey to the ho*M*e of the couple (pair)."

To remember that one out of every five hands dealt will be jacks or better, in the original five cards, think of "Jack's he?? in the whale." In a game where each one of five players are playing, the number of hands possible which are Jacks or higher are 536,100. This may be easily remembered as a *lame shot* from a *seesaw*, if you play foolishly.

The odds against bettering the following may be remembered like this:

Against bettering three of a kind = 8 to 1. Have *tea* for three.
Against bettering a full house = 89 to 1. *Few buy and hit.*
Against bettering four of a kind = 359 to 1. I'll have in *my lap* a beggar's ha*t*.

And if you hold an ace for a "kicker" the odds are:

Against making two pair = 5 to 1. O*il* the au*to* and go home.
Against making three of a kind = 12 to 1. *Tin hut* is where you live when you try this too often.
Against making a full house = 119 to 1. *Deathbed* is where some gamblers wound up when they thought they could make this.
Against making four of a kind = 1080 to 1. A*dhesives* on hea*d*, enough said!
Against bettering your hand at all = 3 to 1. *M*oo and wai*t*!

And these statistics *prove* it doesn't pay to hold an ace for a "kicker." Now, the odds against these hands are also interesting:

Against bettering two pair on a one card draw = 11 to 1. *Death* o*de* you'll sing.
Against bettering one pair in a three card draw = 5 to 2. Ye*ll*ow-ho*n*ey when you get it.
Odds are 7 to 1 against making hand higher than two pair = 7 to 1. We*ak* i*d*ea.
Against making a full house with a two card draw = 15 to 1. The *duel* can wai*t*!
Against making four of a kind with a two card draw = 23 to 1. E*nemy* ha*te*.
Against bettering your hand at all with a two card draw = 9 to 1. *P*ay *d*ue.

If you hold a kicker with three of a kind and draw one card, you have these odds stacked against you:

Against you making a full house = 14 to 1. You need e*ther*, in your ha*t*!
Against you making four of a kind = 46 to 1. Only a *rich* w*idow* can afford this!

Against bettering your hand at all by holding a kicker with three of a kind is 11 to 1, or you are holding *dead* weight!

Of course, your knowledge of the rules of the games and the odds will certainly help you improve your play and enable you to win more than you are presently winning by being ignorant of the percentages and the odds.

Here Are Other Ways to Have Fun with Your Memory Entertaining Audiences

Any good book on magic will provide you with a storehouse of tricks you can memorize. Remember, use your knowledge of the memory system in this book to commit these tricks to memory. For example, you might compose a list of basic words especially for magic and with each, associate a specific idea to help you remember in sequence. Another good way to use your memory power for entertaining at parties is to get a good book on party stunts from the library and plan a number of them which you can use to demonstrate your ability to remember.

The Associated Words Party Game. This is an interesting way for you to meet everyone at a party for the first time and recall their names and the associated words assigned to them when they arrived. Here's how it works:

Each guest upon arriving is given a card which he hangs around his neck. Written on that card is one word. For example, Bread, Butter, Coffee, Cup, Salt and Pepper, etc. Then the couples are paired and introduced. (This is often used in many variations at church socials, single people's clubs, etc.)

You introduce yourself to each person. At an announced time, everyone switches cards and changes places in the room. You then proceed through the room demonstrating your ability to remember faces by telling who was who!

The Well-known Couples Party Game. This is a variation that starts a party off with a lot of laughter. As each male guest enters he is given a name card such as Adam. As each female guest arrives she chooses or is given a name such as Eve. Then you meet each person, associating the name with the face. Later, the couples who came together but who were paired off with others in this amusing way, switch their cards. You then tell who was who, much to their astonishment.

There are many other variations of choosing partners at parties and these can be loads of fun when you use your ingenuity to demonstrate your mental ability to remember. For instance, you might arrive at the party with numbered cards to be hung around the guests' necks. Later on these cards are switched and you tell who was who. A variation of this is a show stealer when you assign numbers to each person, they line up and then, while you are out of the room, switch places. You then replace each person in his or her proper order in the sequence of their seating.

Here's a game nobody but you can win every time! Assign a pre-memorized list of words to people in sequence as they arrive. For example, you meet each person, tell him you are the District Attorney and are going to assign a clue or a murder weapon to him. You then hold out a hat and he draws a folded slip of paper which he hides on his person.

Next, the person who received the slip of paper enters the room and performs a certain charade according to the instruction on the slip of paper he has drawn. Finally, the murder victim is discovered and every-one tries to guess who the "murderer" is. Only *you* can guess.

This is the secret. On each slip of paper drawn out of the hat by everyone is a word representing a "murder weapon" and a "clue" and a charade. Only one slip contains a "black dot." The person getting that is the "murder victim." One other slip contains the word "murderer."

Now here are how the slips are prepared in advance:

1. You are the first suspect. Enter the room, touch the top of your head three times and keep this slip of paper.
2. You are the "murder victim." When the time comes your body will be discovered. Please cooperate.
3. You are the third suspect. Enter the room, touch the top of your head three times and keep this slip of paper.
4. You are the murderer. Enter the room and touch the top of your head four times (or once) and keep this slip of paper.

As you see, each person you remember has something else to do. When the "body" is discovered, everyone is paraded out to perform their charades for everyone else to guess. Of course, no one can do it. You see to it that enough false clue "charades" are performed to throw every-one off.

As you build up to the naming of the victim you may have everyone call out their numbers which you will call out again to them (much to their amazement) as you recapitulate the "crime."

There are many variations of this and other well-known parlor games. By all means *do* use your memory power to have fun, as well as to improve yourself personally, to learn, and to cash in upon.

You'll Never Again Have an Excuse for Saying, "I Forgot!"

The basic elements of all my memory system and its applications were learned in a few hours. The expanded application has been developed in the last eight years. You can now expand the basic principles with the benefit of my experience set down in these pages.

If I had it to do all over again, I would have begun at an earlier age. Perhaps if I had known then, what I know now, I would have accomplished great things with my memory power. *If.*

I hope you will use the secrets and the techniques in this book to good advantage. I hope that you will use your knowledge of the secrets of memory power to inspire our young people to learn and to use their bright minds in the pursuit of learning so that their children's children will live in a world blessed with peace and self-knowledge.

But enough of this philosophizing.

This has been a great satisfaction, teaching you the methods and ideas which have brought me so much success, fun and knowledge. I trust that you will put your memory power to good use.

Now it can be truly said that you will never again have an excuse for saying, "I forgot!"

XX

The Hersey
Number Dictionary

The words you will find in this number dictionary may be used singly, or in combinations in a variety of ways. For instance, if you want to make up a number word for 14,410, you may compose it in any number of ways:

1 441 0 – 14 41 0 – 144 10, etc.
1 441 0 = hat rewards
14 41 0 = tar road icy
144 10 = dryer hothouse

The words you need may be tailored to fit your associations by using a little effort to string them together from these lists. Many words which could have been included in this dictionary are not listed. This has been deliberate, so you might be encouraged to develop the habit of composing your own words. By all means, do this. It's fun.

Number			Number		
0	hose	house	12	tin	heathen
1	hat	tee	13	team	tummy
2	hen	Noah	14	tire	tray
3	ham	hymn	15	tool	hotel
4	hare	row	16	tissue	dish
5	hill	owl	17	tack	duck
6	hedge	ash	18	taffy	TV
7	hook	key	19	tape	tub
8	hive	heavy	20	nose	henhouse
9	hoop	pie	21	net	honeydew
10	toes	hot-house	22	nun	onion
11	tot	diet	23	gnome	name

Number				Number			
24	Nero	Henry		73	comb	gum	
25	nail	Nellie		74	car	choir	
26	Nash	winch		75	coal	keel	
27	nag	nick		76	cage	cash	
28	Navy	knife		77	cake	keg	
29	knob	honeybee		78	cuff	coffee	
30	moose	moss		79	cap	cob	
31	mate	meat		80	fez	vase	
32	moon	money		81	foot	photo	
33	mom	Miami		82	fan	phone	
34	mare	hammer		83	foam	fume	
35	mail	mule		84	fire	fur	
36	match	mooch		85	foil	fly	
37	mike	mug		86	fish	fudge	
38	muff	movie		87	fig	fang	
39	mop	amoeba		88	fife	five	
40	Rose	horse		89	VIP	fop	
41	rat	road		90	bus	bat	
42	rain	heron		91	bat	boot	
43	ram	room		92	bone	pony	
44	error	rower		93	beam	bomb	
45	rail	roll		94	bar	pear	
46	rouge	roach		95	ball	pail	
47	rake	rag		96	beach	pitch	
48	roof	wharf		97	book	pack	
49	rope	rib		98	beef	pave	
50	lace	louse		99	baby	pipe	
51	loot	light		100	thesis	diocese	
52	lion	lane					
53	lime	lamb		000	ice-houses	sissies	
54	lyre	lair		001	icy-sod	wisest	
55	lily	Lulu		002	season	assassin	
56	latch	lodge		003	sesame	icy-swim	
57	lake	lock		004	Caesar	assessor	
58	leaf	laugh		005	sizzle	swizzle	
59	lap	leap		006	ice-shoe	size-shoe	
60	cheese	shoes		007	seasick	ice-sack	
61	chute	shot		008	saucy-waif	ice-safe	
62	ocean	chain		009	icy-subway	ice-sweep	
63	chime	jam		010	sties	hostess	
64	chair	jury		011	statue	estate	
65	Chili	jail		012	stein	Houston	
66	choo-choo	judge		013	steam	stem	
67	check	sheik		014	stair	oyster	
68	chef	Chevvy		015	stool	whistle	
69	chip	shop		016	stage	hostage	
70	case	goose		017	stick	stag	
71	cat	kid		018	stove	Steve	
72	cane	gun		019	step	stub	

Number			Number		
020	sneeze	snooze	069	ice-ship	sew-shop
021	snoot	hacienda	070	skis	sox
022	sign-on	Xenon	071	skeet	Scot
023	ice-anemia	icy-numb	072	skin	Socony
024	senior	Eisenhower	073	Eskimo	skim
025	snail	zonal	074	skewer	whisker
026	snatch	snitch	075	skull	icicle
027	snake	sink	076	Scotch	sketch
028	sniff	son of	077	seacock	easygoing
029	snap	snob	078	skiff	skivvy
030	seams	sea-moss	079	scoop	ice-cap
031	smite	Yosemite	080	sieves	safes
032	simian	seaman	081	Soviet	sift
033	some ham!	icy-mummy	082	siphon	seven
034	smear	Samaria	083	save-me	icy-foam
035	smile	small	084	Savior	Xavier
036	smooch	smudge	085	swivel	civil
037	smog	smock	086	savage	safe-edge
038	wise-move	semi-heavy	087	sea-fog	zoo-havoc
039	zombie	sum-up	088	safe-view	safe-fee
040	sires	seers	089	save-up	wise-veep
041	sword	sort	090	spies	sea-bees
042	sire	siren	091	spade	spud
043	serum	swarm	092	spoon	Spain
044	soarer	zero-hour	093	spam	sweep-home
045	cereal	Israel	094	zebra	spear
046	serge	search	095	spool	spill
047	housework	Sarawak	096	speech	soupy-hash
048	surf	serf	097	spook	zwieback
049	syrup	wise-rabbi	098	spoof	spiffy
050	slice	sluice	099	soup-up	soap-up
051	salad	salute			
052	saloon	solon	100	Diocese	outsize
053	slime	asylum	101	dust	Tuesday
054	sailor	hustler	102	dozen	Disney
055	sea-lily	silly-whale	103	dismay	twosome
056	sledge	slush	104	de-icer	Howitzer
057	slug	sea-log	105	diesel	tassle
058	slave	sleeve	106	dosage	dizzy-Joe
059	slip	sloop	107	desk	tusk
060	sages	sashes	108	adhesive	doze-off
061	ice-shed	satiate	109	auto-swap	toss-up
062	ice-chain	sashay-in	110	duds	idiots
063	seize-Iwo Jima	sea-chum	111	DDT	hot-headed
064	suture	sash-hero	112	Titan	deaden
065	satchel	sea-shell	113	totem	diadem
066	sea-judge	sage-hedge	114	daughter	theatre
067	sea-shack	ice-shake	115	title	detail
068	sea-chef	sea-chief	116	hot-dish	detach

Number

Number

117	tooth-ache	white-duck	166	head-judge	adjudge
118	teed-off	witty-dive	167	white-chalk	hot-jug
119	tied-bow	tidy-up	168	head-chef	white-chief
120	tennis	dunes	169	tea-shop	dish-up
121	tent	donut	170	dog-house	ticks
122	tenon	white-nun	171	ticket	Dagwood
123	town-home	denim	172	deacon	token
124	diner	tenor	173	dogma	outcome
125	tunnel	toenail	174	dagger	tiger
126	Danish	tonnage	175	decal	tickle
127	donkey	tank	176	day-coach	dog-watch
128	white-ivy	wet-navy	177	woodcock	digging
129	Danube	thin-hip	178	DeCafe	take-off
130	dimes	tums	179	tea-cup	whitecap
131	damned	admit	180	doves	advice
132	domino	demon	181	divot	David
133	to-Miami	white-mum	182	divan	typhoon
134	dimmer	tomorrow	183	defame	defy-me
135	white-meal	hot-meal	184	diver	devour
136	DiMaggio	damage	185	devil	duffle
137	tomahawk	atomic	186	white-fish	tough-jaw
138	white-muff	hot-movie	187	defog	white-fog
139	dump	thump	188	white-five	hot-fife
140	dress	terrace	189	divvy-up	tough-boy
141	dirt	turret	190	Topaz	tubs
142	drain	attorney	191	teapot	deputy
143	drum	tram	192	Audubon	thighbone
144	dryer	terrier	193	head-bum	white-puma
145	drill	trowel	194	diaper	dipper
146	dredge	torch	195	table	top-hole
147	drag	turkey	196	white-page	debauch
148	drive	trophy	197	tobacco	hat-bag
149	drape	troop	198	tip-off	white-puff
150	dials	Dallas	199	white-puppy	tip-up
151	toilet	athlete			
152	talon	Tulane	200	nieces	noses
153	hoodlum	Thelma	201	nest	honest
154	dollar	tailor	202	ensign	insane
155	Delilah	Talullah	203	hansom	enzyme
156	deluge	theology	204	answer	nicer
157	talc	wedlock	205	nozzle	nasal
158	tea-leaf	outlive	206	new-sash	wins-show
159	tulip	ad-lib	207	nose-gay	nice-guy
160	duchess	audacious	208	new-safe	nice-wife
161	digit	Dutch-toy	209	newsboy	winesap
162	Dutch-inn	Duchin	210	notice	Andes
163	dodgem	teach-me	211	knitted	nudity
164	dowager	ditcher	212	Indian	antenna
165	hot-July	touch-hole	213	anatomy	entomb

Number			Number		
214	notary	Andria	263	new-chime	wench-whim
215	needle	knothole	264	Nigeria	injury
216	new-dish	Hindu-shah	265	angel	initial
217	India-cow	antique	266	hinge-hatch	new-judge
218	native	endive	267	handshake	honey-cheek
219	Andy-boy	wind-up	268	anchovy	Hawaiian-chief
220	nuns	nines	269	new-ship	enjoy-hobby
221	noon-tea	innuendo	270	nags	nicks
222	Hawaiian-onion	new-nun	271	nugget	necktie
223	union-home	own-name	272	noggin	Nikoyan
224	nunnery	niner	273	honeycomb	enigma
225	union-hall	new-nail	274	Niagara	Hungary
226	new-Nash	unhinge	275	nickle	inkwell
227	win-inning	hen-neck	276	hen-cage	engage
228	Nineveh	new-knife	277	Hancock	new-keg
229	nun-buoy	knee-knob	278	new-cuff	knock-off
230	gnomes	new-homes	279	hencoop	new-cop
231	nomad	inmate	280	knives	novice
232	nominee	honeymoon	281	Nevada	hen-foot
233	new-muumuu	new-mama	282	New Haven	novena
234	enemy-arrow	new-hammer	283	wine-foam	infamy
235	animal	enamel	284	infra	unfair
236	enmesh	hen-mash	285	anvil	navel
237	new-mug	new-hammock	286	knife-edge	navy-shoe
238	nymph	numb-foe	287	Univac	invoke
239	new-mop	new-map	288	naive-wife	enough-ivy
240	nurse	one-horse	289	new-fob	new veep
241	north	unearth	290	knobs	nips
242	hen-run	Nero-wine	291	naphtha	inhabit
243	new-harem	won-army	292	Nippon	Nubian
244	nearer	honorary	293	Napalm	embalm
245	knurl	unruly	294	nipper	neighbor
246	Norge	energy	295	nebula	nipple
247	New York	Newark	296	new-page	knob-hitch
248	nerve	new-wharf	297	hen-peck	new-bag
249	unrap	Nairobi	298	hen-bevy	new-beef
250	annals	analyze	299	new pipe	new-poppy
251	inlet	amulet			
252	nylon	new-alien	300	Moses	masseuse
253	new-loom	hen-lime	301	mast	mist
254	nailer	inhaler	302	mason	Amazon
255	Honolulu	nailhole	303	mazuma	museum
256	knowledge	unlatch	304	miser	Missouri
257	knuckle	unlucky	305	missile	muzzle
258	new-life	new-love	306	message	massage
259	own-lip	no-help	307	mask	music
260	notches	niches	308	missive	massive
261	notched	unshod	309	Mesabi	mishap
262	engine	nation	310	Midas	Medusa

Number				Number			
311	mat-head	imitate		360	matches	images	
312	maiden	madonna		361	machet	emaciate	
313	madam	Mahatma		362	mission	machine	
314	miter	motor		363	my-jam	Mitchum	
315	medal	motel		364	masher	moocher	
316	meat-hash	my-dish		365	Mitchell	my-shell	
317	mattock	medic		366	ham-judge	mesh-shoe	
318	motive	midwife		367	magic	ham-Jack	
319	mudpie	made-up		368	ham-chef	my-shave	
320	mince	moons		369	match-up	much-hope	
321	minuet	Monday		370	Mickies	mugs	
322	minion	May-onion		371	Mikado	maggot	
323	my-name	homonym		372	mahogany	Macon	
324	miner	manure		373	my-comb	make-me	
325	manual	Emmanuel		374	mucker	haymaker	
326	Menjou	menage		375	mangle	Michael	
327	mink	monkey		376	my-cash	mawkish	
328	ham-knife	human-hive		377	mocking	mucky-goo	
329	my-knob	my honey-bee		378	make-off	my-coffee	
330	mums	mimosa		379	magpie	mock-up	
331	mammoth	Mohammet		380	movies	muffs	
332	mammon	May-moon		381	muffet	mufti	
333	my-muumuu	my-mummy		382	muffin	home-phone	
334	mummer	memoir		383	aim-foam	move-hem	
335	mammal	my-mail		384	mover	mayfair	
336	my-match	mom-wash		385	muffle	I'm-full	
337	mimic	home-hammock		386	ham-fish	my-fish	
338	mummify	my-move		387	my-folk	movie-key	
339	mambo	my-mop		388	my-five	mauve-ivy	
340	Mars	mares		389	move-up	mafia-whip	
341	mart	married		390	embassy	mops	
342	moron	Marine		391	moppet	wombat	
343	Miriam	my-room		392	impugn	my-pan	
344	mirror	merry-hour		393	wampum	my-poem	
345	mural	moral		394	umpire	hamper	
346	marsh	Maharajah		395	maple	Mabel	
347	morgue	Morocco		396	ambush	impeach	
348	Murphy	mayor-vow		397	hymn-book	humbug	
349	my-robe	hem-robe		398	my-puff	map-view	
350	mules	Himalayas		399	my-baby	imbibe	
351	mallet	mildew					
352	melon	million		400	roses	rhesus	
353	millium	my-lamb		401	roast	rosette	
354	molar	miler		402	raisin	horizon	
355	mill-wheel	mole-hill		403	resume	worrisome	
356	mulch	militia		404	razor	rosary	
357	milk	Milwaukee		405	wrestle	resole	
358	ham-loaf	Amalfie		406	horse-shoe	wire-sash	
359	my-lap	mail-boy		407	Rusk	airsick	

Number   Number

408	receive	our-sofa	457	rowlock	railing
409	rasp	recipe	458	relief	roll-off
410	radius	radios	459	hare-lip	whirl-up
411	red-head	redwood	460	ridges	riches
412	rataan	red-hen	461	rachet	rouged
413	radium	rhodium	462	Russian	urchin
414	Rotary	radar	463	Hiroshima	regime
415	rattle	hurdle	464	archer	Roger
416	radish	Rhodesia	465	Rachel	Richelieu
417	red-wing	reading	466	hairy-judge	wire-judge
418	ratify	write-off	467	air-chuck	retching
419	redoubt	radio-buoy	468	hairy-chief	air-chief
420	ruins	harness	469	airship	worship
421	runt	rent	470	rugs	Iroquois
422	reunion	renown	471	rocket	regatta
423	our-name	your-name	472	raccoon	organ
424	Ranier	Renoir	473	requiem	recomb
425	Runnell	renewal	474	rocker	rookery
426	ranch	wrench	475	oracle	wrinkle
427	rink	ring	476	air-coach	wreckage
428	run-off	wire-knife	477	rigging	air-cock
429	rainbow	run-up	478	rake-off	our-coffee
430	rooms	reams	479	rack-up	recoup
431	roomette	hermit	480	Orpheus	roofs
432	Roman	harmony	481	raft	rivet
433	our-mom	airy-mum	482	raven	ear-phone
434	armor	reamer	483	airy-foam	arrive-home
435	Rommell	airmail	484	referee	river
436	rummage	rematch	485	rifle	ravioli
437	reaming	remake	486	refugee	refuge
438	remove	ramify	487	raving	revoke
439	rhumba	ramp	488	revive	roof-view
440	warhorse	rowers	489	rev-up	arrive-happy
441	reward	arrow-root	490	air-base	robes
442	rerun	our-reign	491	rabbit	rowboat
443	re-arm	wire-room	492	robin	harpoon
444	hairy-warrior	our-rear	493	air-bomb	raw-opium
445	rural	aurora-halo	494	reaper	robber
446	wire-RUSH!	awry-arch	495	ripple	ruble
447	our-rock	rare-key	496	rubbish	herbage
448	re-roof	rarefy	497	year-book	Roebuck
449	hair-rope	rare-pal	498	rope-off	rebuff
450	rolls	reels	499	hairy-pup	wire-pipe
451	roulette	herald			
452	airline	reline	500	Ulysses	lassies
453	Harlem	heirloom	501	list	lawsuit
454	roller	lawyer	502	lesson	Louisiana
455	royal-lei	our-lily	503	Lyceum	wholesome
456	relish	horology	504	loser	ulcer

Number

Number

505	wholesale	wall-cell	554	oily-lawyer	hill-lair
505	wholesale	wall-cell	554	oily-lawyer	hill-lair
506	yellow-sash	hell-siege	555	hail-hail-hail	halleluiah
507	Alaska	lacing	556	Elijah	allege
508	yellow-sofa	all-safe	557	lilac	yellow-lake
509	lisp	oil-soap	558	whole-loaf	yellow-loaf
510	lighthouse	lettuce	559	lullaby	hilly-alp
511	Yuletide	loaded	560	loges	lashes
512	Latin	Altoona	561	legit	oily-jet
513	yellow-dame	lithium	562	legion	Elgin
514	ladder	leather	563	yellow-comb	yellow-gem
515	ladle	lethal	564	ledger	Alger
516	old-shoe	eel-dish	565	oil-shale	yellow-shale
517	yellow-dog	lathing	566	leash-shy	wheel-judge
518	Latvia	hold-off	567	wheel-chock	wheel-jack
519	let-up	light-up	568	oily-shave	ledge-view
520	lions	lioness	569	oil-ship	leash-ape
521	linit	Holland	570	lugs	legs
522	linen	Lenin	571	locket	liquid
523	lunem	Olney-hymn	572	lagoon	lichen
524	liner	loaner	573	welcome	alchemy
525	Lionel	lonely	574	locker	logger
526	launch	lunch	575	alcohol	illegal
527	link	Hellenic	576	luggage	all-cash
528	yellow-knife	lone-hive	577	legging	looking
529	line-up	lean-waif	578	alcove	liquefy
530	looms	limes	579	lock-up	look-up
531	loomette	helmet	580	levees	loaves
532	lemon	layman	581	loft	lift
533	yellow-mum	Lima-home	582	leaven	liven
534	yellow-mare	Elmer	583	oil-foam	leave-home
535	Lemuel	yellow-meal	584	lever	welfare
536	limoge	yellow-mash	585	level	lawful
537	lemming	liming	586	lavish	yellow-fish
538	lymph	wool-muff	587	laughing	living
539	lamp	lump	588	live-wife	yellow-five
540	lairs	walrus	589	yellow-fob	live-up
541	lariat	lard	590	elipse	loops
542	aileron	Lorraine	591	halibut	whale-boat
543	alarm	Laramie	592	Albany	whalebone
544	lower-row	yellow-horror	593	album	Alabama
545	Laurel	low-rail	594	labor	leper
546	larch	large	595	label	hill-billy
547	lark	lyric	596	Lepage	hole-patch
548	larva	low-reef	597	Alpaca	eloping
549	larrup	oily-rub	598	lop-off	all-beef
550	lilies	hula-hulas	599	hollow-pipe	yellow-poppy
551	lilt	loyalty			
552	Lillian	yellow-lane	600	Jesus	cheeses
553	yellow-loam	holy-lamb	601	joust	chest

Number   Number

602	Jason	chosen	651	child	jeweled
603	juicy-ham	huge-ham	652	Chilean	huge-lion
604	juicer	Chaucer	653	shalom	ash-lime
605	chisel	Jessel	654	jeweler	jailor
606	cheese-show	juicy-hash	655	shillelah	huge-lily
607	juicy-chew	huge-sock	656	geology	chilly-issue
608	Joseph	huge-safe	657	shellac	shilling
609	wash-up	wash-soap	658	shelf	chilly-wife
610	jets	Judas	659	jalopy	julep
611	washtub	jaded	660	judges	choo-choos
612	jitney	shut-in	661	hooch-shot	achieved
613	huge-dam	wash-dame	662	shoe-shine	chilly-ocean
614	shutter	cheater	663	huge-jam	watch-chime
615	shuttle	chattel	664	Cheshire	huge-jar
616	huge-dish	jet-issue	665	huge-jail	watch-shill
617	watch-dog	show-dog	666	chilly-judge	choo-choo-show
618	chew-taffy	shut-off	667	joshing	wash-shack
619	shut-up	shoe-top	668	hash-chef	wash-chief
620	Chinese	chains	669	watch-shop	shoe-shop
621	giant	shanty	670	checks	jacks
622	Shannon	shine-on	671	jacket	choked
623	shun-em	chain-hem	672	chicken	ash-can
624	shiner	January	673	check-me	wash-comb
625	chenille	shiny-halo	674	sugar	joker
626	change	shiny-shoe	675	shackle	jackal
627	junk	shank	676	show-cage	hoochy-coochy
628	Geneva	huge-knife	677	Chicago	jacking
629	join-up	huge-knob	678	check-off	shake-off
630	chemise	James	679	Jacob	check-up
631	wash-maid	jimmied	680	chefs	shaves
632	chow-mein	watchman	681	shaft	cheviot
633	show-mum	huge-mammy	682	chiffon	shove-in
634	shimmer	chimer	683	chilly-foam	wash-foam
635	huge-mule	Ishmael	684	chauffeur	shaver
636	watch-match	ash-match	685	shovel	shuffle
637	Jamaica	huge-Mohawk	686	huge-fish	jew-fish
638	huge-muff	huge-movie	687	shaving	chafing
639	jumbo	chimp	688	shove-off	chilly-five
640	shears	chairs	689	watch-fob	shove-up
641	chart	chariot	690	gypsy	chips
642	churn	Sharon	691	ash-pit	wash-pot
643	charm	Jeremiah	692	jawbone	Japan
644	shearer	juror	693	huge-beam	J-bomb
645	shrill	churl	694	chopper	jobber
646	church	cherish	695	chapel	jubilee
647	shark	jerk	696	sheepish	shoe-patch
648	sheriff	giraffe	697	shoe-bag	wash-bag
649	cherub	shrub	698	chop-off	chip-off
650	shoelace	jellies	699	huge-pipe	show-puppy

Number			Number		
700	kisses	gasses	748	grave	graph
701	cast	cost	749	grape	caribou
702	cousin	caisson	750	class	gallows
703	chasm	exhume	751	cloud	cloth
704	Kaiser	kisser	752	gallon	clan
705	castle	axle	753	clam	column
706	wax-show	gay-sash	754	collar	calorie
707	cask	kiosk	755	ukelele	Galileo
708	gasify	gay-sofa	756	goulash	college
709	gossip	gasp	757	cloak	calico
710	kites	goddess	758	cliff	caliph
711	cadet	coded	759	club	gallop
712	cotton	kitten	760	cages	coaches
713	academy	weak-dam	761	gadget	gashed
714	gator	equator	762	cushion	kitchen
715	cattle	kettle	763	gooey-jam	ketchum
716	gay-dish	Katisha	764	catcher	kosher
717	Kodak	catwalk	765	eggshell	cudgel
718	Godiva	octave	766	key-judge	weak-judge
719	goodbye	giddap	767	gashing	key-jack
720	queens	canes	768	cash-fee	hack-chief
721	candy	Canada	769	ketchup	key-shop
722	canyon	canine	770	cukes	cookies
723	economy	key-name	771	cook-out	coquette
724	canary	gunner	772	cocoon	cockney
725	canal	kennel	773	gingham	Kokomo
726	conch	coinage	774	cocker	Quaker
727	gunk	cognac	775	goggle	cog-wheel
728	convoy	hack-knife	776	caulkage	weak-cage
729	canopy	canape	777	KKK	cake-walk
730	gams	combs	778	kick-off	weak-coffee
731	comet	commode	779	kick-up	key-cop
732	kimono	gamin	780	caves	cuffs
733	gay-Miami	gay-muumuu	781	gift	cavity
734	camera	Gomorrah	782	coffin	cave-in
735	camel	comely	783	cave-home	gay-foam
736	gum-shoe	key-match	784	quiver	coffer
737	gimmick	comic	785	gavel	gay-veil
738	gay-muff	gay-movie	786	gay-fish	go-fetch
739	camp	Gump	787	gaff-hook	giving
740	cross	curse	788	key-five	hock-fife
741	carrot	cart	789	give-up	gay-fop
742	crown	crayon	790	cubs	cops
743	cream	groom	791	cubit	cupid
744	courier	career	792	cabin	cabana
745	gorilla	carol	793	weak-opium	weak-beam
746	garage	crash	794	cooper	copper
747	crock	creek	795	gable	cable

Number   Number

796	cabbage	gay-pooch	844	friar	furrier
797	kapok	Quebec	845	frill	virile
798	keep-off	hook-beef	846	overshoe	forge
799	gay-poppy	weak-pipe	847	frock	frog
			848	verify	heavy-roof
800	fezzes	faces	849	frappe	heavy-wrap
801	fist	fiesta	850	fleece	flies
802	face-in	wave-sign	851	flit	flood
803	heavy-sum	face-me	852	violin	felon
804	visor	officer	853	film	flame
805	vessel	vassal	854	flier	flare
806	visage	office-show	855	fly-wheel	flail
807	facing	heavy-sack	856	village	flesh
808	face-off	heavy-safe	857	flag	flack
809	heavy-soup	face-up	858	fluff	valve
810	vets	foods	859	flap	Philip
811	fat-head	fitted	860	fishes	vicious
812	half-tone	fatten	861	VJ-day	Vashti
813	Fatima	heavy-tome	862	fusion	fashion
814	feather	father	863	Fujiyama	heavy-gem
815	fiddle	vital	864	fissure	voucher
816	footage	heavy-dish	865	vigil	fish-hole
817	fatigue	vodka	866	fish-hatch	heavy-judge
818	votive	wave-TV	867	fish-hook	fishing
819	heavy-tub	fat-boy	868	fish-wife	half-shave
820	Venus	vanes	869	fish-pie	heavy-job
821	vanity	faint	870	fox	fags
822	Finnian	heavy-nine	871	fanged	faggot
823	Euphonium	viney-home	872	Afghan	Vicuna
824	veneer	finer	873	vacuum	half-coma
825	funnel	vanilla	874	vicar	fakir
826	finch	finish	875	vehicle	vocal
827	phoning	funk	876	heavy-cage	half-cash
828	fine-view	heavy-knife	877	Viking	heavy-cake
829	fine-pew	heavy-nap	878	half-coffee	ivy-cafe
830	fumes	foams	879	heavy-cap	half-cape
831	vomit	heavy-mat	880	fives	half-face
832	foeman	heavy-woman	881	fifth	fifty
833	heavy-mammy	wife-hum	882	Vivian	heavy-van
834	femur	few-more	883	five-M	heavy-foam
835	v-mail	female	884	fifer	fiver
836	famish	heavy-image	885	heavy-foil	fife-hole
837	heavy-mug	half-mug	886	heavy-fish	half-fish
838	heavy-muff	half-muff	887	heavy-fog	heavy-heavy-guy
839	vamp	heavy-mop	888	FFV	vivify
840	fires	virus	889	five-buoy	five-pay
841	ford	Fred	890	veeps	few-pies
842	fern	farina	891	hoof-beat	vapid
843	forum	farm	892	Fabian	heavy-bone

Number			Number		
893	half-opium	heavy-beam	941	parade	bride
894	viper	vapor	942	prune	brain
895	fable	feeble	943	broom	Burma
896	heavy-bush	foppish	944	briar	prayer
897	half-back	heavy-bag	945	broil	Brillo
898	heavy-peavey	huff-puff	946	bridge	porridge
899	wave-poppy	heavy-poppy	947	brick	park
			948	proof	brief
900	bases	busses	949	prop	bribe
901	bust	paste	950	bellows	pillows
902	basin	bosun	951	palette	ballot
903	bosom	possum	952	balloon	pylon
904	buzzer	boozer	953	plume	plum
905	pussy-willow	Bissell	954	plier	bowler
906	passage	abusage	955	pole-hole	Belial
907	bazooka	pass-key	956	pledge	polish
908	pacify	pea-sieve	957	bullock	plug
909	busy-bee	pea-soup	958	bailiff	Bolivia
910	boathouse	boots	959	bell-boy	playboy
911	potted	beaded	960	budgies	bushes
912	baton	Bataan	961	beach-head	budget
913	podium	bottom	962	pigeon	potion
914	potter	butter	963	pajama	beach-home
915	poodle	beetle	964	pitcher	badger
916	potash	wipe-dish	965	bushel	poacher
917	paddock	bedding	966	peach-show	bush-hedge
918	epitaph	Batavia	967	bush-hook	pitching
919	pot-pie	boot-up	968	pitch-off	patch-off
920	pines	buns	969	bishop	pie-shop
921	bayonet	bonnet	970	pigs	bikes
922	banana	bunion	971	bucket	pocket
923	Panama	weepy-Naomi	972	Bikini	Pekin
924	banner	pioneer	973	pygmy	Begum
925	panel	pin-wheel	974	baker	beggar
926	banjo	paunch	975	bugle	pickle
927	bank	panic	976	baggage	package
928	Baniff	wipe-knife	977	peacock	boogie-woogie
929	pin-up	wipe-knob	978	pick-off	back-off
930	pumice	bums	979	pick-up	bug-a-boo
931	BMT	happy-maid	980	puffs	paves
932	pie-man	bee-man	981	puffet	pivot
933	happy-mama	weepy-mom	982	buffoon	bovine
934	boomer	puma-area	983	happy-foam	beehive-hum
935	pommel	pummel	984	beaver	Bavaria
936	balmy-joy	buy-match	985	buffalo	bevel
937	wipe-mug	bomb-echo	986	peavish	buy-fish
938	happy-movie	palm-off	987	bivouac	paving
939	pump	Bombay	988	puff-off	puffy-huff
940	pears	brassie	989	puff-up	happy-veep

Number			Number		
990	papoose	babies	996	pea-bush	baby-ish
991	puppet	bob-white	997	pea-bag	Peiping
992	baboon	bobbin	998	pop-off	baby-wife
993	happy-bum	happy-poem	999	pop-up	pay-papa
994	piper	pepper	1000	toy-seesaws	twice-size
995	bubble	Bible